STAGE 3

ADVANCED FINANCIAL ACCOUNTING

First edition February 1987
Sixth edition January 1992

ISBN 0 86277 674 0 (previous edition 0 86277 729 1)

British Library Cataloguing-in-Publication data

A catalogue record for this book is available
from the British Library

Published by

BPP Publishing Limited
Aldine House, Aldine Place
London W12 8AW

We are grateful to the Chartered Institute of Management Accountants,
the Chartered Association of Certified Accountants, the Institute of
Chartered Accountants in England and Wales and the Chartered
Institute of Bankers for permission to reproduce past examination
questions. The suggested solutions have been prepared by BPP
Publishing Limited.

CONTENTS

PREFACE

The examinations of the Chartered Institute of Management Accountants are a demanding test of students' ability to master the wide range of knowledge and skills required of the modern accountant. The Institute's rapid response to the pace of change is shown both in the content of the syllabuses and in the style of examination questions set.

BPP Practice and Revision Kits are designed to supplement BPP's Study Texts with study material for practice and revision tailored to accommodate any recent changes in the style and content of the examination.

The 1992 edition of the Stage 3 Advanced Financial Accounting kit contains:

- the syllabus and the Institute's syllabus guidance notes
- an analysis of recent examination papers, plus summaries of examiners' comments on the exams
- study notes to jog your memory of each area of the syllabus
- updating notes to make sure your knowledge is as current as possible
- a checklist for you to plan your study and keep tabs on your progress
- a test your knowledge quiz
- a question bank divided into topic areas containing:
  - a total of 12 tutorial questions to warm you up on key techniques before starting the examination standard questions (italicised in the index)
  - a total of 48 examination standard questions, most of which come from past examinations, including all examination questions set in at least the last five papers up to and including May 1991
- a full test paper consisting of the November 1991 examination, for you to try out in exam conditions

All questions are provided with full suggested solutions plus tutorial notes prepared by BPP. The tutorial notes to past examination questions contain detailed summaries of the examiner's comments where relevant.

If you attempt all the examination standard questions in the kit, together with the test paper, you will have written answers equivalent to nearly 11 examinations. So if you write good answers to all of them, you should be well prepared for anything you meet in the examination itself. Good luck!

BPP Publishing
January 1992

SYLLABUS

Aim

To test the candidate's ability:

(a) to prepare financial statements for publication in accordance with company law and statements of standard accounting practice;
(b) to analyse and interpret financial accounting statements and recognise their limitations.

Content	Ability required
1. *Company accounts: weighting 50%*	
Preparation of accounts in accordance with the requirements of the Companies Act and Statements of Standard Accounting Practice	4
Treatment of taxation in company accounts; accounting for deferred taxation	3
Consolidated accounts involving one or more subsidiaries and associated companies; inter-company transactions, problems of transfer pricing; acquisition and merger methods	4
Accounting treatment of acquisitions, mergers, capital reconstruction schemes, reduction of share capital, purchase of company's own shares	3
Foreign currency translation: accounting for foreign branches and overseas subsidiaries	3
2. *Income and value measurement: weighting 15%*	
Problems of profit measurement and alternative approaches; extra-ordinary and exceptional items	4
Application of current cost and current purchasing power methods in practice	3
Valuation of assets: alternative bases; stocks and work in progress; investment properties; accounting for leases and hire purchase	3
Recommended accounting practice regarding capitalisation of research and development and interest; treatment of goodwill	3
3. *Interpretation of accounts: weighting 25%*	
Advanced aspects of the interpretation of accounts and the use of ratios; preparation of related reports	4
Preparation and interpretation of statements of source and application of funds for group accounts, including acquisitions and disposals	4
Calculation of earnings per share, price/earnings ratios and other stock market ratios	4

SYLLABUS

<table>
<tr><td></td><td></td><td>Ability
required</td></tr>
</table>

4. *The development of accounting standards: weighting 10%*

The role of the Accounting Standards Board   2

The influence on financial accounting requirements of the
International Accounting Standards Committee, the European
Economic Community, Company Law and the Stock Exchange   1

Exposure drafts   1

The syllabus printed above contains a ranking of the level of ability required in each topic, and a weighting for each syllabus area. The Institute has published the following explanatory notes on these points.

'Abilities required in the examination

The rankings range from 1 to 4 and represent the following ability levels.

*Ranking for
syllabus topics*

Appreciation
To understand a knowledge area at an early stage of learning,
or outside the core of management accounting, at a level which
enables the accountant to communicate and work with other
members of the management team   1

Knowledge
To advise on such matters as laws, standards, facts and techniques
at a level of detail appropriate to a management accounting
specialist   2

Skill
To apply theoretical knowledge, concepts and techniques to the
solution of problems where it is clear what technique has to be
used and the information needed is clearly indicated   3

Application
To apply knowledge and skills where candidates have to determine
from a number of techniques which is the most appropriate and select
the information required from a fairly wide range of data, some of
which might not be relevant; to exercise professional judgement and
to communicate and work with members of the management team and
other recipients of financial reports   4

Study weightings
A percentage weighting is shown against each topic in the syllabus; this is intended as a guide to the amount of study time each topic requires.

All topics in a syllabus must be studied, as a question may examine more than one topic or carry a higher proportion of marks than the percentage study time suggested.

The weightings do not specify the number of marks which will be allocated to topics in the examination.'

THE EXAMINATION PAPER

Paper format

The examination paper contains compulsory questions in section A worth between 65% and 75% of the marks. For all the recent sittings there have been three optional questions in section B, of which two were to be attempted. However, the examiner has indicated that this is not a set pattern. Before November 1989 all questions were compulsory.

There is a significant discussion element in each paper; *at least* 30-40 of the total marks available are allocated to non-computational work.

Analysis of past papers

November 1991	*Marks*

Section A

1.	Consolidated profit and loss account	40
2.	Report analysing financial results of a competitor company	30

Section B

3.	Purchase of own shares	15
4.	Use of EPS as a measure of performance	15
5.	Fair value concept	15

This paper forms the test paper at the end of the kit, so only an outline of its contents is given here.

May 1991		*Marks*	*Question number in this kit*

Section A

1.	Prepare consolidated balance sheet; explain why fair values of assets used in consolidation	40	36
2.	Report to board analysing financial results of a competitor company	30	58

Section B

3.	Capitalisation of brand names	15	10
4.	Depreciation of fixed assets; investment properties	15	23
5.	Closing rate and temporal rate methods of foreign currency translation	15	45

Examiner's comments

The essay questions were not answered as well as the computational questions. 'It is important for candidates to practise answering essay questions during their revision'. Lack of examination technique was demonstrated, particularly where candidates had not stuck to the time allocation. Poor presentation was also a problem. Candidates should cross-reference workings and notes.

Candidates made a fair attempt at the first part of question 1, but the second part was not answered well. Question 2 produced good answers and it should be noted that 'most marks are given for the analysis and interpretation of ratios rather than for the calculation of ratios'. Some candidates had not kept up-to-date enough to answer question 3 and answers to questions 4 and 5 demonstrated a lack of basic knowledge of the SSAPs.

THE EXAMINATION PAPER

		Marks	Question number in this kit
November 1990			
Section A			
1.	Published accounts: P&L account, balance sheet and notes	45	29
2.	Memorandum explaining items in consolidated SSAF	25	53
Section B			
3.	Defined benefit pension scheme: changes to accounting policy and disclosures required by SSAP 24	15	25
4.	Report on accounting for changing price levels	15	12
5.	Discuss influence on financial statements of UK companies of IASC and EC	15	3

> *Examiner's comments*
>
> 'Candidates should be aware that in a company accounts question, some of the marks were awarded for presentation.' Clear scripts, legible and well laid out, will be more easily, and therefore more favourably, marked. Again, candidates were reminded to keep up to date and to answer *four* questions.
>
> Question 1 was reasonably well answered, but many candidates made some basic errors which should not be found at Stage 3. Some candidates answered question 2 very well, but others made fundamental errors, or failed to explain their answers properly.
>
> Question 3 was very unpopular and some who chose to answer it obviously had no knowledge of SSAP 24. Candidates frequently failed to answer the actual question set in 4 and 5.

May 1990			
Section A			
1.	Preparation of projected consolidated profit and loss account; comparison of EPS	45	40
2.	Report for board on competitor's accounts	25	57
Section B			
3.	Discuss benefits of segmental analysis for users of accounts and reasons why preparers resist such disclosures	15	52
4.	Report on off-balance sheet finance using controlled non-subsidiaries	15	9
5.	Discuss whether a consolidated historical cost balance sheet gives a realistic valuation of the group	15	32

> *Examiner's comments*
>
> Question 1 was in a slightly different format than usual but this did not trouble those candidates who understood the concepts behind consolidation. Candidates often failed to answer the second part of the question.
>
> Questions 2 and 3 were well answered but question 4 was very unpopular, even though Exposure Drafts are examinable in this paper.
>
> Question 5 produced some very good but also some very bad answers with candidates overlooking some current topics.

THE EXAMINATION PAPER

		Marks	Question number in this kit

Section A

		Marks	Question number in this kit
1.	Published accounts: P&L account, balance sheet and full notes	40	28
2.	Report on profitability and liquidity of a competitor; explain limitations of analysis from published accounts	20	56
3.	Report explaining purpose, scope and authority of accounting standards	10	2

Section B

		Marks	Question number in this kit
4.	Report on treatment of goodwill in published accounts and problems in treatment of goodwill relating to acquisitions and disposals	15	24
5.	Discuss advantages and disadvantages of historical cost accounting for shareholders	15	11
6.	Memorandum explaining foreign currency translation methods accounting treatment of exchange differences and disclosures required	15	44

Examiner's comments

Some candidates used the wrong format in question 1 and presentation was poor. Some very basic mistakes were made. The answers to question 2 were quite good, but limited. Candidates often ignored part (b).

Answers to question 3 were very vague and sketchy but question 4 produced answers showing candidates were more up to date with topical issues.

Question 5 was not well answered; although questions are no longer set on SSAP 16, candidates should still be familiar with the section on income and value. The first part of question 6 produced good answers, but not the second part.

May 1989

1.	Consolidated balance sheet for a company with a 60% subsidiary and an associated company	35	35
2.	Journal entries and reconstruction account to record management buy-out; opening balance sheet	30	50
3.	Calculation of EPS after prior year adjustment and rights issue; list limitations of EPS	15	60
4.	Report explaining treatment of long-term contract WIP in published accounts and highlighting any possible problems	20	21

THE EXAMINATION PAPER

	November 1988	*Marks*	*Question number in this kit*
1.	Accounting for foreign currency transactions in the accounts of an individual company	35	42
2.	Preparation of consolidated funds statement, and comment on the points highlighted by the statement	35	
3.	Discussion of the information revealed and concealed by consolidated accounts	15	31
4.	Explanation of exceptional and extraordinary items	15	5

May 1988

1.	Preparation of consolidated balance sheet and profit and loss account using the merger accounting method	25	47
2.	Interpretation of accounts by means of inter-firm comparison data	40	
3.	Explanation of the treatment of leases in the accounts of lessee companies	20	8
4.	Discussion of the extent to which accounting standards restrict flexibility in accounting practice	15	1

THE EXAMINATION PAPER

Examiner's comments
Candidates did not use their time well and did not answer all the questions.

Some candidates demonstrated no knowledge of merger accounting in their answers to question 1, although other answers were very good.

The first part of question 2 was quite well answered, although more depth and insight must be shown. The second part produced some very poor answers.

Some candidates had not studied leasing as was apparent by their answers to question 3.

Answers to question 4 were not planned properly: '... it is important to plan the answer, develop a good structure and use the evidence ... to support logical arguments ...'

STUDY GUIDE

Examination technique

Several major problems are identified by examiners over and over again. Here are a few notes to help you overcome them.

(a) *Inadequate preparation.* You can only avoid this by working hard and *effectively*. It is possible to work very hard but not to succeed in learning to *apply* your knowledge in the way the examiner wants, perhaps because you spend too much time on peripheral areas; or because you don't leave time to cover the whole syllabus; or simply because you don't practise past examination questions. The remedies for these problems are to *plan* your studies (and to keep your plan under review so that you can adjust it for unexpected changes); and to use this kit to get a good idea of the depth and breadth of knowledge which you will be expected to show in your exam.

(b) *Poor examination techique.* It cannot be emphasised too strongly that there is nothing to be gained by spending a long time on one question at the expense of all the others. You earn most marks in the early stages of your solution to a question and if you have to rush them you will lose many valuable marks through careless errors. On a three hour paper, each mark deserves 1.6 minutes (making allowance for ten minutes reading time at the start of the paper and ten minutes at the end to look through your work and ensure that all parts of all answers are labelled, your workings are clearly referenced to your answers and so on). For example, a 25 mark question deserves 40 minutes *and no more*. Use of answer plans for written examples helps you to gain some marks if you do run out of time. *Always* show workings.

(c) *Question spotting.* This is a waste of time, as a rule. Question spotters are often badly tripped up. It is particularly futile to prepare essays on likely discussion topics *without* a thorough grasp of the topic. Nothing annoys examiners more than a prepared essay *which does not answer the question set!* You *must* be capable of applying your knowledge to answer the specific requirements of the question.

(d) *Untidiness*

- If your handwriting is very large or poor, write on every other line of the paper and consider printing.

- Clearly label and cross-reference your workings and notes. *Always* use the proper headings for T accounts, published accounts and so on.

- Use tabulated answers for written questions if appropriate.

- Underline important points in written answers (but don't waste time on an elaborate colour coding system).

- Make sure that your numbers are clearly distinguishable from each other.

Most important of all, don't panic! If you are finding the paper hard then it's likely that most other candidates are too. Remember that you would not have reached Stage 3 without a lot of hard work and ability and so you must know something!

STUDY GUIDE

Using this kit

The more practice you can get in answering examination-style questions, the better prepared you will be for the examination itself. But if time is limited, remember that a serious attempt at one question is more valuable than cursory attempts at two. Avoid the temptation to 'audit' the answers: complete your attempt before checking with our solution. When you have had enough practice to be confident of your grasp of the material, try a few questions under exam conditions, timing yourself against the clock. Finally, you should attempt the examination paper at the end of the kit, preferably under examination conditions.

To obtain the greatest benefit from the use of this study material you are recommended to proceed as follows.

(a) Complete a thorough preparation of each subject before attempting the questions on that subject. Answering questions is a test of what you have learnt and also a means of practising so that you develop a skill in presenting your answers. To attempt them before you are ready is not a fair test of your proficiency and the result may discourage you.

(b) Write your answers in examination conditions without referring to books, manuals or notes. Then refer to the suggested answer in this kit. The suggested answers are only suggestions. They are correct and complete on essentials but there is more than one way of writing an answer.

(c) Follow the subdivisions of the kit so that you use the questions to test what you can do after systematic preparation.

(d) Use the Practice and Revision Checklist in the kit to record your progress and to ensure that you have covered all areas.

The questions in this kit are designed to provide a wide coverage of the syllabus. By working through the questions, you should therefore be going over all the topics you ought to learn, and assessing your ability to answer examination-style questions well.

To use this kit properly, you should prepare your own answers to questions first, and then compare the suggested solutions with your own. Look to see how many points of similarity and difference there are between them.

Questions which call for a written answer are difficult to revise with, because it is human nature to be easily bored by writing out lengthy solutions. This is what we would suggest as a possible remedy for this problem.

(a) You should attempt a full written solution to one or two questions, in order to gain experience and familiarity with the task of producing solutions within the timescale allowed in the examination itself.

(b) For other questions you should prepare an *answer plan*. This is a list of the points that you would put into your solution, preferably in the order that you would make them.

(c) You should then read our solution and:

    (i) make a note of points that are new to you and that you think you should learn (perhaps by underlining certain sentences in the solution for future reference);

(ii) prepare an answer plan from our own solution, to make sure that you understand the relevance to the question of the points we raise. This useful discipline will ensure that you absorb the points in the solution more thoroughly.

Notes on specific areas of the syllabus

1. *The development of accounting standards*

   The regulatory regime has undergone a major overhaul. The Accounting Standards Committee (ASC) has been dissolved and has been replaced by the Accounting Standards Board (ASB) which is better staffed and funded and completely independent of the accountancy bodies, unlike the ASC. It should therefore be able to issue or amend standards more quickly. There is now also a Companies Act 1985 requirement that companies must disclose departures from accounting standards and that defective accounts must be revised if necessary by order of the courts. Directors can be fined for approving defective accounts. A Review Panel will be on the watch for defective accounts. Both the ASB and the Review Panel are overseen by an independent Financial Reporting Council (FRC).

   You can usefully revise this area by attempting questions 1 to 3.

2. *Income and value measurement*

   (a) SSAP 6 *Extraordinary items and prior year adjustments*

      (i) This standard defines *extraordinary items* and *exceptional items*. It requires that exceptional items should be included in profit or loss on ordinary activities for the year (but separately disclosed in the notes) whereas extraordinary items are shown after profit or loss on ordinary activities and before dividends. The practical importance of this distinction is that earnings per share (EPS), an important investors' ratio, is calculated on ordinary activities and so an extraordinary loss does not reduce EPS but an exceptional loss does (and *vice versa* for extraordinary and exceptional profits). Note the effect upon SSAP 6 of the Urgent Issues Task Force opinion (see Updating Notes).

      (ii) *Prior year adjustments* as defined by SSAP 6 arise from fundamental errors or charges in accounting policy and are used to restate profits or losses brought forward rather than to reduce or increase profit for the year. The aim of SSAP 6 here is to minimise *reserve accounting* and to ensure that all *realised* profits and losses are reflected in the result for the year as far as possible.

   (b) An important, but difficult, point to grasp is the concept of *capital maintenance*. The preparation of a balance sheet requires that values should be attributed to assets and liabilities outstanding at the end of an accounting period. The amount of an enterprise's net assets (or capital) will depend on the method adopted for calculating these values. Ignoring any capital injected or withdrawn during an accounting period, the profit earned for the period will be the difference between the value of capital at the beginning and the value of capital at the end of the period. Another way of stating this is to say that a company must maintain the value of its capital in order to break even; anything achieved in excess of this represents profit.

There are many systems of attributing values. In conventional historical cost accounting (HCA) assets are valued at historical cost less any amounts provided for or written off in respect of depreciation or diminution in value. A company maintains its capital if the net book value of its net assets remains constant, or increases (making an historical cost profit) over an accounting period.

In current purchasing power (CPP) accounting the value of capital is measured in terms of a stable monetary unit, £CPP. Profit is calculated by comparing opening and closing values of capital, as expressed in this unit. This system provides a measure of how well the business is maintaining its capital against the effects of *general* inflation.

In current cost accounting (CCA) assets are valued at their 'value to the business'. The underlying capital maintenance concept is that of maintaining the 'operating capability' of the business, its ability to provide the same amount of goods and services with its existing resources. CCA provides a measure of how well the business is maintaining its capital against the effects of *specific* inflation.

The theoretical aspects of this problem are discussed in Q 11 *Historical cost accounting* (11/89) and Q 12 *Changing price levels* (11/90). But you should note that the specimen paper included a long compulsory question on CPP computations. To practise the mechanics of CPP and CCA you should attempt questions 13 to 15 of the kit.

3. *Company accounts*

These fall into two types: those testing your knowledge and understanding of particular topics and published accounts questions.

There is very little to published accounts questions beyond rote learning of the statutory and quasi-statutory disclosure requirements. Q 26 *Caxton* helps you to assess your knowledge of the CA 1985 published accounts formats. When you are satisfied that you have the rote-learning under your belt make a careful attempt at a fully comprehensive question. Start with Q 27 *Chapman*, an easy question testing your ability to make elementary adjustments. Then attempt Q 28 *S plc* (11/89). At this stage your object should be to produce an answer which is complete, regardless of how long it takes. Compare your answer carefully with our suggested solution and fill in any gaps in your knowledge which may be revealed.

You should now go on to attempt as many other published accounts questions as you have time for, this time against the clock. Bear in mind that these questions often incorporate frills: for example, they may ask for detailed tax workings.

Questions on specific topics may include the following.

(a) SSAP 4 *Accounting for government grants*
     SSAP 5 *Accounting for value added tax*

     These are probably the most straightforward SSAPs. You can revise them both by tackling Q 17 *Newtrade*.

(b) SSAP 8 *Taxation under the imputation system*
     SSAP 15 *Accounting for deferred tax*

     A simple tax question to get you started is Q 18 *Strachan* (11/87). Then try Q 19 *Binstead*. The important points to remember are as follows.

- ACT quarterly returns and the interaction of franked payments and franked investment income
- Maximum ACT set-off rules
- Grossing up of franked investment income in the profit and loss account
- The components of the tax charge in the profit and loss account
- Treatment of ACT deferred asset
- Calculation of deferred tax provision
- Disclosure of deferred tax
- Treatment of income tax debtors and creditors

(c) SSAP 9 *Stocks and long-term contracts*

This covers two frequently examined topics: stock valuation and valuation of long-term contract WIP. To practise the stock valuation rules, try Q 20 *Miller* (11/83) and to revise long-term contracts do Q 21 *Long-term contracts* (5/89). The test your knowledge quiz also contains computational questions on these topics.

(d) SSAP 12 *Accounting for depreciation*
SSAP 19 *Accounting for investment properties*

These are fairly straightforward areas. You must know the rules laid down in SSAP 19 defining an 'investment property' and be able to write up the 'investment revaluation reserve'. Try Q 22 *Goneril, Regan and Cordelia* and Q 23 *Depreciation of property* (5/91).

(e) SSAP 17 *Accounting for post balance sheet events*
SSAP 18 *Accounting for contingencies*

The first step in working on these SSAPs is to get a clear grasp of the distinction between the two. Then learn the rules for treatment and disclosure of 'adjusting' and 'non-adjusting' post balance sheet events and the various degrees of remoteness for contingent gains and losses. Pay particular attention to the examples given in each SSAP as these are often the model for examination questions. Q 27 *Chapman* tests your ability to comply with these standards (amongst others).

(f) SSAP 22 *Accounting for goodwill*

(i) This SSAP defines goodwill as 'the difference between the value of a business as a whole and the aggregate fair values of its separable net assets'. It can be either *purchased* or *inherent* and may be *negative* (that is, a business might be worth less than the sum of its parts).

(ii) This SSAP has been under review (ED 47 is still in issue on goodwill) but currently it requires that positive purchased goodwill should either be capitalised and amortised over its estimated useful economic life or (the preferred option) it should be written off against (deducted from) reserves. ED 47 sought to enforce the amortisation method (over 20 years as a maximum), but this has proved unpopular.

(iii) Negative goodwill (also known as a capital reserve arising on consolidation) should be credited (added) to reserves.

(iv) Goodwill usually arises when one company purchases another. It would not be shown separately on the parent company's balance sheet which simply shows the cost or valuation of the investment. However, in consolidated accounts this investment is eliminated against its underlying components, that is, the subsidiary's fixed assets, current assets and so on and the parent's share of its post-acquisition profits. In cancelling off the parent's investment against the net assets acquired goodwill emerges as a balancing figure.

This is a very topical area and it is expected that the ASB will tackle the subject in due course. Q 24 *Goodwill* (11/89) covers the ground well.

4. *The accounts of groups of companies*

Group accounts are a major topic in the syllabus and you must develop a thorough understanding and fluency in handling examination questions. You should learn by heart the format of:

(a) a consolidated balance sheet;

(b) a consolidated profit and loss account.

Due to the introduction of FRS 1 *Cash flow statements (* see Updating Notes) you must now learn the format of the cash flow statement laid out in FRS 1, rather than the funds statement in SSAP 10.

Associated companies are a popular topic with examiners and you should ensure that you understand:

(a) how to calculate the balance sheet figure for 'interests in associated companies'; and

(b) how the results of associated companies are brought into and disclosed in the consolidated profit and loss account.

SSAP 1 *Accounting for associated companies*
SSAP 14 *Group accounts*
SSAP 23 *Accounting for acquisitions and mergers*

(i) SSAPs 1 and 14 have been updated by the ASB *Interim statement on consolidated accounts*, because the Companies Act 1985 has been amended by the Companies Act 1989 and much of the legal terminology used in the rules of group accounts has changed. However, the underlying principles are unchanged.

(ii) An investment in under 20% of a company's shares, where the investing company has no *significant influence* over the other company, is a *trade investment* and is not consolidated or treated in any way differently from any other investment.

(iii) A 20% + investment (or a smaller one where there *is* significant influence) is treated as an investment in an *associated company*. (A 20% + investment is presumed to give significant influence but if it can be shown that this does not exist then the investment is a trade investment).

(iv) An investment in >50% of another company's shares usually results in control of that company, which makes it a *subsidiary*. The CA 1989 introduced the idea of a controlled non-subsidiary, requiring such subsidiaries to be consolidated. This description of 'dominant influence' effectively outlawed off balance sheet finance involving such arrangements.

'13. Dominant influence is effective control with or without the legal rights that normally signify control. Control over an undertaking is the ability to direct that undertaking. In the context of consolidated accounts control means the ability of an undertaking to direct the financial and operating policies of another undertaking with a view to gaining benefits from its activities.'

(v) Associated companies are not consolidated. The investment is shown in the balance sheet at cost plus the investing company's share of post-acquisition retained profit. This is analysed in the notes.

	£'000
Group share of net assets	X
Premium paid on acquisition (= goodwill)	X
Value of investment under equity accounting	X

Equity accounting is the name for this treatment.

(vi) Subsidiaries are consolidated. There are two ways of doing this, the *acquisition method* and the *merger method*. See Q 16 *Poynton* for a description of the differences and attempt Q 46 *Newman* which requires you to use both techniques.

(vii) The acquisition method is much more common as few business combinations qualify for the *option* of consolidation under the merger method.

To get you started on consolidated accounts, try Q 33 *Aye and Bee*, which introduces goodwill and Q 34 *Bath* (11/82) which involves intra-group trading.

You should then attempt a comprehensive example without trying to time yourself. Compare your answer in detail with the suggested solution and make sure that you fully understand any errors you made. Best for this purpose are:

Q 35 *ABC* (5/89): balance sheet; and
Q 39 *Duxbury* (5/87): P & L account.

The syllabus also refers to consolidation of foreign subsidiaries. You should familiarise yourself with the techniques involved by attempting Q 43 *Oxford*.

5. *Company reorganisations*

The groundwork for dealing with questions on changes in capital structure consists of studying the accounting treatment of share issues and redemptions. The questions actually set in past CIMA examinations have gone beyond this and have required students to account for share issues and redemptions as one part of a scheme involving, perhaps, the acquisition of an unincorporated business or a reduction of capital. Q 50 *PQR* (5/89) is typical and should be studied carefully.

6. *Interpretation of accounts*

In past years, the examiners have been concerned, not so much with the standard of *calculating* ratios, but with the standard of *interpreting* them. A question on ratio analysis will invariably ask for some discussion based on the ratios you have calculated, so it is essential for you to know what each one signifies.

As a first step, think about which ratios are needed in order to answer the question. There is no point in doing more work than necessary, and the examiner will not be impressed by the calculation of irrelevant ratios. When you have picked out which ratios you need, calculate them and set them out in a table, where they can easily be referred to during the discussion part of the question.

The following is a useful approach to an interpretation of accounts question.

'Candidates should take care when planning their answer to this kind of question. Accountancy is a device for communicating information for decision making and it might help the candidate to see himself/herself in the position of the supplier of the report and the examiner as the recipient who is seeking advice. In other words, it is the job of the candidate to produce a convincing and comprehensible report. If this objective is to be achieved, it will help a great deal to divide the report into appropriate sections and to set out relevant calculations in an appendix to the report. The appropriate sections will depend on the nature of the investigation, but the following provide a reasonable framework.

- Identify recipient of report
- Introduction
- Financial developments
- Liquidity and gearing
- Asset turnover
- Profitability
- Conclusion

Within each of these sections comments should be made about the significance of the information contained in the statement of funds (if any) and an examination of the company's ratios compared with [the norm].'

The *main* ratios to remember (the list below is not exhaustive) are as follows.

(a) *Profitability ratios*

It should go without saying that a company ought to be profitable, and obvious checks on profitability are:

(i) whether the company has made a profit or loss on its ordinary activities;
(ii) by how much this year's profit or loss is bigger or smaller than last year's profit or loss.

Profit on ordinary activities *before* taxation is generally thought to be a better figure to use than profit after taxation, because there might be unusual variations in the tax charge from year to year which would not affect the underlying profitability of the company's operations.

Another profit figure that should be calculated is PBIT: profit before interest and tax. This is the amount of profit which the company earned before having to pay interest to the providers of loan capital. By providers of loan capital, we usually mean *longer term* loan capital, such as debentures and medium-term bank loans, which will be shown in the balance sheet as 'Creditors: amounts falling due after more than one year.'

Profit before interest and tax is therefore:

(i)   the profit on ordinary activities before taxation; *plus*
(ii) interest charges on long term loan capital.

It is impossible to assess profits or profit growth properly without relating them to the amount of funds (capital) that were employed in making the profits. The most important profitability ratio is therefore *return on capital employed* (ROCE), which states the profit as a percentage of the amount of capital employed.

$$\text{ROCE} = \frac{\text{Profit on ordinary activities before interest and taxation (PBIT)}}{\text{Capital employed}}$$

Capital employed = Shareholders' funds plus 'creditors: amounts falling due after more than one year' plus any long term provisions for liabilities and charges

A common variant is *return on equity* which measures profit after interest (and usually after tax) as a percentage of ordinary share capital and reserves.

It is often a good idea to sub-analyse ROCE, to find out more about why the ROCE is high or low, or better or worse than last year.

There are two factors that contribute towards a return on capital employed, both related to sales turnover.

(i)   *Profit margin.* A company might make a high or low profit margin on its sales. For example, a company that makes a profit of 25p per £1 of sales is making a bigger return on its turnover than another company making a profit of only 10p per £1 of sales.

(ii) *Asset turnover.* Asset turnover is a measure of how well the assets of a business are being used to generate sales. For example, if two companies each have capital employed of £100,000, and Company A makes sales of £400,000 per annum whereas Company B makes sales of only £200,000 per annum, Company A is making a higher turnover from the same amount of assets, twice as much asset turnover as Company B, and this will help A to make a higher return on capital employed than B. Asset turnover is expressed as 'x times' so that assets generate x times their value in annual turnover. Here, Company A's asset turnover is 4 times and B's is 2 times.

Profit margin and asset turnover together explain the ROCE, and if the ROCE is the primary profitability ratio, these other two are the secondary ratios. The relationship between the three ratios can be shown mathematically.

Profit margin x Asset turnover = ROCE

$$\frac{\text{PBIT}}{\text{Sales}} \quad x \quad \frac{\text{Sales}}{\text{Capital employed}} = \frac{\text{PBIT}}{\text{Capital employed}}$$

It might be tempting to think that a high profit margin is good, and a low asset turnover means sluggish trading. In broad terms, this is so. But there is a trade-off between profit margin and asset turnover, and you cannot look at one without allowing for the other.

(i)   A high profit margin means a high profit per £1 of sales, but if this also means that sales prices are high, there is a strong possibility that sales turnover will be depressed, and so asset turnover lower.

(ii) A high asset turnover means that the company is generating a lot of sales, but to do this, it might have to keep its prices down and so accept a low profit margin per £1 of sales.

(b) *Debt and gearing ratios*

Debt ratios are concerned with how much the company owes in relation to its size, whether it is getting into heavier debt or improving its situation, and whether its debt burden seems heavy or light.

(i) When a company is heavily in debt, and seeming to be getting even more heavily into debt, the thought that should occur to you is 'This can't go on!' If the company carries on wanting to borrow more, banks and other would-be lenders are very soon likely to say 'No more!' and the company might well find itself in trouble.

(ii) When a company is earning only a modest profit before interest and tax, and has a heavy debt burden, there will be very little profit left over for shareholders after the interest charges have been paid. And so if interest rates were to go up (on bank overdrafts and other borrowings) or the company were to borrow even more, it might soon be incurring interest charges in excess of PBIT. This might eventually lead to the liquidation of the company.

The *debt ratio* is the ratio of a company's total debts to its total assets.

(i) Assets consist of fixed assets at their balance sheet value, plus current assets.

(ii) Debts consist of all creditors, whether amounts falling due within one year or after more than one year.

You can ignore long-term provisions and liabilities, such as deferred taxation.

There is no absolute guide to the maximum safe debt ratio, but as a very general guide, you might regard 50% as a safe limit to debt. In practice, many companies operate successfully with a higher debt ratio than this, but 50% is nonetheless a helpful benchmark. In addition, if the debt ratio is over 50% and getting worse, the company's debt position will be worth looking at more carefully.

The *capital gearing ratio* is a measure of the proportion of a company's capital that is prior charge capital. It is measured as:

$$\frac{\text{prior charge capital}}{\text{total capital}}$$

(i) Prior charge capital = creditors: amounts falling due after more than one year (*including* loan capital, if itemised separately in the balance sheet, and *excluding* long term corporation tax liabilities, since these do not have a claim over any profits in the form of interest) plus preference share capital (if any). There is also a view that a bank overdraft, although shown as a current liability in the balance sheet, is often a permanent feature of a company's debt structure and so is as good as long term debt. If this view is taken, the bank overdraft should also be included as prior charge capital, together with any other short term loans which are likely to be replaced when they mature with a new longer term loan.

(ii) Total capital is ordinary share capital and reserves plus prior charge capital plus any long term liabilities or provisions. We would also include minority interests in group accounts.

It is easier to identify the same figure for total capital as total assets less current liabilities, which you will find given to you in the balance sheet.

As with the debt ratio, there is no absolute limit to what a gearing ratio ought to be. A company with a gearing ratio of more than 50% is said to be highly geared (whereas low gearing means a gearing ratio of less than 50%).

A similar ratio to the gearing ratio is the *debt/equity ratio*, which is the ratio of:

$$\frac{\text{prior charge capital}}{\text{ordinary share capital and reserves}}$$

This gives us the same sort of information as the gearing ratio, and a ratio of 100% or more would indicate high gearing.

The significance of the gearing ratios is that:

(i)   the more highly geared the company, the greater the risk that little (if anything) will be available to distribute by way of dividend to the ordinary shareholders; and

(ii)   a high geared company has a large amount of interest to pay annually (assuming that the debt is external borrowing rather than preference shares). If those borrowings are 'secured' in any way (and debentures in particular are secured), then the holders of the debt are perfectly entitled to force the company to realise assets to pay their interest if funds are not available from other sources. Clearly, the more highly geared a company the more likely this is to occur when and if profits fall.

(c)   *Working capital liquidity ratios*

The 'standard' test of liquidity is the *current ratio*. It can be obtained from the balance sheet, and is the ratio of:

$$\frac{\text{current assets}}{\text{current liabilities}}$$

The idea behind this is that a company should have enough current assets that give a promise of 'cash to come' to meet its future commitments to pay off its current liabilities. Obviously, a ratio in excess of 1 should be expected. Otherwise, there would be the prospect that the company might be unable to pay its debts on time. In practice, a ratio comfortably in excess of 1 should be expected, but what is 'comfortable' varies between different types of businesses.

Companies are not able to convert all their current assets into cash very quickly. In particular, some manufacturing companies might hold large quantities of raw material stocks, which must be used in production to create finished goods stocks. Finished goods stocks might be warehoused for a long time, or sold on lengthy credit. In such businesses, where stock turnover is slow, most stocks are not very 'liquid' assets, because the cash cycle is so long. For these reasons, we calculate an additional liquidity ratio, known as the quick ratio or acid test ratio.

The *quick ratio*, or *acid test ratio*, is $\dfrac{\text{current assets less stocks}}{\text{current liabilities}}$

This ratio should ideally be at least 1 for companies with a slow stock turnover. For companies with a fast stock turnover, a quick ratio can be comfortably less than 1 without suggesting that the company should be in cash flow trouble.

Both the current ratio and the quick ratio offer an indication of the company's liquidity position, but the absolute figures should not be interpreted too literally. It is often theorised that an 'acceptable' current ratio is 1.5 and an 'acceptable' quick ratio is 0.8, but these should only be used as a guide. Different businesses operate in very different ways.

What is important is the trend of these ratios. From this, one can easily ascertain whether liquidity is improving or deteriorating. If a company has traded for the last 10 years (very successfully) with current ratios of 0.43 and quick ratios of 0.12 then it should be supposed that they can continue in business with those levels of liquidity. If in the following year their current ratio were to fall to 0.38 and their quick ratio to 0.09, then further investigation into their liquidity situation would be appropriate. It is the relative position that is far more important than the absolute figures.

Don't forget the other side of the coin either. A current ratio and a quick ratio can get bigger than they need to be. A company that has large volumes of stocks and debtors might be over-investing in working capital, and so tying up more funds in the business than it needs to. This would suggest poor management of debtors (credit) or stocks by the company.

(d) *Working capital turnover ratios*

A rough measure of the average length of time it takes for a company's debtors to pay what they owe is the *'debtor days' ratio*, or average debtors' payment period.

It is only an estimated average payment period, but it is calculated as follows.

$$\frac{\text{trade debtors}}{\text{sales}} \quad \text{x} \quad 365 \text{ days}$$

Sales are usually made on 'normal credit terms' of payment within 30 days. Debtor days *significantly* in excess of this might be representative of poor management of funds of a business. However, some companies must allow generous credit terms to win customers. Exporting companies in particular may have to carry large amounts of debtors, and so their average collection period might be well in excess of 30 days.

The *trend* of the collection period (debtor days) over time is probably the best guide. If debtor days are increasing year on year, this is indicative of a poorly managed credit control function (and potentially therefore a poorly managed company!)

Another ratio worth calculating is the *stock turnover period*, or stock days. This is another estimated figure, obtainable from published accounts, which indicates the average number of days that items of stock are held for. As with the average debt collection period, however, it is only an approximate estimated figure, but one which should be reliable enough for comparing changes year on year.

The number of stock days is calculated as: $\dfrac{\text{stock}}{\text{cost of sales}} \quad \text{x} \quad 365$

The reciprocal of the fraction, $\dfrac{\text{cost of sales}}{\text{stock}}$

is termed the stock turnover, and is another measure of how vigorously a business is trading. A lengthening stock turnover period from one year to the next indicates:

(a) a slowdown in trading; or
(b) a build-up in stock levels, perhaps suggesting that the investment in stocks is becoming excessive.

Finally, make sure you know the limitations of ratio analysis.

Recommended essential practice for this area is Q 56 *C plc* (11/89) and Q 57 *Meteor* (5/90).

Other types of question in this area ask for cash flow statements. As SSAP 10 has now been replaced by FRS 1 you must know the FRS 1 cash flow format by heart and you must be able to interpret the statements you produce. The examiner has said that FRS 1 will be examinable from May 1992 onwards. Questions relating to SSAP 10 have been retained for the sake of completeness and comparability as you may be asked to compare and contrast the information presented in cash flow statements and SSAFs. We have included a tutorial question on cash flow statements as it is unclear what form questions will take in the exam. However, you *must* make sure that you also learn the format for *consolidated* cash flow statements (see Updating Notes).

Value added statements should not be overlooked. Try Q 55 *Value*.

Finally, you must have a good knowledge of SSAP 3 *Earnings per share*. There are three full EPS questions in the kit and you should try all of them. The only way to master SSAP 3 is repeated numerical practice. Try Q 59 *Pilum* and Q 60 *R plc* (5/89).

Here is a list of the UK accounting standards in force at the time of writing (December 1991). The gaps in the list are SSAP 7 (issued in 1974 but withdrawn in 1977), SSAP 11 (replaced by SSAP 15) and SSAP 16 on current cost accounting. SSAP 16 aroused considerable controversy and ASC eventually withdrew it in 1988. SSAP 10 and ED 54 (SSAF and cash flow statments respectively) were replaced by FRS 1 in September 1991.

Number	Title
FRS 1	Cash flow statements
SSAP 1	Accounting for associated companies*
SSAP 2	Disclosure of accounting policies
SSAP 3	Earnings per share
SSAP 4	Accounting for government grants
SSAP 5	Accounting for value added tax
SSAP 6	Extraordinary items and prior year adjustments
SSAP 8	The treatment of taxation under the imputation system in the accounts of companies
SSAP 9	Stocks and long-term contracts
SSAP 12	Accounting for depreciation
SSAP 13	Accounting for research and development
SSAP 14	Group accounts*
SSAP 15	Accounting for deferred tax
SSAP 17	Accounting for post balance sheet events
SSAP 18	Accounting for contingencies
SSAP 19	Accounting for investment properties
SSAP 20	Foreign currency translation
SSAP 21	Accounting for leases and hire purchase contracts
SSAP 22	Accounting for goodwill
SSAP 23	Accounting for acquisitions and mergers
SSAP 24	Accounting for pension costs
SSAP 25	Segmental reporting

*As amended in December 1990 by the ASB's *Interim Statement on consolidated accounts*.

Also at the time of writing, there are several Exposure Drafts which have not been made into standards.

ED 46	Disclosure of related party transactions
ED 47	Accounting for goodwill
ED 48	Accounting for acquisitions and mergers
ED 49	Reflecting the substance of transactions in assets and liabilities
ED 50	Consolidated accounts
ED 51	Accounting for fixed assets and revaluations
ED 52	Accounting for intangible fixed assets
ED 53	Fair value in the context of acquisition accounting
ED 55	Accounting for investments

The ASB is considering the responses to these EDs (see ASB work programme in Updating Notes).

Only two SORPs (on pension scheme accounts and on accounting by charities) were published by the ASC. These have not been adopted by the ASB.

Accounting Standards Board

On 1 August 1990 the Accounting Standards Committee (ASC) was disbanded. It was replaced as a standard setting body by the Accounting Standards Board (ASB). The standard setting process has been strengthened and simplified. At the date of preparation of this kit, the following material has been published by the ASB.

December 1990	Interim statement	Consolidated accounts
April 1991	Discussion draft	Statement of principles
		Presentation of financial information
April 1991	Discussion draft	The structure of financial statements
		Reporting of financial performance
July 1991		Statement of Aims
July 1991	Exposure draft	Foreword to accounting standards
July 1991	Exposure draft	Objectives of financial statements and
		Qualitative characteristics of financial information
September 1991	Financial reporting standard	Cash flow statements

(The last ED will form two chapters of the Board's Statement of Principles.)

The contents of the above documents are discussed in the Updating Notes where applicable. The ASB has also published its intended work programme and pronouncements on a variety of issues.

The ASB adopted all SSAPs extant at 1 August 1990, giving the SSAPs the force of law. All current EDs will be discussed as potential accounting standards. The UK SORPs have not been adopted.

UPDATING NOTES

If you have been studying with the latest edition of the BPP *Advanced Financial Accounting* study text you will already be up to date for developments up to September 1991. Brief notes are given below on developments since then with some extra notes for those who may have older texts. You are recommended to pay close attention to *Management Accounting* and *CIMA Student* for further changes. Remember that the examiner has said that candidates need to be *completely up to date* for the examination.

1. **Accounting Standards Board: work programme**

    The ASB's consultative process leads to the setting of Financial Reporting Standards (FRSs). To produce an FRS, first a working Draft for Discussion (DD) is published to get feedback from people closely involved with or with a direct interest in the standard setting process. The DD, as a result of this process, is converted into a Financial Reporting Exposure Draft (FRED), which has the same status as an ED had when the ASC was in existence. Candidates should be aware of the contents of FRSs and FREDs published by the ASB. The syllabus rule for CIMA examinations is that legislation, standards and so on will be examinable in a year if they were published before 31 December in the previous year.

    In September 1991 the ASB updated its intended work programme, although in general terms and without commitment to specific dates of publication. The following points were raised.

    (a) Of the ASC exposure drafts remaining, four form a natural group and these will be dealt with 'in tandem' where possible. These are as follows.

    -   ED 47 *Accounting for goodwill*
    -   ED 52 *Accounting for intangible fixed assets*
    -   ED 48 *Accounting for acquisitions and mergers*
    -   ED 53 *Fair value in the context of acquisition accounting*

    The ASB feels that these EDs will form the 'focus of its next phase of activity', presumably forming the next two FRSs.

    (b) The two exposure drafts ED 46 *Related party transactions* and ED 55 *Accounting for investments* involve various problems related to current legislation and controversy. It is unlikely that these EDs will be dealt with in the near future. The remaining EDs (49, 50, 51 and 52) are covered by the work programme or documents already published.

    (c) The ASB has also said that 'it seems likely that work will be required in the not too distant future on the following SSAPs.

    -   SSAP 12 *Accounting for depreciation*
    -   SSAP 19 *Accounting for investment properties*
    -   SSAP 15 *Accounting for deferred tax*
    -   SSAP 20 *Foreign currency translation*
    -   SSAP 21 *Accounting for leases and hire purchase contracts*
    -   SSAP 24 *Accounting for pension costs*'

    (d) The ASB also wishes to undertake at least one major project during 1992. Those mentioned in the work programme include the following.

    (i) *Management discussion and analysis (MD & A)*. This is a discussion and analysis by management of the company's financial condition and results of operations. It is already required as part of a company's annual filing in the USA.

(ii) *Historical summaries*. These would cover relevant comparative figures for the last ten years. They were recommended by the Stock Exchange to all listed companies in 1964 but were never made mandatory.

(e) Briefly, the ASB mentions other topics which may be of interest in the near future.

- Capitalisation of interest
- Interim financial reports
- New financial instruments
- Impairment of assets
- Interest rate methods (the use of discounting in financial statements).

Some of these topics are already being studied by international standard-setting bodies or standing-setting bodies in other countries (such as the USA).

You should keep a look out for any other publications from the ASB which appear during your studies.

In July 1991 the ASB published the definitive *Statements of aims* and the following financial reporting exposure drafts.

(a) Foreword to accounting standards.
(b) Statement of principles: the objective of financial statements and the qualitative characteristics of financial information.

2. Statement of aims

The *Statement of aims* is produced here in full as it is very brief.

'*Aims*

The aims of the Accounting Standards Board (the Board) are to establish and improve standards of financial accounting and reporting, for the benefit of users, preparers and auditors of financial information.

Achieving the aims

The Board intends to achieve its aims by:

1. Developing principles to guide it in establishing standards and to provide a framework within which others can exercise judgement in resolving accounting issues.

2. Issuing new accounting standards, or amending existing ones, in response to evolving business practices, new economic developments and deficiencies being identified in current practice.

3. Addressing urgent issues promptly.

Fundamental guidelines

1. To be objective and to ensure that the information resulting from the application of accounting standards faithfully represents the underlying commercial activity. Such information should be neutral in the sense that it is free from any form of bias intended to influence users in a particular direction and should not be designed to favour any group of users or preparers.

2. To ensure that accounting standards are clearly expressed and supported by a reasoned analysis of the issues.

3. To determine what should be incorporated in accounting standards based on research, public consultation and careful deliberation about the usefulness of the resulting information.

4. To ensure that through a process of regular communication, accounting standards are produced with due regard to international developments.

5. To ensure that there is consistency both from one accounting standard to another and between accounting standards and company law.

6. To issue accounting standards only when the expected benefits exceed the perceived costs. The Board recognises that reliable cost/benefit calculations are seldom possible. However, it will always assess the need for standards in terms of the significance and extent of the problem being addressed and will choose the standard which appears to be most effective in cost/benefit terms.

7. To take account of the desire of the financial community for evolutionary rather than revolutionary change in the reporting process where this is consistent with the objectives outlined above.'

3. Exposure draft: Foreword to accounting standards

This FRED is similar in nature to the foreword used by the ASC in relation to SSAPs. The contents are listed briefly here.

(a) *Authority*. This section refers to:

- the legal authority of FRSs in relation to the Act;
- directors responsibilities to prepare accounts showing a true and fair view;
- the responsibility of members of CCAB bodies in industry and practice in relation to financial statements (as preparers or auditors);
- CCAB bodies may investigate non-compliance.

(b) *Scope and application*. The standards apply to:

- financial statements of a reporting entity that are intended to give a true and fair view;
- group accounts in the UK (and Ireland) including any overseas entities.

(c) *Compliance with accounting standards*. The following rules and comments are laid down.

(i) It will normally be necessary to comply with the standards to show a true and fair view.
(ii) In applying the standards, the user should be guided by their spirit and reasoning.
(iii) In *rare* cases it may be necessary to depart from a standard to show a true and fair view.
(iv) Departures should be dealt with objectively according to the 'economic and commercial characteristics of the circumstances'; the departure and its financial effect should be disclosed.
(v) The Review Panel and the DTI have powers and procedures to investigate departures and to require a restatement through the court.

(d) *The public sector.* 'The prescription of accounting requirements for the public sector in the United Kingdom is a matter for the Government'.

(e) *The issue of an FRS.* This section covers the procedures for discussion, consultation and drafting.

(f) *Accounting standards and the legal framework.* Consistency with UK and EEC law is aimed for.

(g) *International accounting standards.* An FRS will contain a section explaining how it relates to the IAS dealing with the same topic. 'The Board supports the IASC in its aims to harmonise international financial reporting'.

As you can see, the foreword merely gives the FRSs a context in relation to other standard setting bodies, company law and users and preparers of accounts.

4. **The objective of financial statements and the qualitative characteristics of financial information**

This FRED forms the first two chapters of the *Statement of principles.* Its contents are very closely associated with the IASC text *Framework for the preparation and presentation of financial statements;* in fact, the wording of the *Framework* is used wherever it is considered satisfactory. The contents of the FRED are listed briefly here.

(a) *Chapter I: the objective of financial statements.* This chapter reproduces terms and ideas introduced by the earlier Discussion Draft *Statement of principles: presentation of financial information.* The main points raised are as follows.

    (i) '12. The objective of financial statements is to provide information about the financial position, performance and financial adaptability of an enterprise that is useful to a wide range of users in making economic decisions.'

    (ii) The limitations of financial statements are emphasised as well as the strengths.

    (iii) All of the components of financial statements (balance sheet, profit and loss account, cash flow statement) are interrelated 'because they reflect different aspects of the same transactions...' The notes to the financial statements 'form an integral part of the financial statements'.

    (iv) The draft emphasises the ways financial statements provide information about the financial position of an enterprise. The main elements which affect the position of the company are:

        ● the economic resources it controls;
        ● its financial structure;
        ● its liquidity and solvency;
        ● its capacity to adapt to changes in the environment in which it operates (called *financial adaptability*).

    The draft discusses the importance of each of these elements and how they are disclosed in the financial statements.

(b) *Chapter II:* Quantitative characteristics of financial statements. The ED gives a diagramatic representation of the discussion, shown overleaf.

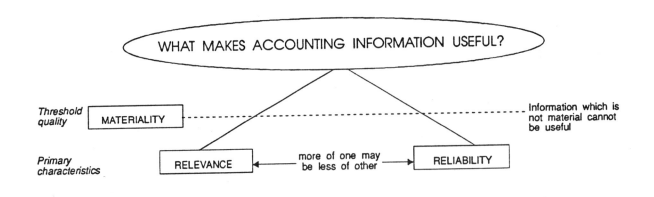

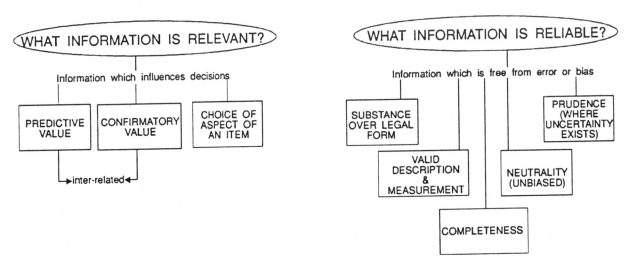

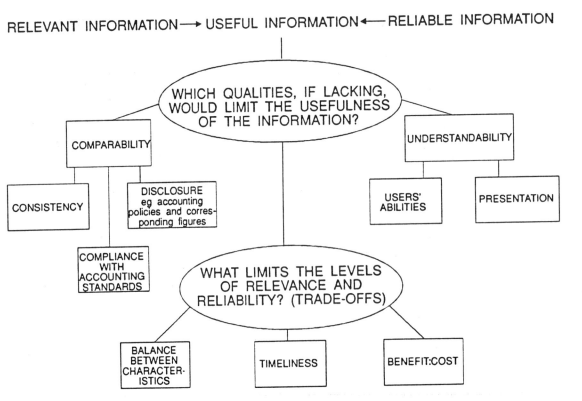

    (i)   *Primary* qualitative characteristics are *relevance* and *reliability*.

    (ii) *Secondary* qualitative characteristics are *comparability* and *understanding*.

The diagram shown here is reasonably explanatory. The ED ends with an appendix which highlights the departures from the IASC text.

You should read the full text of these FREDS and check the extent of knowledge required for each sitting of this examination.

5. Discussion drafts

The ASB have issued two discussion drafts as noted in the introduction to the text; part of one of the DDs was incorporated into the FRED *The objective of financial statements and the qualitative characteristics of financial information* discussed above. We will not discuss the content of these drafts in detail, but you should be aware that the draft on the reporting of financial performance proposes a radical alteration of the profit and loss account format. This would involve separating out results of continuing activities, discontinued activities and acquisitions on the face of the profit and loss account.

6. FRS 1 Cash flow statements

In September 1991 the Accounting Standards Board (ASB) published FRS 1 *Cash flow statements*. The provisions of FRS 1 apply to accounting periods ending on or after 23 March 1992. It supersedes SSAP 10 *Statements of source and application of funds*. The FRS sets out the structure of a cash flow statement and it also sets the minimum level of disclosure. A commentary on the FRS is given here and a tutorial question has been included in the question bank (Q 54). The examiner has said that examination questions could be set on cash flow statements from May 1992, but it is unclear what form these questions will take. A question on funds flow statements has been retained for comparison and completeness.

(a)   The *objective* of the statement is shown here in full.

    '(1)   The objective of the FRS is to require reporting entities falling within its scope to report on a standard basis their cash generation and cash absorption for a period. To this end reporting entities are required to provide a primary financial statement analysing cash flows under the standard headings of 'operating activities', 'returns on investments and servicing of finance', 'taxation', 'investing activities' and 'financing', disclosed in that sequence, in order to assist users of the financial statements in their assessment of the reporting entity's liquidity, viability and financial adaptability. The objective of the standard headings is to ensure that cash flows are reported in a form that highlights the significant components of cash flow and facilitates comparison of the cash flow performance of different businesses.'

(b)   Some of the *definitions* are worth showing in full; in particular, note the definition of cash equivalents.

    '(2)   *Cash*
         Cash in hand and deposits repayable on demand with any bank or other financial institution. Cash includes cash in hand and deposits denominated in foreign currencies.

      (3)   *Cash equivalents*
Short term, highly liquid investments which are readily convertible into known amounts of cash without notice and which were within three months of maturity when acquired; less advances from banks repayable within three months from the date of the advance. Cash equivalents include investments and advances denominated in foreign currencies provided that they fulfil the above criteria.

      (4)   *Cash flow*
An increase or decrease in an amount of cash or cash equivalent resulting from a transaction.'

(c) *Scope.* All 'reporting entities', unless excluded by the paragraphs shown below, must produce a cash flow statement as part of the financial statements. The cash flow statement is called a 'primary statement' which places it on an equivalent level with the balance sheet and profit and loss account.

(d) The exclusions from the requirement to prepare a cash flow statement are as follows.

      '(8)   The FRS applies to all financial statements intended to give a true and fair view of the financial position and profit or loss (or income and expenditure) except those of entities that are:

         (i)   companies incorporated under the Companies Acts and entitled to the exemptions available in Section 246 to 249 of the Companies Act 1985 for small companies when filing accounts with the Registrar of Companies (these sections lay out the definitions of 'small' and 'medium' sized companies.

        (ii)   entities which would have come under category (i) above had they been companies incorporated under companies legislation; or

       (iii)   wholly owned subsidiary undertakings of a parent undertaking which is established under the law of a member Statement of the European Community where:

           (1)   the parent undertaking publishes, in English, consolidated financial statements which include the subsidiary undertaking concerned, drawn up in accordance with United Kingdom or Republic of Ireland companies legislation or the EC Seventh Company Law Directive; and

           (2)   those consolidated financial statements include a consolidated cash flow statement dealing with the cash flows of the group; and

           (3)   that cash flow statement gives sufficient information to enable a user of the financial statements to derive the totals of the amounts required to be shown under each of the standard headings set out in this FRS; or

        (iv)   Building societies......; or

        (v)   Mutual life assurance companies.'

(e) *Preparation of cash flows.* All cash inflows and outflows must be shown in the statements, other than those resulting from the sale or purchase of 'cash equivalents' (because cash equivalents are treated as cash in the statement). 'Transactions which do not result in cash flows .... should not be reported in the cash flow statement.'

(f) *Format for cash flow statements*

'(12) The cash flow statement should list the inflows and outflows of cash and cash equivalents for the period under the following standard headings:

operating activities;
returns on investments and servicing of finance;
taxation;
investing activities; and
financing

in that order and showing a total for each standard heading and a total of the net cash inflow or outflow before financing. '

(g) *Classification of cash flows by standard heading.* The standard lays out the items to be included under each heading and then discusses other items which may cause difficulties in classification. You should note that cash flow must be *material* to be included (it must be relatively large or of importance for some other significant reason). The standard allows further subdivision of the heading and where an item has not been specified in the standard, then it should be included under the most appropriate heading.

The standard does allow departure from the classifications laid out here, but only in rare cases, where to follow the standard would not show a true representation of the activities of the entity.

The illustrative examples shown here is taken from the standard. The content under each heading is self explanatory (when read in conjunction with the notes to the cash flow statement).

(h) *Illustrative example 1: Single company*

XYZ LIMITED
CASH FLOW STATEMENT FOR THE YEAR ENDED 31 MARCH 1992

	£'000	£'000
Net cash inflow from operating activities		6,889
Returns on investments and servicing of finance		
Interest received	3,011	
Interest paid	(12)	
Dividends paid	(2,417)	
Net cash inflow from returns on investments and servicing of finance		582
Taxation		
Corporation tax paid (including advance corporation tax)	(2,922)	
Tax paid		(2,922)
Investing activities		
Payments to acquire intangible fixed assets	(71)	
Payments to acquire tangible fixed assets	(1,496)	
Receipts from sales of tangible fixed assets	42	
Net cash outflow from investing activities		(1,525)
Net cash inflow before financing		3,024
Financing		
Issue of ordinary capital	211	
Repurchase of debenture loan	(149)	
Expenses paid in connection with share issues	(5)	
Net cash inflow from financing		57
Increase in cash and cash equivalents		3,081

UPDATING NOTES

Notes to the cash flow statement

1. Reconciliation of operating profit to net cash inflow from operating activities

	£'000
Operating profit	6,022
Depreciation charges	893
Loss on sale of tangible fixed assets	6
Increase/(decrease) in stocks	(194)
Increase/(decrease) in debtors	(72)
(Increase)/decrease in creditors	234
Net cash inflow from operating activities	6,889

2. Analysis of changes in cash and cash equivalents during the year

	£'000
Balance at 1 April 1991	21,373
Net cash inflow	3,081
Balance at 31 March 1992	24,454

3. Analysis of the balances of cash and cash equivalents as shown in the balance sheet

	1992 £'000	1991 £'000	Change in year £'000
Cash at bank and in hand	529	681	(152)
Short-term investments	23,936	20,700	3,236
Bank overdrafts	(11)	(8)	(3)
	24,454	21,373	3,081

4. Analysis of changes in finance during the year

	Share capital £'000	Debenture loan £'000
Balance at 1 April 1991	27,411	156
Cash inflow/(outflow) from financing	211	(149)
Profit on repurchase of debenture loan for less than its book value		(7)
Balance at 31 March 1992	27,622	–

Illustrative example 2: Group

XYZ GROUP PLC
CASH FLOW STATEMENT FOR THE YEAR ENDED 31 MARCH 1992

	£'000	£'000
Operating activities		
Cash received from customers	195,016	
Cash payments to suppliers	(109,225)	
Cash paid to and on behalf of employees	(56,434)	
Other cash payments	(12,345)	
Net cash inflow from continuing operating activities	17,012	
Net cash outflow in respect of discontinued activities and reorganisation costs	(990)	
Net cash inflow from operating activities		16,022
Returns on investments and servicing of finance		
Interest received	508	
Interest paid	(2,389)	
Interest element of finance lease rentals payments	(373)	
Dividend received from associated undertaking	15	
Dividends paid	(2,606)	
Net cash outflow from returns on investments and servicing of finance		(4,845)
Taxation		
UK corporation tax paid	(2,880)	
Overseas tax paid	(7)	
Tax paid		(2,887)
Investing activities		
Purchase of tangible fixed assets	(3,512)	
Purchase of subsidiary undertakings (net of cash and cash equivalents acquired) (see note 7)	(18,221)	
Sale of plant and machinery	1,052	
Sale of business (see note 8)	4,208	
Sale of trade investment	1,595	
Net cash outflows in respect of unsuccessful takeover bid	(3,811)	
		(18,689)
Net cash outflow before financing		(10,399)
Financing		
Issue of ordinary share capital	(49)	
New secured loan repayable in 1995	(1,091)	
New unsecured loan repayable in 1993	(1,442)	
New short-term loans	(2,006)	
Repayment of amounts borrowed	847	
Capital element of finance lease rental payments	1,342	
Net cash inflow from financing		(2,399)
Decrease in cash and cash equivalents		(8,000)
		(10,399)

33

Notes to the cash flow statement

1. Reconciliation of operating profit to net cash inflow from operating activities

	£'000
Operating profit	20,249
Depreciation charges	3,158
Profit on sale of tangible fixed assets	(50)
Increase in stocks	(12,263)
Increase in debtors	(3,754)
Increase in creditors	9,672
Net cash inflow from continuing operating activities	17,012
Net cash outflow in respect of discontinued activities and reorganisation costs	(990)
Net cash inflow from operating activities	16,022

2. Analysis of changes in cash and cash equivalents during the year

	£'000
Balance at 1 April 1992	78
Net cash outflow before adjustments for the effect of foreign exchange rate changes	(8,000)
Effect of foreign exchange rate changes	(102)
Balance at 31 March 1992	8,024

3. Analysis of the balances of cash and cash equivalents as shown in the balance sheet

	1992	1991	Change in year
	£'000	£'000	£'000
Cash at bank and in hand	1,041	1,279	(238)
Bank overdrafts	(9,065)	(1,201)	(7,864)
	(8,024)	78	(8,102)

4. Analysis of changes in financing during the year

	Share capital (including premium)	Loans and finance lease obligations
	£'000	£'000
Balance at 1 April	10,334	7,589
Cash inflows from financing	49	2,350
Shares issued for non-cash consideration	9,519	
Loans and finance lease obligations of subsidiary undertakings acquired during the year		3,817
Inception of finance lease contracts		2,845
Balance at 31 March 1992	19,902	16,601

(Note to preparers of financial statements

The disclosures set out below in respect of non-cash transactions may be combined with information disclosed elsewhere in the financial statements, for example the disclosure in respect of subsidiary undertakings acquired during the year could be combined with the disclosures required by paragraph 13(5) of Schedule 4A to the Companies Act 1985.)

5. Major non-cash transactions

    (a) During the year the group entered into finance lease arrangements in respect of assets with a total capital value at the inception of the leases of £2,845,000.

    (b) Part of the consideration for the purchases of subsidiary undertakings and the sale of a business that occurred during the year comprised shares and loan notes respectively. Further details of the acquisitions and the disposal are set out below.

6. Purchase of subsidiary undertakings

	£'000
Net assets acquired	
Tangible fixed assets	12,194
Investments	1
Stocks	9,384
Debtors	13,856
Taxation recoverable	1,309
Cash at bank and in hand	1,439
Creditors	(21,715)
Bank overdrafts	(6,955)
Loans and finance leases	(3,817)
Deferred taxation	(165)
Minority shareholders' interests	(9)
	5,522
Goodwill	16,702
	22,224
Satisfied by	
Shares allotted	9,519
Cash	12,705
	22,224

The subsidiary undertakings acquired during the year contributed £1,502,000 to the group's net operating cash flows, paid £1,308,000 in respect of net returns on investments and servicing of finance, paid £522,000 in respect of taxation and utilised £2,208,000 for investing activities.

7. Analysis of the net outflow of cash and cash equivalents in respect of the purchase of subsidiary undertakings

	£'000
Cash consideration	12,705
Cash at bank and in hand acquired	(1,439)
Bank overdrafts of acquired subsidiary undertakings	6,955
Net outflow of cash and cash equivalents in respect of the purchase of subsidiaries	18,221

8. Sale of business

	£'000
Net assets disposed of	
Fixed assets	775
Stocks	5,386
Debtors	474
	6,635
Loss on disposal	(1,227)
	5,408
Satisfied by	
Loan notes	1,200
Cash	4,208
	5,408

The business sold during the year contributed £200,000 to the group's net operating cash flows, paid £252,000 in respect of net returns on investments and servicing of finance, paid £145,000 in respect of taxation and utilised £209,000 for investing activities.

(i) *Changes from SSAP 10*
The most obvious change from SSAP 10 is as follows.

‘4   The FRS requires reporting entities to report cash flows rather than accrual based funds flows and the basic structure of the cash flow statement is prescribed. ’

The standard notes other changes.

(i) SSAP 10 allowed exemption from preparing a funds statement only to those entities with turnover or gross income of less than £25,000. The small company exemption is far more generous in the FRS, leading to a much higher proportion of exemptions.

(ii) The so called 'line by line' method of accounting for subsidiary disposals or purchases is no longer permitted. The purchase or sales consideration must now be shown under investing activities.

(iii) The standard also notes that the funds statement did not provide any new information; it merely rearranged items already included in the balance sheet and profit and loss account. Additionally SSAP 10 did not provide a definition of funds or set out a basic structure for a statement.

(j) *Changes from ED 54*
Briefly, the following changes are mentioned.

(i) *Scope.* The ED 54 had the same exemption rules for preparation of the cash flow statements as SSAP 10 had for funds flow statements. As mentioned above, these exemptions have been relaxed in the FRS.

(ii) *Reporting net cash flow from operating activities.* ED 54 considered two methods, direct and indirect, for reporting net cash flow from operating activities. It was felt that the direct method could be costly and therefore the FRS allows the indirect method, but recommends the direct method.

(iii) *Interest and dividend receipts and payments.* The FRS requires interest received and paid to be shown under 'returns on investments and servicing of finance' rather than under operating activities. Additionally, the FRS does *not* distinguish between interest paid (as contractual) and dividends paid (as discretionary). Dividends received and dividends paid should be shown under 'returns on investments and servicing of finance'.

(iv) *Taxation.* The FRS requires disclosure of cash flows relating to taxation of income and capital gains to be shown in its own separate section rather than as cash flows relating to operating activities as suggested by ED 54. Additionally, the FRS requires cash flows to be disclosed exclusive of VAT, rather than inclusive as suggested by ED 54.

(v) *Cash or net debt.* The FRS satisfies the requirements of those who feel that cash flow statements should analyse the movement in an entity's net cash or debt position. This has been done by 'splitting the servicing of finance from the movement in principal amounts of finance, requiring a total giving the net cash flow before financing and by requiring a reconciliation of the items within the financing section of the statement to the opening and closing balance sheets.'

7. Other matters

(a) The ASB has produced the *Interim statement on consolidated accounts* which enacts various changes to SSAPs 1 and 14 to bring them into line with the CA 1989. These provisions are already incorporated into the questions in this kit and do not require further study. (The July 1991 BPP Study Text was fully updated with these changes.) The statement will provide part of the basis of the ASB's new FRS on consolidated accounts.

(b) In July 1991 the Urgent Issues Task Force (UITF) issued a ruling to stop the practice of accounting for Euro-convertible bonds using a lower rate of interest (the rate paid) rather than the market rate; this was because the holder had an option to redeem these bonds at a large premium if conversion to shares proved unattractive. There was, therefore, a much higher implied rate of interest.

(c) Also in July 1991, the Review Panel wrote to over 100 large companies (and their auditors) informing them that they were not following a key provision of the 1989 Companies Act. This provision states that companies must specifically state in their accounts whether they have been prepared in accordance with accounting standards, and to detail and justify any significant departures from the standards.

(d) *Public Sector Liaison Committee*

The Accounting Standards Board recently announced the formation of its Public Sector Liaison Committee (PSLC).

The committee's terms of reference are:

● as a matter of immediate and important priority to inform itself of the proposals being developed by the ASB for a new approach to the primary financial statements in the private sector and the formation of a new body of principles underlying accounting statements, which the ASB now has in hand;

● to advise the ASB on any proposed public sector statements of recommended practice (SORPs);

- to comment on material issued for comment by the ASB, preferably at the discussion draft stage, from the point of view of the bodies they cover;

- to foster a common developmental philosophy for public and private sector reporting.

The committee held its inaugural meeting on 1 October 1991.

(e)   *SSAP 6*

On 31 October 1991 the UITF issued a document *Restructuring costs* which sought to clarify the definition of extraordinary and exceptional items in SSAP 6 in relation to restructuring costs. Restructuring costs are incurred by groups when the group structure is reorganised (which may involve closing or selling significant parts of the business).

SSAP 6 list the costs associated with the closing down of a significant part of the business as an example of an extraordinary item. However, the UITF has concluded that 'where the cost of restructuring or reorganising business activities needs to be disclosed by virtue of its size or incidence, it should be dealt with as an exceptional item, not an extraordinary item, unless it stems directly from a separate extraordinary event or transaction'. This means that the ASB sees costs associated with restructuring as within the normal course of business for most companies.

THE MEANING OF EXAMINERS' INSTRUCTIONS

The examinations department of the CIMA has asked the Institute's examiners to be precise when drafting questions. In particular, examiners have been asked to use precise instruction words. It will probably help you to know what instruction words may be used, and what they mean. With the Institute's permission, their list of recommended requirement words, and their meaning, is shown below. 'The following instruction words are recommended to examiners as being precise and likely to elicit the required response. The definitions given here are deliberately short and to the point rather than lengthy. It is recommended that examiners do not ring the changes between instructions in order to be literary. If the answers to all questions in a particular paper require discussion, it is felt there is nothing against using the word 'discuss' in each requirement.'

Recommended requirement words are:

Advise/recommend	Present information, opinions or recommendations to someone to enable that recipient to take action.
Amplify	Expand or enlarge upon the meaning of (a statement or quotation)
Analyse	Determine and explain the constituent parts of
Appraise/assess/evaluate	Judge the importance or value of
Clarify	Explain more clearly the meaning of
Compare (with)	Explain similarities and differences between
Contrast	Place in opposition to bring out difference(s)
Criticise	Present the faults in a theory or policy or opinion
Demonstrate	Show by reasoning the truth of
Describe	Present the details and characteristics of
Discuss	Explain the opposing arguments
Distinguish	Specify the differences between
Explain/interpret	Set out in detail the meaning of
Illustrate	Use an example, chart, diagram, graph or figure as appropriate, to explain something
Justify	State adequate grounds for
List	Itemise
Prove	Show by testing the accuracy of
Reconcile	Make compatible apparently conflicting statements or theories
Relate	Show connections between separate matters
State	Express
Summarise	State briefly the essential points (dispensing with examples and details)
Tabulate	Set out facts or figures in a table.

Requirement words which will be avoided

Examiners have been asked to avoid instructions which are imprecise or which may not specifically elicit an answer. The following words will *not* be used.

Comment	
Consider	as candidates could do this without writing a word
Define	in the sense of stating exactly what a thing is as CIMA wishes to avoid requiring evidence of rote learning
Enumerate	list is preferred
Identify	
Outline	as its meaning is imprecise. The addition of the word 'briefly' to any of the suggested action words is more satisfactory
Review	
Specify	
Trace	

PRACTICE AND REVISION CHECKLIST

This page is designed to help you chart your progress through this Practice and Revision Kit and thus through the Institute's syllabus. By this stage you should have worked through the study text, including the illustrative questions at the back of it. You can now tick off each topic as you revise and try questions on it, either of the practice type or of the full examination type. Insert the question numbers and date you completed them in the relevant boxes. You will thus ensure that you are on track to complete your revision before the exam.

The checklist is arranged in topic order, and follows the content of this Revision Kit, the corresponding BPP Study Text and, to a large extent, the Institute's syllabus.

	Revision of study text chapter(s) Ch No/Date Comp	*Tutorial question in kit* Ques No/Date Comp	*Examination style question* Ques No/Date Comp
The development of accounting standards			
Financial reporting	1		
Income and value measurement Asset valuation and profit measurement	2		
Current purchasing power and current cost accounting	3-4		
Company Accounts			
Company accounts	5-11		
Published accounts	5-11		
Group Accounts			
Consolidated balance sheet	12-16		
Consolidated P&L account	17-18		
Foreign subsidiaries	19		
Merger accounting	20		
Company Reorganisations			
Capital transactions	21-22		
Interpretation of accounts			
Additional statements	23		
Ratio analysis	24		
Earnings per share	25		

Test paper

Date completed
[   ]

TEST YOUR KNOWLEDGE: QUESTIONS

Total marks: 75

SSAPs

1 How should a person not accountable for VAT treat any VAT on inputs?   (1 mark)

2 Which of the following presentations is/are acceptable under SSAP 5?

   (a) Turnover (net of VAT)   £6.0m

   (b) Turnover (incl of VAT)   £7.0m

		£m
(c)	Sales inclusive of VAT	7.0
	Less VAT thereon	1.0
	Turnover	6.0

(1 mark)

3 Define 'recoverable ACT'.   (3 marks)

4 Define 'accounting bases'.   (2 marks)

5 What is the correct accounting treatment for a revenue-based grant?   (1 mark)

6 SSAP 4 forbids the use of the deferred credit method of accounting for capital-based government grants. True or false?   (2 marks)

7 Describe the accounting treatment for the following items:

   (a) a series of unusually severe bad debts;
   (b) the writing off of a large amount of goodwill, because of a sudden change in the company's prospects;
   (c) a material underprovision for contract losses in the previous year.   (3 marks)

8 At what amount should stocks and work in progress, other than long-term contract work in progress, be stated in periodic financial statements?   (1 mark)

9 Suggest four situations in which net realisable value is likely to be less than cost.   (4 marks)

10 To what enterprises does FRS 1 apply compared to SSAP 10?   (1 mark)

11 Under what circumstances should freehold land be depreciated?   (2 marks)

12 What are the criteria for deferral of development expenditure?   (4 marks)

13   SSAP 13 states that deferred development expenditure should be separately disclosed and should be included in intangible fixed assets in the balance sheet. What is the exception to this rule?

(3 marks)

14   State whether the following post balance sheet events are adjusting or non-adjusting:

(a)   purchase of an investment;
(b)   a change in the rate of corporation tax, applicable to the previous year;
(c)   an increase in pension benefits;
(d)   losses due to fire;
(e)   a bad debt suddenly being paid;
(f)   the receipt of proceeds of sales or other evidence concerning the net realisable value of stock;
(g)   a sudden decline in the value of property held as a fixed asset;
(h)   a merger.   (4 marks)

15   What is the correct treatment for a material contingent gain?   (2 marks)

16   What exceptions does SSAP 19 admit to the definition of investment properties? (2 marks)

17   In the context of SSAP 19 what does 'current value accounting' involve?   (2 marks)

18   In what circumstances does SSAP 20 suggest the temporal method may be appropriate to translate the results of a foreign subsidiary?   (2 marks)

19   Define a finance lease.   (2 marks)

20   In what way does SSAP 22 differ from Companies Act 1985 in its prescribed treatment of goodwill arising on consolidation?   (3 marks)

21   How does SSAP 25 extend the disclosure requirements relating to segmental reporting?

(4 marks)

Published accounts (1 mark each)

22   What are the items which must be shown on the face of the profit and loss account?

23   Which profit and loss account items may be shown in the notes?

24   What items would you expect to find included in 'cost of sales'?

25   How would profits on the sale of fixed assets be treated?

26 State the disclosures required in respect of interest payable and similar charges.

27 What items must not be treated as assets on any company's balance sheet?

28 Give the prescribed format for the breakdown of creditors.

29 What are the statutory provisions relating to development costs?

30 Give the definition of (a) a small company; and (b) a medium-sized company.

31 State the filing exemptions available to a medium-sized company.

Multiple choice (1 mark each)

32 A Limited is preparing draft accounts for the six months to 30 June 19X6 under the historical cost convention. At 1 January 19X6 its freehold building was such that the land element cost £100,000, and the buildings element had a net book value of £80,000 and was expected to last another forty years. The freehold's current market value at 1 January 19X6 was £200,000. The depreciation charge for the period using the straight line method should be:

A   Nil
B   £1,000
C   £2,000
D   £2,250
E   £5,000

33 B Limited has taken out a 25 year lease on a property for its investment potential, and sublet it to an associated company at an arm's length rental. The lease has 15 years left to run at the balance sheet date. In the context of SSAP 19, which of the following statements best describes the status of the property?

A   The property is an investment property and must be depreciated
B   The property is an investment property and may be depreciated
C   The property is an investment property and should not be depreciated
D   The property is not an investment property and should be depreciated
E   The property is not an investment property and should not be depreciated

34 C Limited has prepared the following schedule of its stocks.

Item	Purchase cost	Attributable production overheads incurred	Attributable distribution overheads still to be incurred	Expected sales price
	£	£	£	£
X	80	10	12	85
Y	50	15	20	70
Z	20	5	10	40
	150	30	42	195

Stocks should be valued at:

A   £148
B   £153
C   £195
D   £222
E   None of the above

35   Which one of the following is permitted by SSAP 22?

A   Amortisation of goodwill over less than its useful economic life
B   Immediate write-off of goodwill on one acquisition and amortisation of goodwill on another acquisition by the same company
C   The upwards revaluation of goodwill
D   An increase in the estimate of the remaining useful life of the goodwill
E   The retention of goodwill arising on consolidation without its amortisation

36   For the year ending 31 March 19X6 the taxable profits of a recently established company were £300,000 including a capital gain of £60,000. A dividend of £238,000 was paid on 30 December 19X5. Taking corporation tax at 35% and basic rate income tax at 30%, what mainstream corporation tax is payable when?

A   £3,000 payable 1 January 19X7
B   £3,000 payable 1 January 19X8
C   £12,000 payable 1 January 19X7
D   £15,000 payable 1 January 19X7
E   None of the above

37   SSAP 3 requires that earnings per share should be computed and disclosed under:

A   the nil and net bases with equal prominence
B   the nil basis, with net also if materially different
C   the nil basis, with net also if $\geqslant$ 5% different
D   the net basis, with nil also if materially different
E   the net basis, with nil also if $\geqslant$ 5% different

38   The different methods which have been developed for applying fundamental accounting concepts to financial transactions are called:

A   generally accepted accounting principles
B   accounting bases
C   accounting practices
D   accounting policies
E   accounting conventions

39 A Ltd has the following profit and loss account for the year ended 31 December 19X3:

	£m	£m
Profit on ordinary activities before tax		89.6
Taxation		
UK corporation tax	20.0	
Irrecoverable ACT	4.2	
		(24.2)
		65.4
Minority interests		(0.8)
		64.6
Extraordinary charge		(4.0)
		60.6
Dividends		
Ordinary (133.3 million shares)	18.0	
Preference (2 million shares)	0.5	
		(18.5)
Retained profit for the year		42.1

Earnings per share under the net basis are:

A   45.09p
B   48.09p
C   48.46p
D   51.24p
E   51.61p

40 A Limited has three assets. Their details (in pounds) are as follows.

Asset	A	B	C
Net replacement cost	30	30	30
Net realisable value	25	25	25
Economic value	20	28	32

The total value to the business of the three assets is:

A   £70
B   £75
C   £83
D   £90
E   None of these

41 Nag plc has undertaken a long-term contract for £4m which is now certified as 75% complete.
Estimated costs to completion:

	£'000
Labour	500
Materials	320
Production overheads	120
Administrative overheads	40

Costs to date are £2.5m. This is the first year in which the contract outcome can be foreseen with certainty. There are no known inequalities of profit in the contract.

What are the turnover and cost of sales figures to be recognised in the profit and loss account?

	Turnover	Cost of sales
A	Nil	Nil
B	Nil	£2.5m
C	£3m	£2.5m
D	£3m	£2.58m
E	£3m	£2.59m

42 Noggin plc is to recognise turnover of £2.9m and cost of sales of £2.7m on a long-term contract. Costs to date are £2.5m.

If progress payments to date are £2.4m, what are the balance sheet disclosures required for this contract?

	Amounts recoverable on contracts	Long-term contract work in progress	Accruals/ creditors
A	Nil	£2.7m	£2.4m
B	Nil	£0.3m	Nil
C	£0.2m	£0.3m	Nil
D	£0.5m	Nil	£0.2m
E	£2.9m	Nil	£2.6m

43 Pettigrew plc has revalued its office building freehold from £100,000 to £500,000. The premises will shortly be sold and leased back and a chargeable gain of £100,000 would be realised if the sales proceeds were £500,000. However, rollover relief is expected to be available for the full amount of the gain so the tax liability is unlikely to crystallise. How should Pettigrew treat this potential tax liability in its financial statements?

A Ignore it

B Insert a note stating the facts as a possible post balance sheet event. No other action is required.

C Insert a note stating that the revaluation does not constitute a timing difference and so no deferred tax liability has been provided for.

D As C, but disclose the unprovided tax.

E Insert a note stating the facts *and* provide in the accounts for the tax.

44 Puce Ltd now proposes a dividend of £100,000. Its draft taxation charge was £200,000, its draft corporation tax creditor was £320,000 and its deferred tax balance (in respect of accelerated capital allowances) was £400,000. Assuming no other tax balances existed, an ACT rate of ⅓ and a corporation tax rate of 35%, which amounts would change to allow for ACT payable on the proposed dividend?

A   Corporation tax payable and taxation charge
B   Corporation tax payable and deferred taxation
C   Taxation charge and deferred taxation
D   Corporation tax payable and ACT recoverable
E   Deferred taxation and ACT recoverable

45 During the year ended 31 December 19X8, Restive plc made a 1 for 2 bonus issue and then a 1 for 5 rights issue, which was fully taken up. The rights price was £1.80 and the market value at that time was £2.00. At 1 January 19X8, Restive's issued share capital was £100,000, consisting entirely of ordinary £1 shares, and its reserves (entirely consisting of retained earnings) were £200,000. Retained profit for 19X8 was £100,000 and there were no other reserve movements. What is the aggregate figure for capital and reserves at the end of 19X8?

A   £436,000
B   £454,000
C   £460,000
D   £486,000
E   £504,000

46 Which of the following is *not* a permissible use of the share premium account?

A   Paying up bonus shares
B   Writing off discounts on issue of shares
C   Providing for a premium on redemption of debentures issued at par
D   Writing off discounts on issue of debentures
E   Writing off preliminary expenses

47 Splodge plc's accounts contain two errors. A £10,000 bad debt to be written off has been deducted from sales and a £20,000 credit note received has been added to sales. Before correction, turnover is £1 million and cost of sales was £800,000. What is the gross profit margin after correction of these errors?

A   17.8%
B   18.8%
C   21.2%
D   22.2%
E   22.8%

TEST YOUR KNOWLEDGE: ANSWERS

SSAPs

1   It should be included as part of the cost of any goods and services to which it applies. In particular, the VAT on fixed assets should be added to the cost of the fixed assets concerned. (SSAP 5 para 2).

2   (a) and (c) are acceptable (SSAP 5 para 8).

3   Recoverable ACT is the amount of ACT paid or payable on outgoing dividends paid and proposed which can be:

(a)   set off against a corporation tax liability on the profits of the period under review or of previous periods; or

(b)   properly set off against a credit balance on deferred tax account; or

(c)   expected to be recoverable taking into account expected profits and dividends – normally those of the next accounting period only. (SSAP 8 para 20).

4   The methods developed for applying fundamental accounting concepts to financial transactions and items, for the purpose of financial accounts, and in particular:

(a)   for determining the accounting periods in which revenue and costs should be recognised in the profit and loss account; and

(b)   for determining the amounts at which material items should be stated in the balance sheet. (SSAP 2 para 15).

5   It should be credited to revenue in the same period in which the revenue expenditure to which it relates is charged (SSAP 4 para 23).

6   False. It permits either the deferred credit method or the netting method to be used but points out that the latter option is, in Counsel's opinion, not available to companies governed by the Companies Act 1985.

7   (a) and (c) are exceptional items and should be included in the calculation of profit for the year before tax. Their nature and size should be disclosed. (b) is an extraordinary item and should be shown separately in the profit and loss account for the year. Its nature and size should also be disclosed.

8   At the total of the lower of cost and net realisable value of the separate items of stock and work in progress or of groups of similar items (SSAP 9 para 26).

9 Possibilities:
  (a) an increase in costs or a fall in selling prices;
  (b) physical deterioration of stocks;
  (c) obsolescence of products;
  (d) a decision as part of the company's marketing strategy to manufacture and sell products at a loss;
  (e) errors in production or purchasing (SSAP 9, appendix 1 para 20).

10 To all financial accounts intended to give a true and fair view of financial position and profit or loss other than those of enterprises which are 'small' or 'medium-sized' as defined by the Companies Act 1985, and some subsidiary companies. SSAP 10 applied in the same way but it only exempted companies with turnover or gross income of less than £25,000 per annum.

11 (a) When it is subject to depletion (for example by mining).

  (b) When there is a reduction in the desirability of its location either socially or in relation to available sources of materials, labour or sales (SSAP 12 para 23).

12 The criteria are stated in para 25 of SSAP 13 as follows:

  (a) there must be a clearly defined project; and

  (b) the related expenditure must be separately identifiable; and

  (c) the outcome of such a project must be assessed with reasonable certainty as to:
    (i) its technical feasibility; and
    (ii) its ultimate commercial viability; and

  (d) the aggregate of the deferred development costs, any further development costs, and related production, selling and administration costs must be reasonably expected to be more than covered by related future revenues; and

  (e) adequate resources must exist for the project to be completed and for any consequential increases in working capital.

13 Where companies enter into a firm contract:

  (a) to carry out development work on behalf of third parties on such terms that the related expenditure is to be fully reimbursed; or

  (b) to develop and manufacture at an agreed price calculated to reimburse expenditure on development as well as on manufacture;

  any such expenditure which has not been reimbursed at the balance sheet date should be dealt with as work in progress (SSAP 13 para 17).

14 (b), (e) and (f) are adjusting, the others are non-adjusting (SSAP 17, appendix).

15   It should not be accrued in financial statements. It should be disclosed only if it is probable that the gain will be realised. (SSAP 18 para 17).

16   Property owned and occupied by a company for its own purposes and property let to or occupied by another group company (SSAP 19 para 8).

17   Investment properties should not be subject to periodic charges for depreciation on the basis set out in SSAP 12, except for properties held on lease which should be depreciated on the basis set out in SSAP 12 at least over the period when the unexpired term is 20 years or less.

Investment properties should be included in the balance sheet at their open market value.

Changes in the value of investment properties should not be taken to the profit and loss account but should be disclosed as a movement on an investment revaluation reserve, unless the total of the investment revaluation reserve is insufficient to cover a deficit, in which case the amount by which the deficit exceeds the amount in the investment revaluation reserve should be charged in the profit and loss account.

The carrying value of investment properties and the investments revaluation reserve should be displayed prominently in the financial statements. (SSAP 19).

18   Where the subsidiary:
   (a)   acts as a selling agency for the holding company; or
   (b)   produces raw materials or sub-components for inclusion in the holding company's products; or
   (c)   is located overseas for tax, exchange control or similar reasons. (SSAP 20 para 24).

19   A finance lease is one which transfers substantially all the risks and rewards of ownership of an asset to the lessee. (SSAP 21 para 15).

20   SSAP 22 says that *all* purchased goodwill should be eliminated from the accounts, either immediately or by amortisation. CA 1985 excludes goodwill arising on consolidation from this requirement.

21   The following disclosure is laid out by SSAP 25.

   (a)   The result as well as turnover for *all* segments must be shown ('result' is profit before tax, minority interests and extraordinary items).
   (b)   Each segments' assets must be disclosed.
   (c)   Segmental turnover must be analysed between sales to customers outside the group and inter-segment sales or transfers.
   (d)   The analysis must be by two types of segment, class of business and geographical.

Published accounts

22 There are three:
   (i) profit on ordinary activities before tax;
   (ii) aggregate transfers to or from reserves;
   (iii) aggregate dividends paid and proposed.

   (Note. These items do not appear in the prescribed formats.)

23 *All* of the items in the prescribed profit and loss account formats may be relegated to the notes, since they are all preceded by Arabic numerals.

24 'Cost of sales' will normally comprise:

   ● opening (less closing) stocks and WIP;
   ● direct materials;
   ● other external charges;
   ● direct labour;
   ● all direct production overheads, and indirect overheads that cannot be related specifically to the distribution and administrative functions;
   ● research and development costs;
   ● cash discounts received;
   ● stock provisions.

   However, there is no statutory definition of the term.

25 A profit on the sale of a fixed asset is probably best treated as 'other operating income', since it derives from the company's normal activities but falls outside the definition of turnover. If it is not material it could be treated as a reduction of the depreciation charge.

26 A note to the profit and loss account should state separately in respect of the figure given for interest payable and similar charges, the amounts for:

   (a) bank loans and overdrafts, and loans made to the company (other than bank loans and overdrafts) which are:

      (i) repayable otherwise than by instalments and fall due for repayment within five years of the end of the financial year; or

      (ii) are repayable by instalments, the last of which falls due for payment before the end of that period; and

   (b) loans of any other kind made to the company (those repayable wholly or in part after more than five years of the end of the financial year).

27 Preliminary expenses, expenses of and commission on any issue of shares or debentures, and costs of research.

28 1   Debenture loans
    2   Bank loans
    3   Payments received on account
    4   Trade creditors
    5   Bills of exchange payable
    6   Amounts owed to group companies
    7   Amounts owed to related companies
    8   Other creditors including taxation and social security
    9   Accruals and deferred income.

29 Development costs (BI 1) (these costs are considered in SSAP 13) may only be included in a company's balance sheet in special circumstances (which are not defined in the Act, but see SSAP 13) and, where they are so included, a note to the accounts must state:

(i)   the period over which the amount of those costs originally capitalised is being or is to be written off; and

(ii) the reasons for capitalising the development costs in question.

30 The conditions (which relate to company size) in respect of each company category may be summarised in tabular form.

Category	Turnover	Gross assets*	Average employees per week
Small company (or group)	Not > £2m	Not > £975,000	Not > 50
Medium company (or group)	Not > £8m	Not > £3.9m	Not > 250

All other companies and groups (including banking and insurance companies and all public limited companies) are classified as large companies.

*Gross assets means the total of items A–D on the pro-forma balance sheet.

31 The directors of a medium-sized company or group must file a full balance sheet and directors' report. All notes to the accounts, with the exception of notes on turnover, must also be given. The profit and loss account may however be modified, to the extent that items 1, 2, 3 and 6 of format I and items 1–5 of format II need not be separately disclosed at all, but can be combined and shown as gross profit (or loss). In addition, a directors' statement (as above) and special auditors' report will not be required.

(*Note.* Both small and medium-sized companies must circulate *full* accounts to shareholders.)

Multiple choice

32 B   6/12 x £80,000/40 = £1,000

33 A   Para 10, SSAP 19: an associated company is not a group company and so this is an investment property, but it must be depreciated because the leasehold has less than 20 years to run.

			£
34	A	X : lower of £90, £73 =	73
		Y : lower of £65, £50 =	50
		Z : lower of £25, £30 =	25
		Total	148

35   B   Paras 41 and 42, SSAP 22

			£'000	£'000
36	D			
		CT @ 35% on £300,000		105
		Less ACT set-off		
		ACT paid	102	
		Maximum set-off	(90)	(90)
		(30% x £300,000)		
		Surplus ACT	12	
		MCT liability		15

37   D   Para 14, SSAP 3

38   B   Para 3, SSAP 2

39   B $\dfrac{64.6 - 0.5}{133.3} = 48.09p$

40   C   Value to the business = lower of net replacement cost and recoverable amount

	A	B	C	
	£	£	£	
NRC	30	30	30	
Recoverable amount	25	28	32	
Value to the business	25 +	28 +	30	= £83

41   D   £3m = 75% of the contract value, or the revenue earned to date. £2.58m = 75% x (£2.5m + £0.5m + £0.32m + £0.12m). If there are no known inequalities of profit, then an accrual is required to increase costs *incurred* to date to the cost of sales *expected* to generate 75% of the profit foreseen on the contract as a whole. SSAP 9 does not allow administrative overheads to be included in stock valuation in normal circumstances.

42   D   'Amounts recoverable on contracts' represents the excess of turnover over progress payments. The long-term contract balance is nil because all costs have been transferred to cost of sales, leaving £0.2m costs to be accrued.

43   C   SSAP 15 specifically states that in these circumstances no tax need be provided nor need the unprovided tax be calculated and disclosed.

44 B ACT payable will be included in the corporation tax creditor. ACT recoverable can here be offset in full against the deferred tax balance ($25/35$ x £400,000 > £100,000 x $\frac{1}{3}$).

45 B Share capital = £100,000 + £50,000 (bonus issue) + £30,000 (rights issue: $1/5$ x £150,000) = £180,000.

Share premium account = £24,000 (rights issue: 80p x 30,000).

Retained earnings = £200,000 - £50,000 (bonus issue) + £100,000 = £250,000.

Aggregate capital and reserves = £180,000 + £24,000 + £250,000 = £454,000.

46 B Shares cannot be issued at a discount, unlike debentures.

47 C

	£'000
Turnover (£1m + £10,000 - £20,000)	990
Cost of sales (£800,000 - £20,000)	780
Gross profit	210

Gross profit margin $= \dfrac{210}{990}$ x 100% = 21.2%

INDEX TO QUESTIONS AND SUGGESTED SOLUTIONS

Italics denote tutorial questions; the purpose of these questions is explained in the preface.

INDEX TO QUESTIONS AND SUGGESTED SOLUTIONS

INDEX TO QUESTIONS AND SUGGESTED SOLUTIONS

QUESTIONS

1   ACCOUNTING STANDARDS I (15 marks)   5/88

. 'Accounting standards have eliminated flexibility in financial accounting practice.'

You are required to discuss this statement, illustrating your answer with examples from at least three statements of standard accounting practice.

2   ACCOUNTING STANDARDS II (10 marks)   11/89, amended

The directors of FG plc, a company engaged in the exploration, extraction and processing of oil, are holding a preliminary meeting to discuss their draft annual statutory financial statements.

You are required to write a report for the directors of FG plc explaining the purpose, scope and authority of statements of standard accounting practice.

3   INTERNATIONAL ACCOUNTING STANDARDS (15 marks)   11/90

Discuss the influence on the published financial statements of British companies of the International Accounting Standards Committee and the European Economic Community.

4   TUTORIAL QUESTION: REVENUE RECOGNITION

Revenue recognition practices generally recognise revenue at the point of sale.

Required

(a) Why is revenue recognition important for the measurement of profit under the conventions of accrual accounting?

(b) What criteria suggest revenue should generally be recognised at the point of sale?

(c) At what other points in the business cycle could revenue be recognised under the conventions of accrual accounting? State the circumstances, if any, in which these other points may be more appropriate for recognising profit than the point of sale.

5   STILES (15 marks)   11/88

You are the chief accountant of Stiles plc, a manufacturing company. The managing director of Stiles plc does not understand what accountants mean by exceptional items and extraordinary items in the profit and loss account.

You are required to prepare a memorandum for your managing director explaining the difference between exceptional items and extraordinary items, giving examples of both and summarising the importance of the distinction between these two items.

6 SSAP 6 (20 marks)

(a) SSAP 6 *Extraordinary items and prior year adjustments* is based on the 'all-inclusive' concept of income rather than the 'current operating' income concept.

Required

Discuss the merits of both the 'all-inclusive' income and the 'current operating' income concepts.

(*Note*. The current operating income approach is sometimes referred to as reserve accounting.) (8 marks)

(b) State, giving your reasons, whether you consider the following items to be extraordinary, as defined in SSAP 6, and comment upon any additional information that may be necessary for a considered opinion on disclosure.

    (i) An additional £1 million contribution paid by the company to the employees' pension fund. (4 marks)

    (ii) Previously capitalised development expenditure written off. (4 marks)

    (iii) Damages for libel paid by the publishers of a satirical magazine. (4 marks)

7 FERGUSON (16 marks)

You have ascertained the following information in relation to the accounts of Ferguson Limited.

1.
Year ended 31 December	19X2 £'000	19X1 £'000
Profit on ordinary activities before tax (before research and development charge)	4,625	4,006
Taxation (the 19X2 charge includes £86,000 relating to 19X1)	1,160	1,106

2. During 19X2 the company decided to change its accounting policy relating to research and development. In previous years it had capitalised research and development expenditure and amortised it over eight years, but now all such expenditure is to be written off in the year in which it is incurred. The following figures are relevant.

	£'000
Balance on research and development on 1 January 19X1	2,250
Expenditure on research and development during 19X1	465
Amortisation of research and development during 19X1	440
Expenditure on research and development during 19X2	865

3. In December 19X2 a decision was taken to cease production of a major product line, the TX, owing to its effective technological obsolescence. The net costs incurred as a result of this decision have so far been £630,000, and it is anticipated that further costs of £330,000 have yet to be incurred in respect of the decision.

4. The dividend for 19X1 was £450,000 and the proposed dividend for 19X2 is £550,000.

5.   The profit and loss account balance brought forward as at 1 January 19X1 was £14,700,000.

You are required to prepare the profit and loss account and statement of retained profits, including notes thereon, for the year ended 31 December 19X1. Your answer should include comparative figures and be in accordance with best accounting practice.

8   LEASING (20 marks)   5/88

You are the accountant in a British company which has just been taken over by an American company. The finance director of this American company has written to you to suggest that in future your company should lease rather than purchase its fixed assets because he understands that leasing is still a form of 'off-the-balance sheet finance' in Great Britain.

You are required to write a report for the finance director of the American company explaining the treatment of leases in the published financial statements of British lessee companies relating to accounting periods beginning on or after 1 July 1987.

9   CONTROLLED NON-SUBSIDIARY (15 marks)   5/90

You are the finance director in a manufacturing company and the managing director has asked about off-balance sheet finance involving the use of a controlled non-subsidiary.

You are required to write a report for your managing director explaining:

(a)   the meaning of off-balance sheet finance involving the use of a controlled non-subsidiary; and   (5 marks)

(b)   the existing and proposed accounting treatment and disclosure requirements for off-balance sheet finance schemes involving the use of a controlled non-subsidiary.
                                                                              (10 marks)

10   BRANDS (15 marks)   5/91

'A case can be made for putting brands on to the balance sheet to disclose to shareholders and others the true value of the assets in the business.' (Pizzey: *CIMA Student*, August 1990)

You are required to discuss the arguments for and against including a value for brand names in the balance sheet.

11   HISTORICAL COST ACCOUNTING (15 marks)   11/89

You are required to discuss the advantages and disadvantages of using historical cost accounting in preparing financial statements which are presented to shareholders.

12 CHANGING PRICE LEVELS (15 marks)   11/90

A manager in your firm has read the following quotation from an article in *Management Accounting* by David Allen, concerning accounting for changing price levels.

'What was required was a comprehensive system which calculated

(i)   the capital maintenance provision by reference to the fall in the value of money; but
(ii) unrealised holding gains by reference to the changes in the specific prices of the particular assets employed by an enterprise.'

You are required to write a report to the manager in your firm:

(a)   explaining the above statement in relation to published financial statements;

(10 marks)

(b)   giving a short, numerical example to illustrate your explanation.   (5 marks)

13 MANUFACTURING COMPANY (15 marks)   11/87

You are the management accountant of a manufacturing company where production is capital-intensive using machinery that is estimated to have a five-year life. The present machinery is now approximately three years old. Whilst raw material stocks have a low turnover because of supply problems, finished goods are turned over rapidly and there is minimal work in progress at any one time. The technology incorporated in the means of production is thought to be stable.

In recent years it has not been possible to increase the price of the company's outputs beyond the rate of general inflation without diminishing market share, owing to keen competition in this sector. The company does not consider that it has cash flow problems. The company is all equity financed. Although a bank overdraft is a permanent feature of the balance sheet this is primarily due to customers being given a 60-day credit period, whilst most suppliers are paid within 30 days. There is always a positive balance of short-term monetary assets.

In the previous financial year, net profit after taxation on a strict historical cost basis was considered very healthy, and the directors felt that they could prudently distribute a major portion of this by way of dividend. The directors are considering whether, and if so how, to reflect price-level changes in their financial statements. They are concerned that this would affect their profit figure, and therefore the amount they could distribute as dividend.

The following price-level changes have been brought to the attention of the directors:

	Retail price index	Index for company's machinery	Raw materials stock index
3 years previously	100	100	100
2 years previously	104	116	102
1 year previously	107	125	108
Present	112	140	120

You are required to prepare a report for your directors setting out in general terms how to explain to the shareholders the likely impact on the historical cost profit of possible methods of accounting for price-level changes.

14   CD   (30 marks)   **Specimen paper**

You are given the following information relating to CD Ltd.

(i)   CD Ltd was formed on 1 April 19X4 with issued and fully paid ordinary share capital of £2 million. The proceeds of the share issue were used to finance the following asset purchases.

At cost on 1 April 19X4

	£'000
Plant and machinery	1,200
Vehicles	500
Stock of goods for resale	250
	1,950

Cash in hand at 1 April 19X4 amounted to £50,000.

(ii)   During the period 1 April 19X4 to 31 March 19X5 the following cash transactions took place.

    (a)   Sales and purchases of goods for resale were spread evenly throughout the period. Invoiced sales of £4.8 million were recorded. Purchases totalled £3.3 million, of which the whole of March 19X5 purchases remained in closing stock at 31 March 19X5.

    (b)   The factory warehouses and distribution centre were rented for the first six months of the year at a charge of £40,000 paid on 30 June 19X4. An option to purchase the complex was exercised per note (c) below.

    (c)   On 1 October 19X4 a five-year loan of £400,000 was raised, the entire proceeds of which were used to purchase the factory buildings on the same day. Interest on the loan, at an annual rate of 14%, is paid semi-annually on 31 March and 30 September each year.

    (d)   Distribution expenses of £75,000 per month, and other cash operating expenses of £14,000 per month, were incurred and paid evenly throughout the year.

    (e)   On 31 March 19X5 an item of plant was sold for £108,000. The cost of this item on 1 April 19X4 was £120,000. The gain/loss on sale is calculated on the net book value of the plant at 31 March 19X5.

(iii) CD Ltd charges depreciation on a straight-line basis at the following annual rates.

Buildings	5%
Plant and machinery	15%
Vehicles	20%

Depreciation is calculated monthly from the date of asset purchase.

(iv) A provision for taxation is required at 31 March 19X5 at 40% of net profit on a historical cost basis.

(v) The movement in the general price index during the first year of CD Ltd's existence was as follows.

At 1 April 19X4	120
At 31 March 19X5	132

Mid-period indices, where required, may be constructed using simple arithmetic averages of those given above.

You are required to prepare for CD Ltd:

(a) the profit and loss account for the year ended 31 March 19X5 with all amounts expressed in units of current purchasing power as at 31 March 19X5;   (20 marks)

(b) the balance sheet as at 31 March 19X5 with all amounts expressed in units of current purchasing power as at 31 March 19X5.   (10 marks)

15   TUTORIAL QUESTION: NORWICH (20 marks)

The following information has been extracted from the accounts of Norwich plc prepared under the historical cost convention for 19X6.

PROFIT AND LOSS ACCOUNT EXTRACTS, 19X6

	£m
Turnover	200
Operating profit	15
Less interest payable	3
Net profit	12

SUMMARISED BALANCE SHEET AT 31 DECEMBER 19X6

	£m	£m
Fixed assets at cost less depreciation		60
Current assets		
Stocks	20	
Debtors	30	
Bank	2	
	52	
Current liabilities	30	
Net current assets		22
Total assets less current liabilities		82
Less 15% debentures		20
		62
Capital and reserves		62

The company's accountant has prepared the following current cost data.

	£m
Current cost adjustments for 19X6	
Depreciation adjustment	3
Cost of sales adjustment	5
Replacement cost at 31 December 19X6	
Fixed assets, net of depreciation	85
Stocks	21

Required

(a) Calculate the current cost operating profit of Norwich plc for 19X6 and the summarised current cost balance sheet of the company at 31 December 19X6, so far as the information permits.

(b) Calculate the following ratios from both the historical cost accounts and current cost accounts:
   (i)   interest cover;
   (ii) rate of return on shareholders' equity;
   (iii) debt/equity ratio.

(c) Discuss the significance of the ratios calculated under (b) and of the reasons for differences between them.

Note. Ignore taxation.

16 TUTORIAL QUESTION: POYNTON

Poynton Ltd was incorporated some years ago. Its trial balance as at 30 June 19X8 contained the following information.

TRIAL BALANCE AT 30 JUNE 19X8

	£'000	£'000
Turnover		7,230
Opening stock: first in first out (FIFO) basis	350	
Manufacturing costs	5,000	
Goodwill at cost	120	
Development expenditure	60	
Distribution and administrative costs	1,380	
Plant and machinery at cost less depreciation	2,050	
Net monetary assets	295	
Share capital		1,400
Retained profit at 1 July 19X7		625
	9,255	9,255

The following additional information is made available.

1. The goodwill arose on the acquisition of the business assets of Hammond & Co on 1 July 19X7. The goodwill is estimated to have a useful economic life of three years from the date of acquisition.

2. The following information is provided relating to Poynton's stock.

	Value at	
	1 July 19X7	*30 June 19X8*
	£'000	£'000
FIFO basis	350	400
Average cost basis	302	336

3. The development expenditure, incurred during the period from April to June 19X8, relates to the refinement of one of the company's established products. This change is expected to improve materially the product's marketability and contribution to the overall profitability of Poynton. The improved product was first sold on 1 July 19X8.

69

Required

(a) Produce summarised profit and loss accounts and appropriation accounts for Poynton Ltd for the year ended 30 June 19X8 and balance sheets at that date, using accounting policies that comply with standard accounting practice and show:

(i) the *highest* reported profit for the year;
(ii) the *lowest* reported profit for the year.

Notes
1. Presentation of the financial statements prepared under (a) should comply with relevant statements of standard accounting practice but need not be in the detailed format necessary for publication purposes.

2. Net monetary assets comprise debtors, cash and creditors.

3. Ignore taxation.

(b) Identify *three* other areas in financial reports (in addition to those considered under (a)) where alternative methods of asset valuation and profit measurement are permissible. To what extent do these alternative methods of asset valuation affect the interpretation of financial statements by banks and other users?

17 TUTORIAL QUESTION: NEWTRADE

Newtrade Limited, a manufacturing company, has prepared draft accounts as on 31 March 19X3 for the purpose of producing its first year's financial statements.

Included in assets is a balance on the suspense account of £165,808 made up as follows.

	£		£
Purchases of:		Grants received:	
plant and machinery	145,567	on cost of plant	
motor lorries	48,898	and machinery	25,316
motor cars	12,259	for employment of	
		local labour	15,600
		Balance	165,808
	206,724		206,724

All the amounts shown for the purchase of assets include VAT at 15%.

The directors wish to deal with capital grants on the deferred credit method and to depreciate all fixed assets at 20% per annum.

Required

Write a short memorandum explaining how you think each of the above items should be treated.

18 TUTORIAL QUESTION: STRACHAN

Strachan Limited was incorporated and commenced business on 1 January 19X5. Its accounting year ends on 31 December and the following details relate to its first two years of operation.

	19X5 £	19X6 £
Taxable profits (no chargeable gains)	400,000	800,000
Interim dividend (paid in June)	50,000	50,000
Final dividend (proposed)	100,000	-
Dividends received (September)	-	15,000

You may assume that:

(i)   the rate of corporation tax is 35%;

(ii)   the basic income tax rate is 25%;

(iii) corporation tax liabilities will be settled within one year of the end of the relevant accounting period;

(iv)   the company does not operate a deferred tax account.

You are required to show the relevant entries in Strachan Ltd's profit and loss accounts and balance sheets for both 19X5 and 19X6.

19 BINSTEAD (22 marks)

Binstead Limited's draft profit and loss account for the year ended 31 December 19X1 shows net trading profit £800,000, dividends received £36,500 (excluding tax credits), and debenture interest payable (gross) £140,000. The depreciation charge for the year is £25,000 on (non-industrial) buildings, and £220,000 on vehicles and equipment (including book gains on disposals, £10,000). Extraordinary items in the books are £15,000 (Debit) before tax relief (which they all attract).

For corporation tax purposes, vehicles and equipment purchased during the year cost £1,200,000, and a writing down allowance of 25% will be claimed. £30,000 was recovered on the sale of old machinery on which 100% capital allowances had originally been claimed. Expenses of £20,000, charged in the 19X1 accounts, are expected to be disallowed for tax purposes.

Dividends for the year 19X1 are: preference paid, £40,000; ordinary interim paid, £50,000, final proposed, £100,000. The 19X0 final dividend was £80,000.

The corporation tax rate for financial years 19X0 and 19X1 was 35%. The income tax basic rate for 19X0-X1 and 19X1-X2 was 25%. Mainstream corporation tax was payable 9 months after the year end. The mainstream tax for 19X0, provided in that year at £120,000, was agreed and paid in 19X1 in the sum of £110,000. The deferred taxation account had a credit balance at 31 December 19X0 of £250,000. Full provision for deferred taxation on all timing differences is to be made in 19X1.

All calculations are to be made to the nearest pound.

Required

(a) Draft an extract from Binstead Limited's profit and loss account for the year ended 31 December 19X1, beginning with 'net profit before taxation' and ending with 'net profit for year'. You are to show in rough your computations of all figures in the extract, other than sub-totals. (14 marks)

(b) State the balances, as at 31 December 19X1, of the deferred taxation account and the corporation tax account, showing your computations in rough. (8 marks)

20 TUTORIAL QUESTION: MILLER

Miller Limited is a manufacturing company which has always valued its stock on the basis of direct cost. However, in order to avoid further audit qualifications, the directors of Miller Limited have decided to comply with the requirements of SSAP 9 *Stocks and long-term contracts* in the year ended 31 December 19X2.

From the information given below you are required to prepare a report for the directors of Miller Limited summarising the effects on Miller Limited's financial statements of this change in stock valuation.

Workings should be shown and taxation is to be ignored.

1. The stock valuation on the balance sheet as at 31 December 19X1 was £54,000.

2. During the year ended 31 December 19X2, the first year in which SSAP 9 is to be applied, Miller Limited incurred production overheads of £324,000 (leaving the production overhead applicable to each unit unchanged from the previous year at £6.00) and other overheads of £210,000.

3. On 1 December 19X2 the direct cost per unit increased, for the first time in two years, from £9.00 to £10.00.

4. Production was constant throughout 19X2 and a FIFO stock issue price basis was used.

5. 55,000 units were sold for £25.00 each during the year ended 31 December 19X2.

6. Retained profits at 1 January 19X2 were £247,400.

21 LONG-TERM CONTRACTS (20 marks)   5/89

Your credit control manager is assessing a potential new customer, FG plc, which specialises in long-term contracts such as building power stations. The credit control manager has a copy of the financial statements of FG plc and has asked you to explain how such long-term contracts would be treated in the annual financial statements. In particular, the credit control manager cannot understand why FG plc has negative work-in-progress.

You are required to write a report for the credit control manager explaining the treatment of long-term contract work-in-progress in published financial statements and highlighting any possible problems in the treatment of such work-in-progress.

22 GONERIL, REGAN AND CORDELIA (21 marks)

Goneril Limited and Regan Limited are manufacturing companies and Cordelia Limited is a property investment company. All three companies have recently acquired and disposed of freehold properties which were identical in every respect. Details of the properties are as follows.

3 June 19X4   Each company bought its property for £300,000. The buildings element in the cost of each property was estimated at £120,000 with an estimated useful life of 40 years.

30 June 19X5   Each property was revalued at £380,000 (including buildings element £160,000). The estimated remaining useful life at this date was revised to 50 years.

30 June 19X6   Each property was revalued at £290,000 (including buildings element £100,000).

29 June 19X7   Each property was sold for £320,000.

Goneril Limited and Regan Limited both used their properties for their business operations and both provided a full year's depreciation (straight line) in the year of acquisition and none in the year of disposal. Goneril Limited always incorporates property revaluations into its historical cost accounts, whereas Regan Limited never does.

Cordelia Limited leased its property to produce a rental income negotiated at arm's length.

All three companies have accounting periods ending on 30 June.

Required

(a) Show how the properties would be dealt with in the historical cost accounts (19X4-19X7) of each company separately. The rental income of Cordelia Limited should be ignored. You should answer in accordance with all relevant SSAP's.   (15 marks)

(b) Outline the main reasons for the SSAP 19's prescribed treatment of investment properties.   (6 marks)

23 DEPRECIATION OF PROPERTY (15 marks)   5/91

The managing director of your company has always been unhappy at depreciating the company's properties because he argues that these properties are in fact appreciating in value.

Recently he heard of another company which has investment properties and does not depreciate those properties.

You are required to write a report to your managing director explaining:

(a) the consequences of not depreciating the company's existing properties;   (2 marks)

(b) the meaning of investment properties; and   (5 marks)

(c) the accounting treatment of investment properties in published financial statements.   (8 marks)

24 GOODWILL (15 marks)   11/89

Your managing director attended a conference where the following comment was made.

'Accountants do not know what goodwill is or how to value it and therefore cannot agree how to account for goodwill'.

You are required to write a report for your managing director explaining the treatment of goodwill in published financial statements and highlighting any problems in the treatment of goodwill relating to acquisitions and disposals of businesses.

25 SSAP 24   (15 marks)   11/90

At present your company operates a defined benefit pension scheme and charges the annual contributions payable to this pension scheme as the pension cost in each accounting period.

Required

(a) Write a report for your managing director explaining any change required by SSAP 24.
(5 marks)

(b) Summarise the necessary disclosures in respect of a defined benefit pension scheme.
(10 marks)

26 TUTORIAL QUESTION: CAXTON

Rewrite Caxton Ltd's profit and loss account for the year ended 31 December 19X1 and balance sheet as at 31 December 19X2 (shown below) in Companies Act 1985 format and in accordance with best practice.

	£'000	£'000
Sales		4,679
Cost of goods sold	2,051	
Administration costs	627	
Distribution and sales expenses	495	
Dividends from shares in associated companies	(100)	
Interest paid	25	
Sundry operating income	(112)	
Provisions against investments	50	
		3,036
Profit for the financial year		1,643
Tax on ordinary activities		552
Profit after tax on ordinary activities		1,091
Dividends payable		(567)
Extraordinary expenses	(66)	
Extraordinary revenues	120	
Tax on extraordinary items	(15)	
		39
Profit transferred to reserves		563

	£'000	£'000
Investments		600
Loans		250
Tangible assets		
Plant and equipment	2,106	
Land and buildings	114	
Fixtures, fittings and furniture	98	
		2,318
Intangible assets		
Goodwill	120	
Patents	59	
Research and development costs	602	
		781
		3,949
Current assets		
Cash at bank and in hand	127	
Stocks		
Work in progress	107	
Raw materials	48	
Finished goods	94	
Debtors	567	
Prepayments	12	
	955	
Current liabilities		
Bills of exchange payable	404	
Bank loans and overdrafts	210	
Trade creditors	290	
	904	
Net current assets		51
		4,000
Creditors: amounts falling due after one year		578
Provisions		
Deferred tax		320
Accruals and deferred income		196
		2,906
Financed by		
Ordinary shares		1,500
Share premium		250
Retained profits		1,037
Capital redemption reserve		52
Surplus on revaluation		67
		2,906

27 TUTORIAL QUESTION: CHAPMAN (30 marks)

The accountant of Chapman Ltd has prepared the draft accounts for the year to 31 March 19X7.

PROFIT AND LOSS ACCOUNT
FOR THE YEAR ENDED 31 MARCH 19X7

	£	£
Turnover		2,150,000
Less cost of sales		1,200,000
Gross profit		950,000
Less: distribution costs	36,000	
administrative expenses	527,000	
		563,000
Operating profit		387,000
Less taxation		112,000
		275,000
Dividends proposed		75,000
Retained profit for the year		200,000
Retained profit at 1 April 19X6		736,000
		936,000

BALANCE SHEET AS AT 31 MARCH 19X7

	£	£
Fixed assets		
Intangible assets		
Goodwill		36,000
Research and development		64,000
Tangible assets		
Freehold property		500,000
Plant and machinery		1,194,000
		1,794,000
Current assets		
Stocks	321,000	
Debtors	197,000	
Cash at bank and in hand	3,000	
	521,000	
Creditors: amounts falling due within one year		
Trade creditors	104,000	
Taxation	95,000	
Dividends	75,000	
	274,000	
Net current assets		247,000
Total assets less current liabilities		2,041,000
Provisions for liabilities and charges		
Deferred taxation		(105,000)
		1,936,000
Capital and reserves		
Called up share capital		1,000,000
Retained profit		936,000
		1,936,000

The following additional information is provided.

1. Advance corporation tax is to be provided in respect of the proposed dividend at the rate of $^{25}/_{75}$.

2. The goodwill arose on the acquisition of the business assets of a supplier on 1 October 19X6. It is estimated that the goodwill has a useful economic life of three years from the date of acquisition.

3. The balance of research and development expenditure consists of research expenditure, £50,000, and development expenditure, £14,000. The expenditure was incurred developing a new product which was launched on 1 May 19X7 and is proving a great success.

4. The freehold property is stated at cost less depreciation. The property was professionally revalued at £900,000 on 1 April 19X6 and it has now been decided to use this figure for the purpose of the accounts. The depreciation charge for the year must be increased from £12,000 to £22,000 to take account of this change.

5. On 30 April 19X7 the company was informed that one of its major customers, Mansfield Ltd, had gone into liquidation. It is not expected that the £50,000 owed by Mansfield Ltd, at 31 March 19X7, will be recoverable.

6. The company issued a £100,000 12% debenture on 6 May 19X7.

7. The company has guaranteed repayment of a loan of £90,000 made to one of its suppliers, Groves Ltd. A receiver was called in during March 19X7 to manage the affairs of Groves Ltd, and it is not expected that the company's assets will enable more than £32,000 of the loan to be repaid.

8. Chapman is suing Bridge Ltd for supplying defective goods which have been written off as valueless. The directors and their advisers are confident that Bridge will soon agree to a settlement of £36,500.

Required

Prepare the profit and loss account of Chapman Ltd for the year ended 31 March 19X7 and the balance sheet at that date redrafted to take account, where necessary, of the additional information. The accounting statements should comply, as far as possible, with the Companies Act 1985 and relevant SSAPs. You should, where necessary, explain the adjustment, indicate permissible alternatives and refer to the relevant SSAP.

Notes

1. Notes to the accounts are *not* required.
2. The tax implications of adjustments to take account of additional information 2-8 should be ignored.

28 S PLC (40 marks)   11/89

The trial balance of S plc at 31 December 19X7 is given below.

	Note	£'000	£'000
Fixed assets	1	907,722	
Aggregate depreciation			108,000
Intangible assets	2	120,000	
Stocks and work in progress	3	120,700	
Debtors	4	168,120	
Provision for doubtful debts			620
Cash		100	
Creditors	5		127,450
Bank overdraft	6		50,754
Debentures	7		200,000
Bank loan	8		270,000
Corporation tax	9		47,500
Share capital	10		60,000
Retained profits			119,046
Sales			1,574,500
Cost of sales	11	670,396	
Salaries and wages	12	238,720	
Selling and distribution expenses		86,560	
Administrative expenses		165,592	
Interest charges	13	79,960	
		2,557,870	2,557,870

Notes

1. Details of fixed assets at 1 January 19X7 are as follows.

	Cost £'000	Aggregate depreciation £'000
Freehold property	500,000	–
Plant and equipment	200,000	90,000
Office equipment	107,722	18,000
	807,722	108,000

(i)   The company has not previously provided depreciation on freehold property. The directors have been advised that this treatment is in conflict with SSAP 12 and have agreed to provide depreciation this year. The property, a new factory building, was purchased on 1 January 19W8 with the land costing £350 million and the building £150 million. This building has an expected life of fifty years from that date.

(ii) Depreciation at 15% on the straight-line basis is to be charged on plant and equipment including a full year's depreciation on the £100 million of equipment purchased during 19X7.

(iii) Depreciation at 10% on the reducing balance method is to be charged on office equipment. No new office equipment was purchased during the year, but the board has decided to replace the company's computer at a cost of £8 million. The contract for this new computer has not yet been placed.

2. Intangible assets consist of expenditure during the year on research which may result in reducing the cost of maintenance of road bridges.

3. Details of stocks and work-in-progress are as follows.

	£'000			£'000
Stock at cost				
Material A	12,000	(realisable value		13,700)
Material B	3,000	(realisable value		2,400)
Material C	5,300	(realisable value		6,800)
	20,300			22,900
Work in progress				
Materials	40,500			
Labour	47,900			
Production overhead	9,000			
Administrative overhead	3,000			
	120,700			

The above work in progress includes items with a cost of £6 million which are now considered to be valueless because of obsolescence.

4. The directors propose that the provision for doubtful debts be increased to 5% of debtors.

5. All creditors are payable within one year.

6. The bank overdraft bears interest at 4% per annum over base rate.

7. The 12½% debentures, which are secured over the freehold property, are redeemable in 19Y9 at par.

8. The bank loan is repayable in ten equal annual instalments of £30,000,000 commencing on 31 December 19X7. The loan is secured by a floating charge on the assets of the company.

9. The figure of £47,500,000 represents the estimated corporation tax charge for the previous year. This liability has now been agreed at a figure of £45,000,000. The directors estimate the tax charge for operations for the current year to be £85,000,000.

10. The authorised share capital consists of 100,000,000 ordinary shares of £1 each, of which 60,000,000 have been issued fully paid at par.

11. The cost of sales includes rationalisation costs of £120,000,000, incurred when a plant was closed. A tax saving of £30,000,000 is anticipated on these costs. At a board meeting on 20 January 19X8, it was decided to close another factory with anticipated rationalisation costs of £40 million with an associated tax saving of £5 million.

12. Details of salaries and wages are as follows.

	£'000
Factory wages	125,510
Warehouse wages	32,716
Office salaries	79,780
Directors' remuneration	714
	238,720

13. The interest charges are as follows.

	£'000
Bank overdraft interest	25,460
Bank loan interest	42,000
Debenture interest (half year)	12,500
	79,960

14. The directors have recommended an ordinary dividend of 35 pence per ordinary share. The advance corporation tax is ⅓.

You are required to prepare, in a form suitable for presentation to the shareholders of S plc:

(a) the profit and loss account for the year ended 31 December 19X7;   (15 marks)

(b) the balance sheet at 31 December 19X7; and   (10 marks)

(c) the notes to accompany these two financial statements.   (15 marks)

29 COMPREHENSIVE (45 marks)   11/90

The following trial balance has been extracted from the books of M plc at 31 May 19X2.

	Notes	£'000	£'000
Freehold land and buildings at cost	1	187,500	
Patents	2	5,000	
Factory plant and machinery at cost		112,500	
Goodwill	3	124,125	
Research and development expenditure	4	37,500	
Fixtures and fittings at cost		37,500	
Motor vehicles at cost		56,250	
Accumulated depreciation at 31 May 19X2			
Plant and machinery			51,375
Fixtures and fittings			11,813
Motor vehicles			18,750
Trade debtors		133,223	
Advance corporation tax paid	5	3,600	
Closure and redundancy costs	6	14,000	
Stock of raw materials at cost at 1 June 19X1		84,800	
Purchase of raw materials		545,450	
Overdraft interest		7,875	
Stock of work in progress at 1 June 19X1		24,563	
Administrative expenses		118,575	
Selling and distribution costs		87,600	
Provision for doubtful debts at 31 May 19X2			4,313
Stock of finished goods at 1 June 19X1		138,375	
Manufacturing wages		187,500	
Manufacturing overhead (including depreciation for the year on plant, fixtures and vehicles)		93,750	
10% debentures (19X7-19X9)	7		75,000
Creditors			73,125
Bank overdraft			38,438
Rents received			15,000
Sales			1,105,063
Share capital	8		300,000
Deferred tax account			37,500
Share premium account			60,000
Retained profits at 1 June 19X1			209,309
		1,999,686	1,999,686

Notes

1. Freehold land and buildings at cost were as follows.

	Notes	£'000
Land	(a)	50,000
Buildings	(a)	95,000
Investment property	(b)	42,500
		187,500

    (a) The land and buildings were purchased on 1 June 19X1, at which time the company vacated its old premises. On 31 May 19X2 the buildings were valued on an open market basis by Messrs A, B and C, Chartered Surveyors, at a figure of £105,000,000 and the directors wish this figure to be incorporated into the accounts. If the buildings were sold at their valuation a tax liability of £3,000,000 would arise. The buildings are to be depreciated over 50 years on a straight-line basis; 25% of the buildings are used as administrative offices.

    (b) The investment property has an open market value of £62,500,000 according to Messrs A, B and C. The rental has been negotiated at arms' length with a company which is not related to M plc in any way.

2. The company acquired patents during the year at cost of £5,000,000. These patents have an unexpired life of ten years.

3. Goodwill has previously been written off over its expected useful economic life. The directors have now decided that it should be written off immediately as a change in accounting policy.

4. Research and development costs related to market research studies in an effort to identify new areas of business which might prove attractive.

5. The ACT paid relates to the dividend proposed for the year to 31 May 19X1. The directors recommend that a dividend of 3.5 pence per share should be paid on the ordinary share capital. The standard rate of income tax is 25p in the £.

6. The figure of £14,000,000 represents closure and redundancy costs incurred when the company discontinued a segment of its business. The estimated tax saving is £4,900,000 which has not yet been included in the corporation tax calculation.

7. A full year's interest on the debentures is to be provided.

8. The company has an authorised share capital of 1,000,000,000 ordinary shares of £1 each of which 300,000,000 have been issued fully paid.

9. Corporation tax on the profits of the year is estimated at £15,000,000 and is due for payment at 1 March 19X3. The directors have decided to make a transfer of £12,000,000 to the deferred tax account.

10. Stocks at 31 May 19X2 at the lower of cost or new realisable value were as follows.

	£'000
Raw materials	70,000
Finished goods	206,000
Work in progress	25,000

11. The debentures are secured on the freehold land and buildings.

You are required to prepare, in a form suitable for presentation to the shareholders (as far as the information permits):

(a) the profit and loss account and the related notes for M plc for the year ended 31 May 19X2;

(25 marks)

(b) the balance sheet and the related notes for M plc at 31 May 19X2.   (20 marks)

30   WALSH   (35 marks)   5/87

Walsh plc is a manufacturing company which has been operating for many years. The following information was extracted from its books for the year to 31 March 19X7.

	£m
Work in progress 1 April 19X6	150
Bank overdraft	80
Dividends received net of tax	14
Land and buildings (net book value)	200
Staff costs: wages and salaries	264
social security costs	10
other pension costs	2
Sundry debtors	5
Trade creditors	120
4% debenture repayable 19Y4/Y6	250
Goodwill at written down value	520
Sales	750
Amortisation of goodwill and patents for current year	50
Finished goods 1 April 19X6	100
Depreciation on buildings and plant for current year	50
Share capital (called up)	700
Patents at written down value	200
Operating charges (see note 1)	200
Interest paid	23
Investments	100
Pension provisions	70
Raw materials and consumables 1 April 19X6	20
Plant and machinery (net book value)	100
Retained profits at 1 April 19X6	10

Notes

1. Operating charges comprise the following.

	£m
Purchases of raw materials and consumables	80
Other operating costs	120
	200

2. The following figures relate to stocks held at 31 March 19X7.

	£m
Raw materials and consumables	30
Finished goods	120
Work in progress	50
	200

3. During the year new plant was developed using the company's own labour and materials, costed at £7 million and £4 million respectively. This development is now to be capitalised and no depreciation is to be charged for the year ended 31 March 19X7.

4. The 4% debenture is secured by a floating charge over all the assets of Walsh plc.

5. An independent organisation has conducted a social audit of the activities of Walsh plc. This revealed that the company anticipates a court case over pollution traceable to its production process, with estimated compensation costs of £100 million.

6. On 31 March 19X7 Walsh plc sold to a developer for £5 million an old licensed restaurant which was situated on a city centre site. This was the only restaurant operated by Walsh plc. The book value of this restaurant was £1 million, and a special tax of £2 million is payable on the gain. Contracts have been exchanged but no entries have been made in the company's books.

7. Corporation tax of £35 million is to be provided.

8. A dividend of £50 million has been proposed for the year ended 31 March 19X7. The income tax rate is 25%.

Required

(a) Prepare the profit and loss account and the related notes for Walsh plc for the year ended 31 March 19X7 in a form suitable for publication using format 2 (by type of expenditure).
(15 marks)

(b) Prepare the balance sheet and the related notes for Walsh plc at 31 March 19X7 in a form suitable for publication using format 1 (a 'vertical' format).
(15 marks)

(c) Comment briefly on the financial position of Walsh plc.
(5 marks)

31 CONSOLIDATED FINANCIAL STATEMENTS (15 marks) 11/88

'The consolidation of financial statements hides rather than provides information.'

You are required to discuss this statement.

32 CONSOLIDATION AND REALITY (15 marks) 5/90

A consolidated historical cost balance sheet gives a realistic valuation for that group.

Discuss.

33 TUTORIAL QUESTION: AYE AND BEE

Aye plc purchased 1,450,000 ordinary shares in Bee plc in 19X0, when the general reserve of Bee plc stood at £400,000 and there was no balance of unappropriated profit.

The balance sheets of the two companies as at 31 December 19X4 are set out below.

	Aye plc £'000	Aye plc £'000	Bee plc £'000	Bee plc £'000
Fixed assets				
Tangible assets				
Buildings	5,000		1,000	
Plant	3,396		543	
Vehicles	472		244	
		8,868		1,787
Investment				
Shares in Bee plc at cost		1,450		–
		10,318		1,787
Current assets				
Stock	1,983		1,425	
Debtors	1,462		1,307	
Cash	25		16	
	3,470		2,748	
Creditors: amounts due within one year				
Overdraft	1,176		840	
Trade creditors	887		1,077	
Tax	540		218	
Dividend	280		–	
	2,883		2,135	
Net current assets		587		613
Total assets less current liabilities		10,905		2,400
Creditors: amounts due after more than one year				
10% debentures		(4,000)		–
15% debentures		–		(500)
		6,905		1,900
Shareholders' funds				
Ordinary shares of 50p each		5,000		1,000
Share premium account		500		–
General reserve		1,200		800
Unappropriated profit		205		100
		6,905		1,900

At the balance sheet date the current account of Aye plc with Bee plc was agreed at £23,000 owed by Bee plc. This account is included in the appropriate debtors and trade creditors balances shown above.

Required

(a) Prepare a consolidated balance sheet for the Aye Bee Group.

(b) Show the alterations necessary to the group balance sheet if the inter-company balance owed by Bee plc to Aye plc represented an invoice for goods sold by Aye to Bee at a mark-up of 15% on cost, and still unsold by Bee plc at 31 December 19X4.

34 TUTORIAL QUESTION: BATH

Bath Limited acquired 80% of the ordinary share capital of Jankin Limited on 1 January 19X1 for the sum of £153,000 and 60% of the ordinary share capital of Arthur Limited on 1 July 19X1 for the sum of £504,000.

From the information given below you are required to prepare the consolidated balance sheet of Bath Limited at 31 December 19X1.

Comparative figures, notes to the accounts and an auditor's report are not required.

Workings must be shown.

1. The balance sheets of the three companies at 31 December 19X1 are set out below.

	Bath Limited £	Jankin Limited £	Arthur Limited £
Share capital			
Ordinary shares of £0.25 each	750,000	100,000	400,000
Share premium	15,000	–	–
Profit and loss account			
1 January 19X1	191,000	19,400	132,000
Retained profits for 19X1	37,000	3,000	54,000
Taxation	78,000	24,000	56,000
Creditors	162,000	74,400	149,000
Bank overdraft: Bank A	74,000	–	–
Depreciation			
Freehold property	9,000	–	40,000
Plant and machinery	87,000	39,000	124,600
Dividends proposed	30,000	15,000	24,000
Current account	–	9,800	–
	1,433,000	284,600	979,600
Freehold property, at cost	116,000	–	200,000
Plant and machinery, at cost	216,000	104,000	326,400
Investments in subsidiaries			
Jankin Limited	153,000	–	–
Arthur Limited	504,000	–	–
Trade investment	52,000	–	–
Stocks and work in progress	206,000	99,000	294,200
Debtors	172,200	73,000	95,000
Bank balance: Bank B	–	7,900	62,800
Cash	1,100	700	1,200
Current account	12,700	–	–
	1,433,000	284,600	979,600

2. No interim dividends were declared or paid in 19X1 out of 19X1 profits. Bath Limited has not yet accounted for dividends receivable from its subsidiary companies.

3. A remittance of £1,700 from Jankin Limited in December 19X1 was not received by Bath Limited until January 19X2.

4. An invoice for £1,200 for stock material (including £240 profit) had been included in sales in 19X1 by Bath Limited but it was not received by Jankin Limited until 19X2.

5. In Jankin Limited's stock at 31 December 19X1, were goods to the value of £8,000 ex Bath Limited on which the latter had taken profit of £1,600.

6. Profits of Arthur Limited are deemed to have accrued equally throughout the year.

7. Any goodwill arising on consolidation is to be amortised over four years.

35 ABC (35 marks)   5/89

You are given the following information.

1. On 30 June 19X4, ABC plc acquired 60% of the ordinary share capital of DEF Limited. At this time DEF Limited's retained profits were £3,000,000.

2. On 1 January 19X5, DEF Limited made a rights issue of 1 for 4. The issue was fully subscribed with ABC plc taking up its full share of the rights.

3. On 1 January 19X6, ABC plc acquired 25% of the ordinary share capital of GHI Limited. At this time GHI Limited's retained profits were £4,000,000.

4. On 28 December 19X7, ABC plc recorded a credit sale of £500,000 to DEF Limited. The items sold had cost ABC plc £200,000. DEF Limited had not recorded the purchase of these items by 31 December 19X7.

5. At the respective dates of acquisition of ABC plc's interests in DEF Limited and GHI Limited, the book value of these two companies' assets closely approximated their fair value with the following exceptions.

   (a) Stock held by DEF Limited had a fair value of £800,000 in excess of its book value. This stock was sold during 19X4.

   (b) The transport fleet of DEF Limited had a fair value of £3,500,000. The book value was £2,500,000. All of the vehicles in the fleet at the date of acquisition are still owned by DEF Limited. They are depreciated at 20% per annum on the reducing balance method.

   No adjustment has been made to the books of DEF Limited to reflect these fair valuations.

6. Goodwill on consolidation is amortised on a straight-line basis over 4 years. A full year's amortisation is charged in the year of acquisition.

7. The summarised balance sheets at 31 December 19X7 were as follows.

	ABC plc £'000	DEF Ltd £'000	GHI Ltd £'000
Tangible fixed assets	26,427	9,832	6,271
Investment in DEF Ltd (at cost)	7,000	–	–
Investment in GHI Ltd (at cost)	1,500	–	–
Trade debtors	12,105	4,216	3,814
Stock	14,629	6,834	4,223
Bank	384	244	287
	62,045	21,126	14,595
Trade creditors	10,196	3,894	2,987
Tax payable	1,054	480	408
Long-term loans	20,000	5,000	4,000
Ordinary share capital	10,000	5,000	1,000
Share premium*	–	1,000	–
Retained profits	20,795	5,752	6,200
	62,045	21,126	14,595

* Relates to DEF Limited's rights issue on 1 January 19X5.

You are required to prepare the consolidated balance sheet at 31 December 19X7 for the shareholders of ABC plc.

36   PQR PLC   (40 marks)   5/91

You are given the following information.

1. On 1 January 19X8 PQR plc acquired 80% of the ordinary share capital and voting rights of STU Ltd.

2. STU Limited acquired 75% of the ordinary share capital and voting rights of VWX Limited on 1 January 19X6.

3. The summarised balance sheets of these three companies at 31 December 19X9 were as follows.

	PQR plc £'000	STU Ltd £'000	VWX Ltd £'000
Tangible fixed assets	1,840	863	520
Investment in subsidiary (at cost)	1,452	500	–
Stock	350	212	108
Debtors	213	127	82
Bank	234	26	19
	4,089	1,728	729
Trade creditors	162	101	52
Taxation payable	112	47	27
Dividends payable	100	50	40
Ordinary share capital	500	200	100
Retained profits	3,215	1,330	510
	4,089	1,728	729

4. At the dates of share purchases the following information is known.

Company	Date	Ordinary share capital £m	Retained profits £m
STU Limited	1.1.19X6	200	560
STU Limited	1.1.19X8	200	800
VWX Limited	1.1.19X6	100	240
VWX Limited	1.1.19X8	100	320

5. During 1990 the following intra-group trading took place.

Selling company	Buying company	Sales at transfer price £m	Profit on sales
STU Limited	PQR plc	280	40% on cost

25% of these trades are held as stock at 31 December 19X9.

6. With the following exceptions, the fair value of the assets of investee companies closely approximated their book value at the relevant acquisition dates.

Company	Asset	Book value £m	Fair value £m
STU Limited	Stock *	147	197
STU Limited	Equipment **	200	400

* All of this stock had been sold by 31 December 19X8.

** This equipment was purchased in 19X7 and is depreciated over its five-year life on a straight-line basis. It is still held by STU Limited.

7. STU Limited has levied a management charge of £10 million per annum on VWX Limited for services which it provides. In 19X9 VWX Limited has neither paid this charge nor accrued it as outstanding.

8. No dividends receivable have been accrued by parent companies.

9. Group accounting policies are as follows.

   (a) Only goodwill pertaining to the parent company is included in the consolidated financial statements.
   (b) Goodwill is written off on a straight-line basis over five years.
   (c) In the year of purchase, a full year's depreciation is provided in respect of fixed assets.

You are required:

(a) to prepare the consolidated balance sheet of ABC plc at 31 December 19X9 for presentation to the shareholders;   (35 marks)

(b) to explain why the fair value of a company's assets is used in the preparation of consolidated financial statements.   (5 marks)

37 WHITESIDE (40 marks) 11/87

You are given the following information relating to the Whiteside Group.

(i) On 1 January 19X1 Whiteside plc acquired 80% of the ordinary share capital of McClair Ltd. This latter company already owned 75% of the ordinary share capital of Olsen Ltd which it acquired on 1 September 19X0. On 1 July 19X4 Whiteside plc acquired 30% of the ordinary share capital of O'Brien Ltd.

(ii) The following information is available on the retained profits of the above companies.

Date	Whiteside plc £'000	McClair Ltd £'000	Olsen Ltd £'000	O'Brien Ltd £'000
1 September 19X0	1,820	1,200	820	218
1 January 19X1	1,947	1,450	940	244
1 July 19X4	2,464	1,526	1,123	300

(iii) SUMMARISED BALANCE SHEETS AT 31 DECEMBER 19X6

	Whiteside plc £'000	McClair Ltd £'000	Olsen Ltd £'000	O'Brien Ltd £'000
Land	750	400	850	140
Equipment	1,045	345	250	110
Investment in McClair Ltd (at cost)	2,500	-	-	-
Investment in O'Brien Ltd (at cost)	250	-	-	-
Investment in Olsen Ltd (at cost)	-	1,500	-	-
Stock	634	423	241	146
Debtors	921	647	407	198
Bank	713	232	353	68
	6,813	3,547	2,101	662
Creditors	843	1,047	311	142
Loan (19X8)	1,000	-	-	-
Ordinary share capital	2,000	750	500	100
Retained profits	2,970	1,750	1,290	420
	6,813	3,547	2,101	662

(iv) At the relevant dates of acquisition the fair values of the net assets of McClair Ltd, Olsen Ltd and O'Brien Ltd closely approximated their balance sheet values with the exception of the land held by McClair Ltd which had a market value £350,000 in excess of its balance sheet value. This land is still held by McClair Ltd.

(v) The following inter-company transactions took place during 19X6.

	Sold by	Sold to	Sales value £'000	Original cost £'000
January 19X6	Whiteside plc	Olsen Ltd	380	200
June 19X6 *	Olsen Ltd	McClair Ltd	250	150
December 19X6*	O'Brien Ltd	Whiteside plc	300	250

*Only in these cases were the goods received by McClair Ltd and Whiteside plc still held by these companies at 31 December 19X6.

(vi) During 19X4 McClair Ltd transferred a machine to Whiteside plc for £500,000. At the time of this transfer the machine's written down value in McClair Ltd's books was £400,000 (cost £800,000, aggregate depreciation £400,000, useful life 8 years and depreciation rate of 12½% per annum straight line). It is a group policy to provide a full year's depreciation on assets in their year of purchase.

(vii) *Accounting policies*

    (a) Goodwill on consolidation is calculated as the parent company's share of any goodwill arising on group acquisitions.

    (b) Goodwill arising on consolidation is written off over 8 years on a straight-line basis.

    (c) Intra-group profits earned by subsidiaries are eliminated, where appropriate, proportionately against the majority and minority interests in the group.

You are required to prepare the consolidated balance sheet for the Whiteside Group at 31 December 19X6 in a form suitable for publication.

38 GREATER COMBINATIONS (30 marks)

Greater Combinations Limited and its subsidiary Cooperative Limited, have produced the following summarised balance sheets as on 30 November 19X9 and profit and loss accounts for the year ended on that date.

SUMMARISED BALANCE SHEETS AS AT 30 NOVEMBER 19X9

	Greater Combinations £'000	Cooperative Limited £'000
Called up share capital: ordinary shares of £1	500	100
Reserves and unappropriated profits	800	260
Deferred taxation	100	90
	1,400	450
Tangible fixed assets	600	100
Shares in subsidiary: 75,000 shares of £1	25	–
Patents and trade marks	75	20
Net current assets	700	330
	1,400	450

SUMMARISED PROFIT AND LOSS ACCOUNTS FOR THE YEAR ENDED 30 NOVEMBER 19X9

	Greater Combinations £'000	Cooperative Limited £'000
Trading profit	225	60
Taxation at 40%	90	24
	135	36
Proposed dividend	75	20
Retained	60	16

Further information

1. The entire issued share capital of Cooperative Limited was acquired on 1 August 19X0 at £1 per share. At this date total reserves and unappropriated profits of Cooperative Limited were equivalent to £0.80 per share. There have not been any changes in the issued share capital since that date.

2. On 31 May 19X9, 25,000 shares of Cooperative Limited were sold at £3 per share (provision for corporation tax to be made at an effective rate of 30%).

3. The sale had been recorded in the books of Greater Combinations Limited by crediting the receipt against the cost of purchase.

4. Trading and profit of Cooperative Limited arise evenly throughout the year.

5. Greater Combinations Limited sells to Cooperative Limited on the normal trade terms of cost plus 25% goods to the value of £100,000 per month. Stock held by Cooperative Limited at the end of the year represents one month's purchases.

6. Both companies maintain the deferred taxation account under the liability method.

7. Greater Combinations Limited does not take credit in its own accounts for dividends until they have been received.

Required

(a) Prepare a consolidated balance sheet at 30 November 19X9 which complies with the best current practice in so far as the information provided will allow.

(15 marks)

(b) Prepare a detailed analysis of the movements in the group 'reserves and unappropriated profits'. (15 marks)

39 DUXBURY (35 marks) 5/87

You are given the following information relating to Duxbury plc, Albiston Ltd and Moran Ltd:

1. PROFIT AND LOSS ACCOUNTS FOR THE YEAR ENDED 31 DECEMBER 19X6

	Duxbury plc £'000
Turnover	17,000
Cost of sales	8,000
Gross profit	9,000
Distribution costs	2,400
Administrative expenses	1,780
Operating profit	4,820
Income from shares in group companies	120
Income from shares in associated companies	25
Profit on ordinary activities before taxation	4,965
Taxation	2,200
Profit on ordinary activities after taxation	2,765
Extraordinary charges	200
Taxation on extraordinary charges	100
Profit after extraordinary items	2,665
Dividend paid	300
Retained profit for year	2,365

	Albiston Ltd £'000	Moran Ltd £'000
Turnover	7,400	3,400
Change in stocks of finished goods and work in progress	380	(800)
	7,780	2,600
Raw material cost	1,050	400
Labour cost	1,700	700
Production overhead costs	1,300	500
Distribution costs	200	300
Administrative expenses	300	100
	3,230	600
Taxation	1,500	200
Profit on ordinary activities after taxation	1,730	400
Extraordinary charges	100	50
Taxation on extraordinary charges	50	20
	1,680	370
Dividends paid	200	100
Retained profit for year	1,480	270

2. Duxbury plc acquired a 60% interest in Albiston Ltd in 19X5 and a 25% interest in Moran Ltd in 19X3. At the dates when these interests were acquired the retained profits of Albiston Ltd and Moran Ltd were £5,000,000 and £1,600,000 respectively.

3. Finished goods stock costing £100,000 was held by Albiston Ltd at the date when Duxbury plc acquired its 60% interest in the company. The fair value of this stock, at that time, was £200,000. This stock was sold externally during 19X6 for a sum exceeding £200,000. You may assume that the book values of the other assets of both Albiston Ltd and Moran Ltd approximated their fair values at the respective dates of acquisition.

4.   The stock held by Duxbury plc at 31 December 19X6 included items costing £400,000 which had been bought from Albiston Ltd during 19X6. This stock had cost Albiston Ltd £200,000.

5.   Retained profits for the companies at 1 January 19X6 were as follows.

Duxbury plc	£9,500,000
Albiston Ltd	£6,000,000
Moran Ltd	£2,000,000

Required

(a)   Prepare the consolidated profit and loss account for the year ended 31 December 19X6 for the shareholders of Duxbury plc. Present this profit and loss account in the format adopted by the parent company in preparing its own profit and loss account.

(25 marks)

(b)   Compute the retained profits figure which would appear in the consolidated balance sheet of the Duxbury group at 31 December 19X6.

(10 marks)

40   PROJECTION   (45 marks)   5/90

The board of ABC plc, a retail organisation, is considering the acquisition of an 80% interest in the ordinary share capital of its main wholesale supplier, DEF plc on 1 January 19X1. You are given the following information.

PROJECTED PROFIT AND LOSS ACCOUNTS FOR THE YEAR ENDING 31 DECEMBER 19X0

	ABC plc £m	DEF plc £m
Turnover	800	200
Cost of sales	500	120
Gross profit	300	80
Distribution costs	90	3
Administration expenses	50	5
Profit on ordinary activities before taxation	160	72
Taxation	60	32
Profit on ordinary activities after taxation	100	40
Dividends	30	10
Retained profit for the year	70	30

Notes

1.   The interest in DEF plc will be acquired for £100 million. This will be financed by raising a new 12% fixed interest loan. £40 million of this loan will be convertible to ordinary shares after 19X1 at the rate of one ordinary 25p share in ABC plc for every £1 of loan stock. At the date of acquisition the shareholders' interest in DEF plc will be as follows.

	£m
Ordinary share capital	20
Retained profits	35
Fair value revaluation reserve*	20
	75

*This reserve, which will be created only for purposes of consolidation, comprises the following individual revaluations.

	£m
Stock	5
Depreciable sales vehicles	15
(with an average remaining life of five years)	
	20

2. ABC plc purchases one quarter of its supplies from DEF plc. This pattern of purchases is mirrored exactly in stockholdings. ABC plc maintains its stock level at 20% of its preceding annual cost of sales.

3. Both companies pursue a uniform 'cost plus' pricing policy based on a standard gross margin for all their customers and consistently distribute, as dividends, 30% (ABC plc) and 25% (DEF plc) of profits available for distribution.

4. ABC plc writes off goodwill, as an administration expense, on a straight-line basis over five years. All other assets are also depreciated on a straight line basis.

5. ABC plc's issued share capital consists of £50 million of 25p ordinary shares.

6. The following assumptions can be made for 19X1.

    (i)   Sales of both companies will grow in volume by 5% in 19X1. Their unit selling prices will be unchanged and existing cost plus pricing policies will be maintained.

    (ii) ABC plc will continue to purchase one quarter of its supplies from DEF plc. Stockholding policies will not change.

    (iii) The expenditures for administration, selling and distribution shown in the 19X0 profit and loss accounts will be repeated in 19X1.

    (iv) Tax charges in 19X1 will be 30% of the profit before tax figure for each company.

    (v)   The 19X1 dividend cover will also be maintained.

    (vi) ABC plc will acquire an 80% interest in the ordinary share capital of DEF plc on 1 January 19X1.

You are required to prepare for the board of ABC plc:

(a) the projected consolidated profit and loss account for ABC plc for the year ending 31 December 19X1;   (40 marks)

(b) a comparison of ABC plc's 19X0 and 19X1 earnings per share.   (5 marks)

41   THOPAS (40 marks)   5/85

Thopas Limited has one partly-owned subsidiary Melibee Limited and a 25% interest in Prudence Limited. The interest in Prudence Limited was acquired on 31 December 19X2, at which date the owner's interest in Prudence Limited comprised ordinary share capital of £150,000 and retained profits of £150,000.

You are given the following information relating to the Thopas Group.

1. Consolidated balance sheets in working schedule form of the parent company Thopas Limited and its only subsidiary Melibee Limited.

	As at 31 December	
	19X4	19X3
	£'000	£'000
Tangible fixed assets	5,030	4,327
Goodwill on consolidation*	100	200
Investment in Prudence Limited at cost	750	750
Stock	527	342
Debtors	216	194
Bank	48	73
	6,671	5,886
Trade creditors	(204)	(201)
Net assets	6,467	5,685
Minority interests	490	440
Ordinary share capital	2,000	1,500
Revaluation reserve	500	-
Retained profits	3,477	3,745
	6,467	5,685

*Goodwill on consolidation is written off at 20% per annum on a straight-line basis.

2. The consolidated profit and loss accounts for the year ended 31 December 19X4.

	Consolidation of Thopas Ltd and Melibee Ltd	Prudence Ltd
	£'000	£'000
Sales	7,660	3,500
Cost of sales	6,238	2,315
	1,422	1,185
Administration costs	1,790	205
	(368)	980
Income from shares in associated company	10	-
	(358)	980
Taxation	150	(440)
	(208)	540
Minority interest	60	-
	(268)	540
Dividend paid	-	40
	(268)	500
Retained profits from previous years	3,745	220
Retained profits carried forward	3,477	720

3. Note on fixed assets supporting the consolidated balance sheet of Thopas Limited and Melibee Limited.

	Land and buildings 19X4 £'000	Plant and machinery 19X3 £'000
At cost at 1 January 19X4	2,400	4,209
Purchases at cost	-	761
Revaluation	500	-
	2,900	4,970
Sales at cost*	-	300
At cost or valuation at 31 December 19X4	2,900	4,670
Aggregate depreciation at 1 January 19X4	1,000	1,282
Aggregate depreciation on sales	-	300
	1,000	982
Depreciation charge for year	100	458
Aggregate depreciation at 31 December 19X4	1,100	1,440

*The plant and machinery sold during 19X4 realised £65,000.

You are required to prepare:

(a) revised balance sheets for the Thopas Group (incorporating Prudence Limited in accordance with standard accounting practice) at 31 December 19X3 and at 31 December 19X4;

(15 marks)

(b) a revised profit and loss account for the Thopas Group (incorporating Prudence Limited in accordance with standard accounting practice) for the year ended 31 December 19X4;

(10 marks)

(c) a statement of source and application of funds for the Thopas Group for the year ended 31 December 19X4 in a form suitable for presentation to shareholders.

(15 marks)

42 CRERAND (35 marks)   11/88

During the year ended 31 December 19X7 Crerand plc, a UK registered company operating in several overseas locations, carried out the following transactions denominated in foreign currencies.

(i) Transactions with a French supplier of raw materials were as follows.

19X7		French francs FFr
1 January	Balancing outstanding	50,000
1 May	Purchases	280,000
1 August	Payment	(300,000)
1 November	Purchases	320,000
31 December	Balance outstanding	350,000

(ii) In 19X6 Crerand plc purchased an 8% equity investment in a Belgian customer for 3,600,000 Belgian francs. The rate of exchange ruling at the date of purchase was £1 = BFr64. As a hedge against future exchange rate fluctuations, Crerand plc financed this investment with the proceeds of a German DM-denominated loan of DM 180,000 raised on the same date, when the rate of exchange was £1 = DM3.15. In 19X7 a dividend of BFr38,000 was payable to Crerand plc. This amount had not been remitted at 31 December 19X7. Sales to this customer are billed in sterling amounts.

(iii) The company is the owner of a hotel situated in an Italian resort. This hotel is treated as an independent branch operation. The local management is responsible for all income and expenditure in local currency (Lira) with surplus cash being remitted to the UK from time to time.

The following financial statements, received from the hotel management, summarise the operations during 19X7.

BALANCE SHEETS

	31 December 19X7 Lira (000)	31 December 19X6 Lira (000)
Property and fittings	520,000	520,000
Net current assets	106,000	84,000
	626,000	604,000
Loan from Italian bank	400,000	400,000
Head office capital account	100,000	100,000
Surplus retained	126,000	104,000
	626,000	604,000

PROFIT AND LOSS ACCOUNT
FOR THE YEAR ENDED 31 DECEMBER 19X7

	Lira (000)
Income from hire of rooms and sundry services	746,000
Less operating expenses	483,000
	263,000
Less local taxes	91,000
	172,000
Less remittances to Crerand plc	150,000
Surplus retained	22,000

The company received £69,450 from the branch during the year. No cash was in transit at the year ends.

Crerand plc accounts for its foreign currency transactions in accordance with the provisions of SSAP 20, with profit and loss accounts being translated at the average rate for the year. The company considers that its accounting for foreign currency transactions reflects their economic substance as far as possible within the provisions of SSAP 20.

Exchange rates prevailing during 19X7 were as follows.

Value of pound sterling (£) against:

19X7	French franc FFr	Belgian franc BFr	German mark DM	Italian lira Lira
At 1 January	9.60	62.50	3.12	2,050
1 May	9.45	-	-	-
1 August	9.50	-	-	-
1 November	9.50	-	-	-
31 December	9.65	60.10	3.05	2,130
Average for year	-	-	-	2,080

Required

(a) Prepare the journal entries necessary to reflect the foreign exchange aspects of the above transactions in the books of Crerand plc for the year ended 31 December 19X7.

(20 marks)

(b) State the amounts which would appear in the balance sheet of Crerand plc at 31 December 19X7 in respect of the above items, including comparatives where possible.

(10 marks)

(c) Explain how the specific exchange differences arising during the year would be dealt with in Crerand plc's financial statements.

(5 marks)

43 OXFORD (40 marks)

The draft financial statements of Oxford plc and its subsidiary, Bonn GmbH are set out below.

Balance sheets at 31 December 19X5

	Oxford plc £'000	Bonn GmbH DM'000
Tangible fixed assets	3,240	4,860
Investment in Bonn	470	-
Stocks	1,990	8,316
Debtors	1,630	4,572
Cash	240	2,016
Creditors	(5,030)	(4,356)
Loans	(1,920)	-
	620	15,408
Share capital (£1/DM1)	118	1,348
Profit and loss account	502	14,060
	620	15,408

Profit and loss accounts for year ended 31 December 19X5

	Oxford plc £'000	Bonn GmbH £'000
Turnover	40,425	97,125
Cost of sales	35,500	77,550
Gross profit	4,925	19,575
Distribution and administration	4,400	5,850
Investment income	277	-
Profit before tax	802	13,725
Tax	300	4,725
Profit after tax	502	9,000
Dividends	700	3,752
Retained	(198)	5,248

The following additional information is given.

1. Exchange rates

	DM to £
31 December 19X2	4.40
31 December 19X3	4.16
31 December 19X4	4.00
15 May 19X5	3.92
31 December 19X5	3.60
Average for 19X5	3.75

2. Oxford acquired 1,011,000 shares in Bonn for £470,000 on 31 December 19X2 when Bonn's profit and loss account stood at DM 2,876,000.

3. Bonn paid an interim dividend of DM 1,448,000 on 13 May 19X5 and proposed to pay a final dividend of DM 2,304,000. Oxford has not yet accounted for the dividend receivable.

4. Oxford's accounting policy is to translate the profit and loss accounts of overseas subsidiaries at an average rate of exchange and to deal with exchange differences including those relating to dividends as a reserve movement.

Required

(a) Prepare the consolidated balance sheet at 31 December 19X5.

(15 marks)

(b) Prepare the consolidated profit and loss account and statement of reserves for the year ended 31 December 19X5. (25 marks)

44 T GROUP (15 marks)   11/89

You are the group accountant in the T Group which has just acquired its first foreign subsidiary. The T Group has financed the acquisition of this new overseas subsidiary by foreign currency borrowing. Your managing director has asked you to explain how the financial statements of this foreign subsidiary will be translated in £ sterling.

You are required to write a memorandum to your managing director explaining:

(a) the choice of foreign currency translation methods;   (3 marks)

(b) the treatment of foreign exchange differences;   (8 marks)

(c) the disclosure required of the foreign exchange translation method and of the treatment of foreign exchange differences.   (4 marks)

45 FOREIGN EXCHANGE (15 marks)   5/91

Your managing director has been studying the accounts of two similar groups with overseas subsidiaries. He is puzzled by the different notes on accounting policies relating to foreign exchange transactions which read as follows.

Company 1
'Overseas assets and liabilities are translated at the closing rate of exchange. Results for the year are translated at the average rate of exchange. Gains and losses arising in translation are dealt with in accordance with SSAP 20.'

Company 2
'The accounts of overseas subsidiaries are translated using the temporal method applied in accordance with SSAP 20. Results for the year are translated using average rate.'

You are required to write a report for your managing director:

(a) explaining the concepts on which the closing rate and temporal methods are based; and
                                                                                   (6 marks)

(b) discussing the factors which will be considered when a group is choosing between the closing rate and temporal methods.   (9 marks)

46 TUTORIAL QUESTION: NEWMAN

The summarised balance sheets of Newman Limited and Gilbert Limited as at 30 September 19X8 are as follows.

	Newman Limited £'000	Gilbert Limited £'000
Freehold properties	–	210
Other fixed assets	3,650	420
Net current assets	1,160	51
	4,810	681
Ordinary share capital (£1 shares)	2,000	300
Reserves at 1 October 19X7	2,600	221
Net profit reported for 19X7/X8	210	160
	4,810	681

Newman Limited acquired the entire share capital of Gilbert Limited on 30 September 19X8 for £900,000. The consideration took the form of five newly issued ordinary shares in Newman Limited for every three shares currently held in Gilbert Limited. This transaction has not yet been recorded in the books of Newman.

Gilbert Limited's freehold properties possessed a fair value of £325,000 on 30 September 19X8. There were no significant differences between the book value and fair value of Gilbert's remaining assets at that time.

Required

(a) Prepare the consolidated balance sheet of Newman Limited and its subsidiary Gilbert Limited at 30 September 19X8 in accordance with the acquisition method of accounting specified in SSAP 14.

(b) Prepare the consolidated balance sheet of Newman Limited and its subsidiary Gilbert Limited at 30 September 19X8 in accordance with the merger method of accounting specified in SSAP 23.

Notes
1. Show all workings.
2. Ignore taxation.
3. The balance sheet should be framed, as far as possible, in the format given in the question, so as to show the group net profit reported for 19X7/X8.

47 STEPNEY (25 marks)   5/88

You are given the following information.

(i) On 30 June 19X7 Stepney plc obtained acceptance by 100% of the ordinary shareholders of Brennan plc of its offer of one new ordinary share in Stepney plc for every one ordinary share in Brennan plc. The offer was also declared unconditional on 30 June 19X7 and arrangements were made for the share exchange to take place within the next few days. On 30 June 19X7 the ordinary shares of Stepney plc had a market value of £8.50 each. The newly-formed group became known as the Stepney Group plc.

(ii) It may be assumed that profits before extraordinary items of both companies accrue evenly over the year. The extraordinary charge in the accounts of Stepney plc relates to an event occurring in March 19X7.

(iii) Stepney plc uses the average cost method of stock valuation while Brennan plc has used the FIFO method in preparing its 19X7 financial statements. The directors of the new group have agreed to standardise accounting practice by using average cost throughout the group. This change would have affected Brennan plc's stock values as shown below.

	Stock values (Brennan plc)	
	FIFO basis	Average cost basis
	£'000	£'000
Stock (31 December 19X6)	2,748	2,528
Stock (31 December 19X7)	3,826	3,014

(iv) SUMMARISED BALANCE SHEETS AT 31 DECEMBER 19X7

	Stepney plc £'000	Brennan plc £'000
Fixed assets	61,376	24,299
Investment in Brennan plc	2,000	-
Current assets	22,685	8,623
	86,061	32,922
Current liabilities	12,472	5,461
Ordinary share capital	15,000 *	1,000 **
Retained profits	58,589	26,461
	86,061	32,922

* called-up share capital in ordinary shares of £1.00 each
** called-up share capital in ordinary shares of £0.50 each.

(v) SUMMARISED PROFIT AND LOSS ACCOUNTS
FOR THE YEAR ENDED 31 DECEMBER 19X7

	Stepney plc £'000	Brennan plc £'000
Turnover	41,456	15,396
Cost of sales	18,221	5,492
Gross profit	23,235	9,904
Administration expenses	2,694	1,063
Selling and distribution costs	4,143	1,824
Profit on ordinary activities before taxation	16,398	7,017
Taxation	5,240	2,076
Profit on ordinary activities after taxation	11,158	4,941
Extraordinary items less taxation	2,616	-
	8,542	4,941
Dividend	2,000	-
Retained profit for year	6,542	4,941
Retained profits at 1 January 19X7	52,047	21,520
Retained profits at 31 December 19X7	58,589	26,461

You are required to prepare, on a merger accounting basis, the consolidated balance sheet at 31 December 19X7 and the consolidated profit and loss account for the year ended 31 December 19X7 of the Stepney Group plc.

48   RESTART (25 marks)

The draft balance sheet of Restart Limited at 30 September 19X7 was as follows.

	£	£
Fixed assets		
Intangible assets		
Development costs	24,000	
Patents and trade marks	34,000	
		58,000
Tangible assets		
Freehold properties (cost)	70,000	
Plant and machinery (NBV)	120,000	
		190,000
Shares in subsidiary company (cost)		120,000
		368,000
Current assets		
Stocks	124,000	
Debtors	160,000	
Amount due from subsidiary company	42,000	
	326,000	
Creditors: amounts falling due within one year		
Bank overdraft	104,000	
Sundry creditors	220,000	
Loans from directors	30,000	
	354,000	
Net current liabilities		(28,000)
		340,000
Capital and reserves		
Called up share capital (authorised: £700,000)		
320,000 8% £1 cumulative preference shares fully paid		320,000
320,000 £1 ordinary shares 75p paid		240,000
		560,000
Profit and loss account (debit balance)		(220,000)
		340,000

Note to balance sheet: arrears of preference dividends amount to £25,600.

A scheme for reconstruction was duly approved with effect from 1 October 19X7 under the following conditions.

(i)   The unpaid capital on the ordinary shares will be called up.

(ii)   The arrears of preference dividend will be cancelled and each preference shareholder will accept a reduction of 25p per share. The dividend rate on new preference shares is to be raised to 9%.

(iii) The ordinary shareholders will accept a reduction of 75p on each share held.

(iv)   Patents and trade marks are to be reduced to £24,000; a provision for doubtful debts of £30,000 is to be created; £50,000 is to be written off plant and machinery and £20,000 off shares in subsidiary.

(v)   Freehold properties are professionally valued and are to be written up to £190,000.

(vi) Development costs are to be eliminated.

(vii) The directors agreed to take ordinary shares at the new par value of 25p each in settlement of loans outstanding.

(viii) The debit balance on profit and loss account is eliminated.

(ix) New capital is allotted for cash and is fully paid as follows:

   (1) each ordinary shareholder (including directors, in respect of their new holdings) to take up two new ordinary shares for every one held;

   (2) each preference shareholder to take up one new preference share for every four held.

The resolution for the reduction of capital, provided for the restoration of the authorised capital to £700,000.

Assume that all these transactions were completed on 1 October 19X7.

Required

(a) (i)   Show the necessary ledger entries in the capital reduction and reconstruction account, the share capital accounts and the bank account.

     (ii) Show the balance sheet of the company after the reconstruction.
                                                                    (18 marks)

(b) State briefly what object is served by a scheme for reduction of capital where a company has incurred heavy losses. By whom should such losses be borne and why?
                                                                    (7 marks)

49 ROBERT (35 marks)

Robert Ltd was incorporated with an authorised share capital of £250,000 divided into 600,000 ordinary shares of 25p each and 100,000 £1 10% cumulative preference shares to take over the existing businesses including cash of Alpha Ltd and Beta Ltd at 31 December 19X2.

The draft balance sheets of Alpha Ltd and Beta Ltd at 31 December 19X2 showed the following.

	Alpha £	Beta £		Alpha £	Beta £
Capital: ordinary			Freehold property		
shares of £1 each	30,000	20,000	at cost	28,000	12,000
Reserves	18,000	6,500	Plant at cost	32,000	25,000
Trade creditors	13,000	26,000	Less depreciation	(10,000)	(8,000)
Bank	14,000	–	Development expenditure	–	10,000
			Stock	15,000	7,500
			Debtors	10,000	2,000
			Bank	–	4,000
	75,000	52,500		75,000	52,500

You are given the following information.

1. The purchase consideration for the business acquired is to be the amount which Robert Ltd would have to invest at 15% per annum to yield the weighted average profit of the past three years. The weights are to be 1,2,3 respectively.

   Profits, which have been adjusted to take account of the adjustments required in note 4 following, were as follows.

	Alpha Ltd £	Beta Ltd £
19X0	8,000	17,000
19X1	14,000	13,000
19X2	16,500	6,500

2. The fixed assets have a fair value at 31 December 19X2 as follows.

	Alpha Ltd £	Beta Ltd £
Freehold property	35,000	18,000
Plant	17,500	22,000

3. The development expenditure of £10,000 has been reviewed. The project it relates to is technically viable but unless the new company is formed to acquire Beta Ltd and provide additional funds, there is doubt as to whether Beta Ltd is a going concern. However, subject to the amalgamation, it is felt that the carrying value should remain at £10,000.

4. Provision is to be made as follows.

	Alpha Ltd	Beta Ltd
(a) Obsolete stock	5% of balance sheet value	-
(b) Doubtful debts	3% of debtors	2½% of debtors
(c) Warranty claims	£6,000	-

5. The purchase consideration is to be satisfied as follows.

   (a) Preference shares are to be issued to the value of the freehold property.

   (b) 75% of the remaining purchase consideration is to be satisfied by the issue of ordinary shares in Robert Ltd at a premium of 5p per share.

   (c) The remainder of the purchase consideration is to be satisfied by cash.

6. Robert Ltd is to issue sufficient ordinary shares at a premium of 5p per share to establish a liquidity ratio of 1:1.

7. The shares received by Alpha and Beta are to be divided to the nearest whole number. If not exactly divisible the balance is to be sold for cash and the cash proceeds distributed.

Required

(a) Prepare journal entries to close the books of Beta Ltd. (10 marks)

(b) Calculate for a shareholder with 100 £1 shares in Alpha Ltd what consideration he would receive from Robert Ltd showing clearly the breakdown between shares and cash.
(7 marks)

(c) Prepare the balance sheet of Robert Ltd immediately after the amalgamation. (Ignore taxation). (18 marks)

50   PQR   (30 marks)   **5/89**

PQR Ltd, a wholly owned subsidiary of a major public company, has experienced losses for several years. The senior managers of PQR Ltd are confident that the company could be revived if further funds were to be invested but have failed to convince the parent company. In early August 19X7, the parent company was the target of a successful take-over bid and the new owners commenced a programme of selling parts of the group which did not fit into its new structure.

Senior managers of PQR Ltd felt that this was an ideal opportunity for a management buy-out and quickly drew up a business plan which received the backing of a firm which specialised in providing venture capital. Buy-out terms were agreed with the parent company in late December 19X7.

The balance sheet of PQR Ltd at 31 December 19X7, the date of the buy-out, was as follows.

	£'000	£'000
Fixed assets		
Tangible assets		
Property (at cost)		380
Plant and equipment (net)		420
Intangible assets		
Patents (at cost *less* amounts written off)		150
		950
Current assets		
Stock and work-in-progress	255	
Debtors	124	
	379	
Creditors: amounts falling due within one year		
Trade creditors	390	
Loan from parent company	388	
Bank overdraft	107	
	885	
Net current liabilities		(506)
		444
Capital and reserves		
Called up share capital		
Ordinary shares of £1 each, fully paid		1,000
Retained profits (debit balance)		(556)
		444

Details of the buy-out and reconstruction were as follows.

1. The parent company has agreed to its ordinary shares being converted into 1,000,000 10% preference shares of £1 each, fully paid. It further agreed to write off the loan.

2. In order to provide additional capital, a new issue was made of 1,000,000 ordinary shares of £1 each, fully paid. The senior managers, who would form the new board of directors, are to subscribe for 200,000 of the new shares and the balance is to be taken up via a Business Expansion Scheme managed by the venture capital firm.

3. The following scheme was put into effect by 1 January 19X8.

    (i)   One of the factories was sold for £600,000, the original cost being £250,000. The remaining factory was revalued at £450,000.

    (ii)   The workforce at the factory which was sold were offered a transfer to the remaining factory or redundancy. Redundancy costs amounts to £175,000 in respect of the employees who chose to accept the redundancy offer.

    (iii) Plant and equipment at the factory which was closed was sold for £150,000. Its net book value was £160,000. New specialist plant was purchased for £300,000 and contracts for further equipment and factory modernisation were approved amounting to £500,000.

    (iv)   Patents were considered to be worthless.

    (v)   £35,000 of obsolete stocks were written off and £15,000 of debtors were also written off as bad debts.

    (vi)   The debit balance on retained profits was written off.

    (vii) Costs of the reconstruction totalling £60,000 were paid.

Required

(a) Show the appropriate journal entries and reconstruction account in the books of PQR Ltd.
                                                                          (20 marks)
(b) Prepare the opening balance sheet of PQR Ltd at 1 January 19X8.   (10 marks)

51 MOSES (15 marks)   5/87

You are the finance director of Moses plc. The marketing director of the company has told you that he only realised recently the amount of information about Moses plc's competitors available in their annual reports. The marketing director considers that he understands much of the annual report of each competitor except for the published financial statements.

You are required to write a report for the marketing director of Moses plc explaining:

(a) the information which can be provided from an analysis of a competitor's published financial statements and which would be particularly relevant for the marketing director;
                                                                          (10 marks)

(b) the limitations of such information.   (5 marks)

52 SEGMENTAL ANALYSIS   (15 marks)   5/90

You are required to discuss:

(a) the benefits, to readers of financial statements, of including segmental financial information in a group's annual report;

(b) the reasons why a group may resist disclosing such detailed segmental financial information in its annual report.

53 CONSOLIDATED FUNDS STATEMENT   11/90

You are the group accountant in LM plc. You have the following information relating to the LM Group.

(a) SUMMARISED CONSOLIDATED PROFIT AND LOSS ACCOUNT FOR THE YEAR ENDED 31 DECEMBER 19X1.

	£'000	£'000
Operating profit		20,750
Income from shares in associated company		1,225
Profit on ordinary activities after taxation		21,975
Taxation: group	9,875	
associated company	525	
		10,400
Profit on ordinary activities after taxation		11,575
Minority interests		1,938
Profit attributed to shareholders of LM plc		9,637
Proposed dividend		2,625
Retained profit for the year		7,012
Retained profit brought forward	9,000	
Goodwill on consolidation written off	(500)	
		8,500
Retained profit carried forward		15,512

(b) SUMMARISED CONSOLIDATED BALANCE SHEETS AT 31 DECEMBER

	19X1		19X0	
	£'000	£'000	£'000	£'000
Fixed assets				
Tangible assets		26,500		21,125
Investment in associated company		7,750		7,125
		34,250		28,250
Current assets				
Stocks	20,750		15,250	
Debtors	17,625		10,875	
ACT recoverable	1,125		750	
Cash in hand and at bank	62		1,806	
	39,562		28,681	
Creditors: amounts falling due within one year				
Trade creditors	9,625		7,250	
Taxation	11,375		6,125	
Proposed dividend	2,625		1,750	
Bank overdraft	1,600		-	
	25,225		15,125	
Net current assets		14,337		13,556
		48,587		41,806
Creditors: amounts falling due after more than one year				
12% debentures 19X9		2,019		6,250
		46,568		35,556
Capital and reserves				
Share capital (£1 shares)		17,500		16,250
Share premium		3,306		2,056
Retained profit		15,512		9,000
		36,318		27,306
Minority interests		10,250		8,250
		46,568		35,556

(c) On 1 July 19X1 LM plc acquired 80% of the issued share capital of S Limited, whose net assets at that date were as follows.

	£'000
Fixed assets	3,250
Stocks	1,375
Debtors	1,225
Creditors	(1,725)
Taxation	(375)
	3,750

The purchase consideration of £3,500,000 was partly funded by the issue of 1 million £1 ordinary shares at £2.50. The balance was paid in cash. The policy of the group is to write off goodwill on consolidation to reserves at the date of acquisition.

(d) Depreciation charged during 19X1 amounted to £2,750,000. There were no disposals of fixed assets during the year.

(e) SUMMARISED GROUP STATEMENT OF SOURCE AND APPLICATION OF FUNDS
FOR THE YEAR ENDED 31 DECEMBER 19X1

	£'000	£'000
Source of funds		
Profit before taxation		21,975
Adjustments for items not involving the movement of funds		
Depreciation	2,750	
Income from associated company	(1,225)	
		1,525
Funds generated from operations		23,500
Funds from other sources		
Issue of shares in part payment for acquisition of subsidiary		2,500
Dividend from associated company		75
		26,075
Application of funds		
Purchase of S Limited	3,500	
Capital expenditure	4,875	
Dividends paid:		
to parent company shareholders	1,750	
to minority shareholders in subsidiaries	688	
Taxation paid	5,375	
Redemption of debentures	4,231	
		20,419
		5,656
Increase/(decrease) in working capital		
Stocks		4,125
Debtors		5,525
Creditors		(650)
Movement in net liquid funds		
Cash in hand	(1,744)	
Bank overdraft	(1,600)	
		(3,344)
		5,656

STATEMENT OF THE EFFECTS OF THE ACQUISITION OF S LTD

	£'000		£'000
Fixed assets	3,250	Shares	2,500
Stocks	1,375	Cash	1,000
Debtors	1,225		
Goodwill	500		
Creditors	(1,725)		
Taxation	(375)		
Minority interest	(750)		
	3,500		3,500

(f)   You have received the following memorandum.

From: Chairman
To: Group accountant
Subject: *Source and application of funds statement for 19X1*

I thought I had mastered funds flow statements but obviously the purchase of S Ltd during the year has introduced complications. In particular, I do not understand the following four points.

(i)   'Income from associated company: £1,225,000'. You have shown this as a deduction from 'Profit before tax' but surely this is a source of funds? Also, I cannot see where you got the figure of £75,000 in 'Funds from other sources'. Finally, what happened to the figure of £525,000 for 'Taxation – associated company'? I cannot find this in the funds statement.

(ii)   'Minority interests'. The figure in the group profit and loss account is £1,938,000 but you have shown £688,000 in the funds statement. Why is this shown as an application?

(iii) How did you calculate the stocks, fixed assets and taxation? What is the purpose of the note on the 'Summary of the effects of the acquisition of S Ltd' at the foot of the funds statement?

(iv)   I have looked at SSAP 10 but can find no real guidance on the above points. What is your justification for your treatment of the above items?

You are required to write a memorandum to the Chairman explaining the above four points raised in the Chairman's memorandum.

54   TUTORIAL QUESTION: CASH FLOW STATEMENTS

The directors of Arc Limited have decided to implement the terms of FRS 1 *Cash flow statements* in the accounts at the earliest opportunity. The following information is available.

PROFIT AND LOSS ACCOUNTS FOR THE YEARS TO 31 DECEMBER

	19X0	19X1
	£'000	£'000
Operating profit	9,400	20,640
Interest paid	–	(280)
Interest received	100	40
Profit before taxation	9,500	20,400
Taxation	(3,200)	(5,200)
Profit after taxation	6,300	15,200
Dividends		
Preference (paid)	(100)	(100)
Ordinary: interim (paid)	(1,000)	(2,000)
final (proposed)	(3,000)	(6,000)
Retained profit for the year	2,200	7,100

BALANCE SHEETS AT 31 DECEMBER

	19X0	19X1
Fixed assets	£'000	£'000
Plant, machinery and equipment, at cost	17,600	23,900
Less accumulated depreciation	9,500	10,750
	8,100	13,150
Current assets		
Stocks	5,000	15,000
Trade debtors	8,600	26,700
Prepayments	300	400
Cash at bank and in hand	600	–
	14,500	42,100
Current liabilities		
Bank overdraft	–	16,200
Trade creditors	6,000	10,000
Accruals	800	1,000
Taxation	3,200	5,200
Dividends	3,200	6,000
	13,000	38,400
	9,600	16,850
Share capital		
Ordinary shares of £1 each	5,000	5,000
10% preference shares of £1 each	1,000	1,000
Profit and loss account	3,000	10,100
	9,000	16,100
Loans		
15% debenture stock	600	750
	9,600	16,850

Additional information

1. The directors are extremely concerned about the large bank overdraft as at 31 December 19X1, and they attribute this mainly to the increase in trade debtors as a result of alleged poor credit control.

2. During the year to 31 December 19X1, fixed assets originally costing £5,500,000 were sold for £1,000,000. The accumulated depreciation on these assets as at 31 December 19X0 was £3,800,000.

Required

(a) Prepare a cash flow statement for the year to 31 December 19X1 using the format laid out in FRS 1.

(b) Compare FRS 1 with SSAP 10 and state whether you feel the use of cash flow statements will improve the standard of financial reporting, with reference to your answer in (a).

55 VALUE (25 marks)

The consolidated profit and loss account of Value Limited has been drafted for the year ended 30 June 19X2 with supporting notes as set out below.

	£'000	£'000
Sales		7,293
Value added tax		432
		6,861
Trading profit (note 1)		537
Deduct		
Depreciation	71	
Interest (note 2)	40	
		111
		426
Add		
Investment and rent income (note 2)	12	
Surplus on property disposal	4	
		16
Profit before tax		442
Taxation		105
Profit after tax		337
Deduct (note 3)		
Foreign currency differences	3	
Extraordinary items	7	
		10
		327
Dividends		141
Retained profit		186

Notes

1. *Trading profit*

	£'000
Trading profit is stated after charging the following.	
Directors' emoluments	3
Auditors' remuneration	1
Hire of equipment	56

2. *Interest, investment and rent income*

	£'000
Interest paid on bank loans and overdrafts	43
Interest received	(3)
	40
Rent from let properties	12

3. *Extraordinary items*

	£'000
Surplus on sale and leaseback of properties	8
Reduction of interest in subsidiary to book value	(15)
	(7)

4. Payment to employees for wages and pension contributions totalled £1,071,000.

Required

(a) Prepare a value added statement for the year ended 30 June 19X2.   (15 marks)

(b) Select three of the items that appear in a statement of value added and briefly discuss possible alternative methods of disclosing these items within the statement.

(10 marks)

56 C PLC (20 marks)   **11/89**

You are the management accountant of C plc.

F plc is a competitor in the same industry and it has been operating for many years. You have the following information relating to F plc.

(i) SUMMARISED PROFIT AND LOSS ACCOUNTS
     FOR THE YEAR ENDED 31 DECEMBER

	19X6 £m	19X6 £m	19X7 £m	19X7 £m	19X8 £m	19X8 £m
Turnover		3,120		2,700		3,000
Materials	630		480		600	
Labour	480		480		600	
Overhead	390		420		450	
		1,500		1,380		1,650
Gross profit		1,620		1,320		1,350
Administrative expenses	780		690		720	
Distribution costs	750		570		690	
		1,530		1,260		1,410
Profit on ordinary activities before taxation		90		60		(60)

(ii) EXTRACTS FROM THE BALANCE SHEETS AT 31 DECEMBER

	19X6 £m	19X6 £m	19X7 £m	19X7 £m	19X8 £m	19X8 £m
Fixed assets (net book value)		1,170		1,110		1,050
Raw materials	300		300		300	
Work in progress and finished goods	480		450		480	
Debtors	390		420		450	
		1,170		1,170		1,230
		2,340		2,280		2,280
Creditors: amounts falling due within one year (including bank overdraft)		810		810		870
Capital employed		1,530		1,470		1,410

(iii) You may assume that the index of retail prices has remained constant between 19X6 and 19X8.

(iv) No fixed assets were purchased or sold by F plc between 19X6 and 19X8.

You are required to write a report for the board of directors of C plc:

(a) analysing the profitability and liquidity of F plc and showing any calculations in an appendix to this report; and (15 marks)

(b) explaining the limitations of your analysis of the performance of F plc. (5 marks)

57 METEOR (25 marks) 5/90

GHI plc is a retailer of women's clothes. It was founded in London and still operates one shop there with more shops being opened in other cities. GHI plc has operated for five years and has gained a reputation for fast growth. Summaries of GHI plc's profit and loss accounts and balance sheets for the previous three years are given below.

SUMMARISED PROFIT AND LOSS ACCOUNTS
FOR YEARS ENDED 31 DECEMBER

	19X7 £m	19X8 £m	19X9 £m
Turnover	3.70	7.10	18.72
Cost of sales	2.50	5.03	14.85
Gross profit	1.20	2.07	3.87
Distribution costs	0.42	0.92	1.61
Administration expenses	0.25	0.31	0.38
Profit on ordinary activities before taxation	0.53	0.84	1.88
Taxation	0.23	0.31	0.62
Profit on ordinary activities after taxation	0.30	0.53	1.26
Dividends	-	-	0.50
	0.30	0.53	0.76

SUMMARISED BALANCE SHEETS AT 31 DECEMBER

	19X7 £m	19X8 £m	19X9 £m
Fixed assets			
Property (note 1)	1.21	3.62	9.59
Fixtures and fittings	0.74	1.32	2.04
Vehicles	0.18	0.24	0.32
Current assets			
Stock	0.57	1.82	4.16
Debtors	0.08	0.84	3.28
Bank	0.26	-	-
	3.04	7.84	19.39

Creditors: amounts falling due within one year			
Bank overdraft	–	1.65	3.04
Trade creditors	1.48	2.02	3.18
Taxation	0.20	0.28	0.52
Creditors: amounts falling due after more than one year			
Debenture loans	–	2.00	10.00
Shareholders' interest			
Ordinary share capital	0.50	0.50	0.50
Retained profits	0.86	1.39	2.15
	3.04	7.84	19.39

Note. GHI plc owns the freehold of all its shops. It does not depreciate its property.

You are an accountant with JKL plc, a competitor of GHI plc.

Required

(a) Prepare a report to the board of JKL plc on the performance of GHI plc concluding with a clear identification of areas requiring further investigation. (20 marks)

(b) Provide an indication of any information on these areas which would be available in the full annual report of GHI plc. (5 marks)

58 M PLC (30 marks)

You are given the following summarised financial statements of M plc which is a competitor of your company.

PROFIT AND LOSS ACCOUNTS
FOR THE YEAR ENDED 31 DECEMBER

	19X6	*19X7*	*19X8*	*19X9*
	£m	£m	£m	£m
Turnover	35,100	39,000	41,700	42,900
Cost of sales	22,800	25,800	28,200	30,300
Gross profit	12,300	13,200	13,500	12,600
Distribution costs	1,800	2,100	2,400	3,000
Administration costs	5,400	5,700	6,900	5,700
	7,200	7,800	9,300	8,700
Operating profit	5,100	5,400	4,200	3,900
Interest	150	600	1,200	1,500
Profit before taxation	4,950	4,800	3,000	2,400
Taxation	750	150	300	450
Profit after taxation	4,200	4,650	2,700	1,950
Retained profits brought forward	720	1,320	2,070	2,370
	4,920	5,970	4,770	4,320
Dividend	3,600	3,900	2,400	1,500
Retained profits carried forward	1,320	2,070	2,370	2,820

BALANCE SHEETS AT 31 DECEMBER

	19X6 £m	19X7 £m	19X8 £m	19X9 £m
Fixed assets	4,596	6,672	8,586	8,268
Current assets				
Stocks	4,800	5,400	5,100	4,500
Debtors	6,300	7,800	9,000	9,600
Bank	204	-	-	-
	11,304	13,200	14,100	14,100
Creditors: amounts falling due within one year				
Trade creditors	2,160	2,400	2,220	2,106
Other creditors	2,610	2,190	2,010	1,584
Bank overdraft	-	1,902	3,276	2,748
	4,770	6,492	7,506	6,438
Net current assets	6,534	6,708	6,594	7,662
Total assets less current liabilities	11,130	13,380	15,180	15,930
Creditors: amounts falling due after more than one year				
Loans	-	1,500	3,000	3,300
Net assets	11,130	11,880	12,180	12,630
Capital and reserves				
Ordinary share capital	6,900	6,900	6,900	6,900
General reserve	2,910	2,910	2,910	2,910
Retained profits	1,320	1,902	7,506	6,438
	11,130	11,880	12,180	12,630

You are required to prepare a report for the board of directors of your company interpreting the financial statements of M plc from 19X5 to 19X8 including an analysis of its profitability and financial position.

59   PILUM   (30 marks)

The draft profit and loss account of Pilum plc for the year ended 31 December 19X4 is set out below.

DRAFT PROFIT AND LOSS ACCOUNT
FOR YEAR ENDED 31 DECEMBER 19X4

	£	£
Profit before tax and extraordinary items		2,530,000
Less taxation		
Corporation tax	1,058,000	
Under provision for 19X3	23,000	
Irrecoverable advance corporation tax	69,000	
		1,150,000
		1,380,000
Extraordinary loss	207,000	
Tax on extraordinary loss	92,000	
		115,000
		1,265,000
Transfer to reserves	115,000	
Dividends		
Paid preference interim dividend	138,000	
Paid ordinary interim dividend	184,000	
Proposed preference final dividend	138,000	
Proposed ordinary final dividend	230,000	
		805,000
Retained profit		460,000

On 1 January 19X4 the issued share capital of Pilum plc was 4,600,000 6% preference shares of £1 each and 4,140,000 ordinary shares of £1 each.

Required

Calculate the earnings per share (on basic and fully diluted basis) in respect of the year ended 31 December 19X4 for each of the following circumstances. (Each of the five circumstances (a) to (e) is to be dealt with separately).

(a)   On the basis that there was no change in the issued share capital of the company during the year ended 31 December 19X4.   (6 marks)

(b)   On the basis that the company made a bonus issue on 1 October 19X4 of one ordinary share for every four shares in issue at 30 September 19X4.   (4 marks)

(c)   On the basis that the company made a rights issue of £1 ordinary shares on 1 October 19X4 in the proportion of 1 for every 5 shares held, at a price of £1.20. The middle market price for the shares on the last day of quotation cum rights was £1.80 per share.
                                                                              (8 marks)

(d)   On the basis that the company made no new issue of shares during the year ended 31 December 19X4 but on that date it had in issue £1,150,000 10% convertible loan stock 19X8 - 19Y1. This loan stock will be convertible into ordinary £1 shares as follows.

19X8   90 £1 shares for £100 nominal value loan stock
19X9   85 £1 shares for £100 nominal value loan stock
19Y0   80 £1 shares for £100 nominal value loan stock
19Y1   75 £1 shares for £100 nominal value loan stock   (6 marks)

(e) On the basis that the company made no issues of shares during the year ended 31 December
     19X4 but on that date there were outstanding options to purchase 460,000 ordinary £1 shares
     at £1.70 per share.   (6 marks)

Assume where appropriate that:
(i)   corporation tax rate is 50%;
(ii) the quotation for 2¼% Consolidated Stock was £25.

60   R PLC (15 marks)   5/89

You are given the following information relating to R plc.

	Year to 31 December	
	19X7	19X8
	£'000	£'000
Trading profit before taxation	1,700 CR	2,400 CR
Taxation	700 DR	1,000 DR
Extraordinary items	400 DR	600 DR
Preference dividends	100 DR	100 DR
Ordinary dividends	250 DR	300 DR
Prior year adjustment (note 1)	-	200 DR

Notes

1. The prior year adjustment relates to an accounting policy change affecting the trading
    profit of R plc. The 19X7 information given above does not reflect this change.

2. On 30 June 19X8, a fully subscribed 1 for 4 rights issue at £1.50 per share was made by R
    plc. The market price before the rights issue was £2.00.

3. The issued ordinary share capital of R plc at 1 January 19X7 was 2 million shares of 10
    pence each. No changes, other than the above rights issue, were made to R plc's ordinary
    share capital in 19X7 and 19X8.

Required

(a) Calculate for R plc, in accordance with the requirements of SSAP 3:

     (i)   the earnings per share for the year ended 31 December 19X7;
     (ii)   the earnings per share for the year ended 31 December 19X8;
     (iii) the adjusted earnings per share for the year ended 31 December 19X7 to be included as
            a comparative figure in the 19X8 financial statements.   (10 marks)

(b) List the limitations of earnings per share as a measure of corporate performance.
                                                                            (5 marks)

SUGGESTED SOLUTIONS

1   ACCOUNTING STANDARDS I

Accounting standards (SSAPs) are often accused of eliminating flexibility or otherwise turning accounting into a mechanical exercise, the mere application of rules. Because SSAPs set out a predetermined approach to the accounting treatment and disclosure of events or transactions, they are accused of preventing accountants from exercising discretion and judgement in their work.

SSAP 21, for instance, requires assets which are the subject of finance leases to be accounted for as if they were owned by the lessee. The SSAP lays down a long list of accounting and disclosure requirements, covering asset valuation, the treatment of finance charges and the disclosure of leasing commitments in future years. This very detailed set of requirements may be onerous, particularly in the case of small private companies, where management are also shareholders and neither want nor need all this information. The existence of the SSAP prevents the accountant in such a situation from limiting disclosure to what he considers to be useful.

It could also be argued that SSAPs tend to discourage experimentation and stifle debate. Once an accounting standard has been formulated, there is little incentive to continue with the search for a better solution. For instance, the debate about the accounting treatment of research and development was suspended for some years after the introduction of SSAP 13, although there were still difficulties in that area. It must, however, be pointed out, that a new exposure draft on that subject (ED 41) was issued in 1987 and eventually led to a very slight revision of the standard in January 1989. Standards may require modification as circumstances change, and a number of standards have been revised. One of the latest revisions has been to SSAP 4. This was thought to conflict with the 1985 Companies Act by allowing companies to state their fixed assets at less than cost. The revision to this SSAP has not eliminated the problem, because it permits the netting method although pointing out that it is not a permissible treatment for limited companies to adopt.

It might plausibly be suggested that SSAPs are *too* flexible. SSAP 16 for instance, was withdrawn as a result of the continuing opposition of many members of the profession. This is regrettable, given the support which it had attracted among academics and a number of large preparers of accounts, including nationalised industry. One of the problems with the old standard-setting process was that the ASC appeared to be more influenced by the acceptance given to a standard by members than by its theoretical backing.

In practice, many SSAPs, despite their alleged inflexibility, offer users a wide range of alternatives. SSAP 23, for instance, on merger and acquisition accounting, has been accused of being too laxly drawn, so that business combinations which are in effect acquisitions can qualify technically as mergers. SSAP 22 allows alternative treatments of goodwill: immediate elimination from the accounts or write-off over a number of years. Companies can choose their preferred alternative. Both these standards came under review shortly after issue.

Such flexibility can be regarded as commercially sensible in allowing companies to choose the accounting method best suited to their business activities. It can also, however, be criticised as allowing results to be manipulated in order to present the picture that management wishes to portray.

It is open to argument whether standards are inflexible or not. In some respects, in particular their application to all companies, they can be accused of inflexibility. It could also be claimed, however, that the number of options they offer and their susceptibility to accounts preparers' exploitation of loopholes make them too flexible to be a real discipline.

The new Accounting Standards Board (ASB) will publish Financial Reporting Standards (FRSs) rather than SSAPs. The first, FRS 1 *Cash flow statements,* was published in September 1991 and it replaces SSAP 10. It is too early to say what the impact of the FRSs will be, but in the meantime the ASB has adopted all the SSAPs currently in force.

2   ACCOUNTING STANDARDS II

Tutorial note. The examiner was disappointed as most candidates knew very little about the standard-setting regime and processes. Also, the authority of the SSAPs was not appreciated, particularly the audit implications of non-compliance.

Suggested solution

To: The board of directors of FG plc
From: Financial controller, FG plc
Subject: *Accounting standards*

Statements of standard accounting practice (SSAPs) are mandatory for those enterprises whose financial statements are intended to give a true and fair view (both under historical and current cost conventions). They cover topics of fundamental importance and general applicability and lay down both accounting method and required disclosure. They should be applied to the financial statements of overseas subsidiaries before consolidation. SSAPs need not be applied to immaterial items.

SSAPs have been issued covering most of the main topics in accounting and disclosure. Each SSAP is intended to narrow the differences in accounting practice for the relevant topic. While many SSAPs are very detailed, such as those on stock valuation and deferred tax provisions, they cannot attempt to set detailed rules to cover all possible combinations of circumstances and, to ensure the widest applicability, each sets out the reasoning on which its conclusions depend. Thus, it is intended that the spirit of each SSAP will guide accountants, directors and auditors to apply comparable accounting in comparable circumstances.

The intention of the Accounting Standards Committee (ASC) in developing SSAPs was that the usefulness and comparability of financial statements should be enhanced by making explicit the standard method or range of methods on which the statements are based. While recognising that disclosure is no substitute for poor accounting, the ASC's statements were also intended to ensure that the greatest amount of information is consistent with commercial confidentiality.

The ASC has now been dissolved and replaced by an independent Accounting Standards Board (ASB), better funded and able to issue Financial Reporting Standards (FRSs) on its own authority, unlike the ASC which had to obtain the approval of all six CCAB bodies for each SSAP. This caused delay as well as compromising the ASC's independence. The FRS will replace the SSAP but all SSAPs currently in force have been adopted by the ASB.

SSAPs have direct legal authority in that the CA 1985 now requires that all companies should disclose whether or not they have complied with all relevant accounting standards and, if not, why not. Defective accounts must now be revised by court order if not done voluntarily. The presumption has now become established that, in the absence of statutory provision, compliance with SSAPs provides the required true and fair view.

A further tier of standard-setting is the International Accounting Standards Committee (IASC). However, its standards are not mandatory on UK companies. It influences UK practice because its provisions are incorporated into SSAPs as far as possible where not already required by statute. Its aim is the harmonisation of accounting standards.

In practice, SSAPs are enforced by the individual members of the accounting bodies acting in their roles as company accountants, directors and auditors. Members of the CCAB bodies who are responsible for the preparation of financial statements are expected to ensure compliance with SSAPs whether or not they are directors; where they are directors they are required to draw the attention of their board colleagues to the provisions of SSAPs. Only where the application of a SSAP would prevent the presentation of the true and fair view may another accounting treatment be used in which case the departure from the standard and its financial effect, if material, should be disclosed.

Auditors are required to ensure compliance with SSAPs except where, as above, this would depart from the true and fair view. Where an auditor does not agree with the departure from the provisions of a SSAP and the effect is material he must qualify his audit report accordingly.

3 INTERNATIONAL ACCOUNTING STANDARDS

Tutorial note. This question was not answered well in the examination. You should be aware of the influence of international bodies on UK accounting standards.

Suggested solution

The objectives of the International Accounting Standards Committee (IASC) and the European Economic Community (EEC) as regards accounting issues are, in general, the same. These are to harmonise the accounts of those enterprises to which their pronouncements apply so as to reduce the areas of difference in accounting treatment and disclosures.

Their powers to enforce their standards are, however, very different. The IASC is essentially a voluntary body whose influence is based on co-operation and persuasion. The EEC, on the other hand, is, through the means of Directives issued by the European Commission, able to produce pronouncements that have the force of law.

All the major accounting bodies in the UK are members of the IASC. As such they are entitled to take part in the process of research, consultation and discussion which precede the issue of an International Accounting Standard (IAS) by the IASC and are obliged to publish IASs in the UK when they are issued. Moreover they are obliged to use their best efforts to ensure that UK accounting standards are consistent with IASs and that published financial statements in the UK comply with IASs.

IASs cover a considerable range of topics and deal with both accounting method and disclosures. In general, since they post-dated the corresponding UK standard on each topic and because they are intended for widespread use, they do not conflict with UK standards. It is, therefore, difficult to assess the extent to which they influence published financial statements in the UK. Overall, it is likely that they are not very influential since, if they did conflict, the influence of UK standards and/or legislation would always override the provisions of an IAS. In addition, IASs have frequently allowed a number of alternative treatments which has weakened their influence, although the IASC has now announced a programme of revision which is intended to reduce the differences in permitted accounting methods. A number of UK companies state in their accounting policies that they follow IASC standards but their determination to continue to do so will not be properly tested until a major conflict arises.

Member states of the EEC are required, under the terms of the Treaty of Rome, to implement the provisions of EC Directives into national law within a prescribed timescale. The EC has to date issued a number of Directives which affect published accounts of which two are of particular importance: the Fourth Directive on the accounts of individual companies and the Seventh on consolidated accounts.

Both of these Directives have had a significant influence over the accounts of UK companies, although the Fourth produced more significant changes than the Seventh. The Fourth Directive prescribed the layout and content of profit and loss accounts and balance sheets although it did not cover funds flow statements. In addition, it set out the valuation principles that were to apply to accounts in a more prescriptive form than UK company law had hitherto. The Seventh Directive introduced the notion of control rather than ownership as the principal criterion for the identification of subsidiary companies in consolidated accounts. Both of these have now been enacted into UK company law.

The provisions of EC Directives are much less detailed than IASC standards and no attempt is made to deal with specific accounting issues. Rather, the basic principles of valuation and recognition are covered together with comprehensive rules regarding disclosure and format. Thus, while EC Directives are mandatory for published accounts in the UK, a great deal of discretion is left to the UK accounting standard setters to deal with specific matters and to the directors of UK companies as to how they apply those standards to their particular circumstances.

The IASC's greatest chance to influence UK accounting standards may come from the adoption of its conceptual framework for use in developing UK standards. The ASC intended to do this and used it in ED 49 and ED 51. The ASB has also adopted this strategy, as demonstrated by the content of the first Discussion Drafts and Exposure Drafts it has issued.

4   TUTORIAL QUESTION: REVENUE RECOGNITION

(a) Accrual accounting is based on the matching of costs with the revenue they generate. It is crucially important under this convention that we can establish the point at which revenue may be recognised so that the correct treatment can be applied to the related costs. For example, the costs of producing an item of finished goods should be carried as an asset in the balance sheet until such time as it is sold; they should then be written off as a charge to the trading account. Which of these two treatments should be applied cannot be decided until it is clear at what moment the sale of the item takes place. The decision has a direct impact on profit since under the prudence concept it would be unacceptable to recognise the profit on sale until a sale had taken place in accordance with the criteria of revenue recognition.

(b) Revenue is generally recognised as earned at the point of sale, because at that point four criteria will generally have been met.

(i) The product or service has been provided to the buyer.

(ii) The buyer has recognised his liability to pay for the goods or services provided. The converse of this is that the seller has recognised that ownership of goods has passed from himself to the buyer.

(iii) The buyer has indicated his willingness to hand over cash or other assets in settlement of his liability.

(iv) The monetary value of the goods or services has been established.

At earlier points in the business cycle there will not in general be firm evidence that the above criteria will be met. Until work on a product is complete, there is a risk that some flaw in the manufacturing process will necessitate its writing off; even when the product is complete there is no guarantee that it will find a buyer.

At later points in the business cycle, for example when cash is received for the sale, the recognition of revenue may occur in a period later than that in which the related costs were charged. Revenue recognition would then depend on fortuitous circumstances, such as the cash flow of a company's debtors, and might fluctuate misleadingly from one period to another.

(c)   The following are examples of accounting procedures which are common in practice and where revenue is recognised other than at the point when a sale is completed.

    (i)   *Recognition of profit on long-term contract work in progress.* Under SSAP 9, credit is taken in the profit and loss account for 'that part of the total profit currently estimated to arise over the duration of the contract ... which fairly reflects the profit attributable to that part of the work performed at the accounting date.' Owing to the length of time taken to complete such contracts, to defer taking profit into account until completion may result in the profit and loss account reflecting not so much a fair view of the activity of the company during the year but rather the results relating to contracts which have been completed by the year end. Revenue in this case is recognised when production on, say, a section of the total contract is complete, even though no sale can be made until the whole is complete;

    (ii)   *Sales on hire purchase.* Title to goods provided on hire purchase terms does not pass until the last payment is made, at which point the sale is complete. To defer the recognition of revenue until that point, however, would be to distort the nature of the revenue earned. The profits of an HP retailer in effect represent the interest charged on finance provided and such interest arises over the course of the HP agreement rather than at its completion. Revenue in this case is recognised when each instalment of cash is received.

5   STILES

To: Managing director
From: Chief accountant
Date: 25 January 19X9
Subject: *Extraordinary items and exceptional items*

In general, all income and expenditure relating to a business should be reported in its profit and loss account. Despite this general rule, however, it is recognised that reported results might be distorted if certain unusual events were hidden away in the profit and loss account without additional disclosure. Two categories of such events are widely recognised by accountants.

(a)   Exceptional items are items which, although they form part of a company's normal activities, are exceptional because of their size. Examples might include:

    (i)   abnormal charges for bad debts;
    (ii)   abnormal write-offs of stocks or work in progress;
    (iii) abnormal provisions for losses on long-term contracts.

(b) Extraordinary items are defined as being 'material items which derive from events or transactions that fall outside the ordinary activities of the business and which are therefore expected not to recur frequently or regularly'. Examples might include:

(i)   the costs of closing down a significant part of the business;
(ii) the profit or loss on selling an investment not acquired with the intention of resale;
(iii) the expropriation of overseas assets by a foreign government.

The difference between extraordinary and exceptional items is therefore whether or not the transaction is outside or within the ordinary activities of the business. Inevitably, there will be a problem of different interpretations, so that one analyst might consider a transaction extraordinary, whereas another analyst might consider the same transaction exceptional. Examples such as making a special provision for pensions, expenses of reorganisation, deficits on the revaluation of fixed assets and profits or losses on the sale of fixed assets or investments have been treated as both exceptional and extraordinary, depending on the outlook of the companies concerned. An item which is clearly extraordinary to one business might be equally obviously exceptional to another. For example, a company which regularly sells off fixed assets (such as second hand motor vehicles) might consider one particular sale to provide an exceptionally large profit or loss, but a company which rarely sells off any fixed assets would regard a large profit or loss as an extraordinary item.

It is important to be clear as to whether an item is exceptional or extraordinary, because different accounting treatments are prescribed for the two categories.

(a) Exceptional items, since they derive from the company's normal activities, should be reported as part of the current year's profit on ordinary activities before taxation. If the amount involved is very large it may be necessary, in the notes to the accounts, to give enough detail for users of the accounts to understand the item's significance.

(b) Extraordinary items are not part of the company's normal activities and cannot be shown as part of the profit or loss on ordinary activities. Instead, after arriving at the figure of profit after taxation without taking account of extraordinary items, the next caption in the profit and loss account will show the gross amount of any extraordinary charges or income. Any tax charge or credit arising from the extraordinary item is shown as a deduction from the gross amount.

The Urgent Issues Task Force (UITF) published a consensus opinion on 31 October 1991 concerning restructuring costs. The opinion sought to clarify matters relating to SSAP 6 in advance of any formal revision to the standard (or the issuing of a new standard). The UITF concluded that 'where the cost of restructuring or reorganising business activities needs to be disclosed by virtue of its size or incidence, it should be treated as an exceptional item, not an extraordinary item, unless it stems from a separate extraordinary event or transaction.' This ruling would appear to halt the practice of classifying such costs as exceptional or extraordinary on the basis of which will enhance the company accounts.

6   SSAP 6

(a)   The all-inclusive income approach is based on the idea that the profit and loss account should include *all* of a company's income and expenditure.

The current operating income approach is based on the idea that the profit and loss account should reflect only the normal, recurring transactions of a business, and only to the extent that they relate to the year under review. All other transactions are dealt with through reserves.

The two approaches differ when transactions occur which either:

(i)   are abnormal or non-recurring; or
(ii)   relate to prior years.

These two categories correspond to the extraordinary items and prior year adjustments of SSAP 6. SSAP 6 adopts the all-inclusive approach and requires that extraordinary items should be taken to profit and loss account, with separate disclosure. Under the current operating income approach, such items would be dealt with through reserves.

The merits of the all-inclusive income approach are as follows.

(i)   It reduces the subjectivity involved in preparing accounts. Since *all* items of income and expenditure must pass through the profit and loss account there is less temptation to manipulate the earnings figure by classifying large debits as reserve movements, while taking large credits to the profit and loss account. It is true, however, that some scope remains for such manipulation since items classified as extraordinary are excluded from the figure of earnings per share under SSAP 3.

(ii)   It makes comparisons between different companies easier.

(iii) It means that the company's successive profit and loss accounts are a complete record of its income and expenditure throughout its history.

(iv)   It is better suited to meet the information needs of accounts users, since no income or expenditure is masked in reserve movements.

The merits of the current operating income approach are as follows.

(i)   Current operating income is a figure of great interest to management, investors and potential investors. It is arguably a more reliable indicator both of the efficiency of management and of future earnings potential.

(ii)   It presents a simpler picture of the company's profit or loss for the period, without the confusion which may be caused by disclosing extraordinary items as part of profit, but excluding them from earnings per share.

(b)   SSAP 6 defines extraordinary items as 'those items which derive from events or transactions outside the ordinary activities of the business and which are both material and expected not to recur frequently or regularly'. In the three specific items which are mentioned in the question we are given no information regarding materiality and this is one item of additional information that would be needed in each case.

(i) Payments to an employees' pension fund are part of a company's ordinary activities and should not be regarded as extraordinary. It may, however, be appropriate to make separate disclosure of the item, if it is material, as an exceptional item.

(ii) Again, development expenditure is incurred in the normal course of a company's activities and a write-off is not an extraordinary item. However, if the write-off arises as a result of a fundamental error in prior years, or as a result of a change of accounting policy, disclosure as a prior year item may be appropriate. Alternatively, it may be necessary to disclose it as an exceptional item. Further information is needed about the reasons for the write-off.

(iii) In most businesses, libel damages might be regarded as an abnormal and non-recurring event. In the case of a satirical magazine that may not be so. In particular, the test of frequency and regularity might indicate that the item is not extraordinary.

7 FERGUSON

PROFIT AND LOSS ACCOUNT FOR THE YEAR ENDED 31 DECEMBER

	19X2	19X1
	£'000	£'000
Turnover	X	X
Cost of sales	X	X
	X	X
Distribution costs	X	X
Administrative costs	(X+865)	(X+465)
Profit on ordinary activities before taxation (note 1)	3,760	3,541
Tax on profit on ordinary activities (note 2)	1,160	1,106
Profit on ordinary activities after taxation	2,600	2,435
Extraordinary items (note 3)	960	–
Profit for the financial year	1,640	2,435
Dividends	550	450
Retained profit	1,090	1,985

	19X2		19X1	
	£'000	£'000	£'000	£'000
Statement of retained profits				
Retained profits at beginning of year				
As previously reported (W1)	16,710		14,700	
Prior year adjustment (note 4) (W2)	2,275		2,250	
As restated		14,435		12,450
Retained profit for the year		1,090		1,985
Retained profits at end of year		15,525		14,435

Notes (extracts)

		19X2	19X1
1.	Profit on ordinary activities before taxation is stated after charging:	£'000	£'000
	Expenditure on research and development	865	465

		19X2	19X1
2.	Tax on profit on ordinary activities	£'000	£'000
	Corporation tax on the profit for the year at 35%	1,074	1,106
	Underprovision in previous years	86	–
		1,160	1,106

3. The extraordinary item relates to costs of terminating production of TX's.

4. The prior year adjustment relates to the change of accounting policy adopted by the company in respect of research and development. In previous years the company capitalised such expenditure and amortised it over eight years but now all such expenditure is written off in the year in which it is incurred.

Workings		£'000
1.	Retained profits as at 1 January 19X1	14,700
	Add profit on ordinary activities	4,006
	Less: R & D amortisation	(440)
	taxation	(1,106)
	dividend	(450)
	Retained profits as previously reported as 1 January 19X2	16,710

2. *Prior year adjustments*

			£'000
19X1	Balance on deferred development expenditure b/f, written off in full		2,250
19X2	As 19X1		2,250
	Add R & D expenditure in 19X1		465
	Less amortisation of development expenditure charged in 19X1		(440)
			2,275

8 LEASING

To:	J Smith/Finance Director, A Co Inc
From:	B Brown/Accountant, B Co Ltd
Subject:	*Accounting treatment of leases*

The accounting treatment of leases is regulated in the UK by an accounting standard, Statement of Standard Accounting Practice 21. SSAP 21 is of importance because compliance with SSAPs is regarded as essential if accounts are to disclose a true and fair view of a company's results. Hence, accounting treatment and disclosure of leases must comply with SSAP 21.

SSAP 21 defines two types of lease.

(i)   A finance lease transfers the risks and rewards of ownership to the lessee. The lessee pays an amount under the leasing contract which totals at least 90% of the purchase price of the asset. In substance, though not in form, a finance lease equates to the purchase of the asset by the lessee, financed by a loan.

(ii)   An operating lease is any lease which is not a finance lease. An operating lease is effectively a rental agreement. The lessor continues to enjoy the risks and rewards of ownership of the asset; for instance, the lessor must repair and maintain the asset. Typically, operating leases are for short periods only.

SSAP 21 requires different accounting treatments to reflect the two different kinds of lease. In the case of an operating lease, the lessee charges the amounts paid to the profit and loss account as expense items. A finance lease, however, is accounted for by treating the leased asset as if it had been purchased by the lessee on credit. Thus, a finance lease is represented by an asset account and a liability account in the name of the lessor. The amount recorded is usually the fair value of the asset, which is the amount that would be paid for it in a cash transaction. Strictly, the standard requires capitalisation of the present value of the minimum lease payments discounted at the interest rate implicit in the lease. However, in practice the fair value is usually a good approximation to the present value.

Each rental payment is then apportioned between capital cost and interest. Acceptable methods for making this apportionment include:

- the level spread method, spreading interest evenly over the life of the lease;
- the sum of the digits method, which tends to allocate most of the interest to the earlier years of the lease;
- the actuarial method, which has the same trend as the sum of the digits method.

SSAP 21 requires the following disclosure of leasing contracts by lessees.

(i)   Lessees must disclose the gross amounts of assets held under finance leases, together with the accumulated depreciation. If this information is consolidated with that relating to owned assets, the net amount of leased assets must be shown separately.

(ii)   Obligations under finance leases must be shown separately from other creditors, analysed between current liabilities, amounts payable in two to five years and amounts payable thereafter.

(iii) Aggregate finance charges for the period relating to finance leases must be disclosed.

(iv) For operating leases, the amount charged for lease payments must be shown, split between that for plant and machinery hire and other rentals. Operating lease commitments should be disclosed, analysed between those agreements expiring within one year, two to five years and later than five years from the balance sheet date.

Before SSAP 21 appeared, it could be said that finance leasing was a form of off balance sheet finance in the UK. This is no longer the case, given the very extensive accounting and disclosure requirements outlined above. Companies are required to reflect the substance of the finance lease transaction in their balance sheets and to give the user of accounts considerable information about the extent of leasing.

9   CONTROLLED NON-SUBSIDIARY

Tutorial note. Candidates avoided this question in the examination and the examiner has pointed out that Exposure Drafts *are* examinable at stage 3.

Suggested solution

From:	Finance director
To:	Managing director
Subject:	*Off-balance sheet financing involving the use of a controlled non-subsidiary*

(a)   Off-balance sheet finance is a term which refers to borrowings or other forms of finance from which a company or a group of companies benefits but which is not reflected in their balance sheet. The purpose of avoiding disclosure of the borrowings is to make the balance sheet appear stronger than it really is.

One method of off-balance sheet finance is to arrange for the borrowing to be undertaken by a company that is controlled by the parent company of a group but which is not technically a subsidiary. The 'controlled non-subsidiary' does not need to be consolidated and its borrowings, therefore, are not incorporated into the group balance sheet. There are two principal forms of controlled non-subsidiary.

The first utilises the exemption currently granted by the Companies Acts from consolidating subsidiaries whose activities are markedly dissimilar from those of the remainder of the group. This provides an opportunity for channelling borrowings into a 'finance' or 'banking' subsidiary which can then be claimed to be different in nature from the rest of the group. Its results and the parent's net investment will then be included in the consolidated balance sheet on an equity basis, thus disguising the borrowings. This does not affect the group net income or net assets but improves the balance sheet ratios.

The second method involves reducing the group investment in the subsidiary to below 50% by selling shares to a merchant bank. Effective control is retained by a contract which prevents the bank from selling the shares other than back to the parent and obliges the bank-nominated directors to abstain from voting at board meetings. Because the parent owns less than 50% of the shares in the controlled company, it is not a subsidiary and need not be consolidated but is equity-accounted.

(b)   Currently neither accounting standards nor company law provide fully effective means for outlawing the above practices either by specifying consolidation or by adequate disclosure. Some may consider that the requirement for accounts to provide a true and fair view implies that disclosure is required of the existence and financial effect of a controlled non-subsidiary. On the other hand, it is common practice to rely on the letter of the law to avoid this.

There are, however, moves to outlaw the practice on two fronts. The ASB (carrying on the work of the ASC) clearly intends to strengthen the principle of 'substance over form' by introducing new definitions of liabilities that will require recognition of most forms of off-balance sheet financing including the use of a controlled non-subsidiary. ED 49 would require recognition of the true economic and commercial effects of such transactions regardless of the form that they take.

Secondly, the 1989 Companies Act, which implements the EC Seventh Directive on consolidated accounts, has amended the Companies Act 1985 so that it will now apply tests regarding control over rather than ownership of another company determine whether or not it should be consolidated. This will deal with the second of the techniques mentioned in (a) above where control is exercised even in the absence of majority ownership. These changes have been incorporated into SSAPs 1 and 14 by the ASB's *Interim statement on consolidated accounts.*

These moves indicate that there is decreasing sympathy in the accounting profession and in the business community for off-balance sheet financing. Thus, we can expect the auditors to take a firmer line on this topic than in the past and a more attentive attitude given to it by the investment community and the financial press.

10   BRANDS

The brand names owned by a company provide it with an opportunity to differentiate its branded products from those that are similar and thereby extract a premium on the selling price. It is the net present value of these streams of future 'super-profits' that constitute the value of a brand. In many ways, therefore, the issues surrounding accounting for brands are similar to those relating to accounting for goodwill.

Arguments for inclusion in balance sheets

The principal argument for the inclusion of the value of brands in balance sheets is that this is useful information to provide to the users of accounts. It is argued that, for many companies, the future cash flows that they can expect issue from the brands they have developed, and excluding these items from the balance sheet seriously reduces the value of the financial statements. Against this it could be argued that there are many other 'omitted assets', such as the value of the employees and inherent goodwill, and that there is no particular reason to treat brands differently from these items.

A development of this argument is that the inclusion of brands in balance sheets would deter predators from acquiring companies with valuable brands at less than their true value and the case of Rowntrees' takeover by Nestle is cited as an example. There may be some merit in this argument in respect of unquoted companies but it would seem unlikely that, in a liquid and developed securities market, the income-producing capacity of valuable brands would remain significantly under-valued for long.

The most convincing arguments for brand accounting are those that reflect the cosmetic and technical changes that this practice could have on financial statements. For example, the assignment of value to brands on a take-over could reduce or eliminate the value of goodwill charged against reserves on acquisition or subsequently amortised against profits.

Where brands are accounted for other than on an acquisition it can be argued that this treatment will increase reported shareholders funds. This should improve the gearing and result in an increased valuation of the firm. This argument discounts the validity of the efficient market hypothesis which research has shown to exist at least in the semi-strong form. In practice, there is little evidence that those quoted companies that have included the value of brands in their balance sheets (notably Cadbury's) have benefited from any subsequent increase in their share price as a result.

Arguments against inclusion in balance sheets

The strongest argument against the inclusion of brands in balance sheets relates to the subjective nature of the assessment. Since generally no transaction has taken place, there is no obvious objective basis on which to value the brands. Even where a transaction has taken place, it is unlikely that an explicit value will have been put on the brands, nor will it usually be possible to separate brands from other elements of goodwill.

The other arguments against inclusion are mostly the counter-arguments to those in favour. It would seem unlikely that the practice of accounting for brands would add useful information and the opportunities it provides for 'creative accounting' could be detrimental to the reputation in the financial community of those companies that attempt to practice it.

11   HISTORICAL COST ACCOUNTING

Tutorial note. You should read this solution carefully as it is a useful summary of the issues involved in this topic, still of concern in spite of SSAP 16's withdrawal. The examiner said this question was *not* well answered in the examination.

Suggested solution

Historical cost (HC) accounting is a system whereby the assets and liabilities of a business and the income and expenditure that arise from its operations are recorded and presented at the actual money amounts of the transactions involved. This system is almost universally used in the UK for the presentation of published company accounts.

Since HC accounting is well established, the conventions and assumptions on which it is based are well understood and generally accepted. In the absence of any indication to the contrary it will normally be assumed by the reader of accounts that these principles have been applied and company law recognises HC accounting as the norm.

A further advantage of HC accounting is that, as it is based on transactions that have actually occurred, its results are relatively easy to verify by the process of audit. Consequently, whatever the other disadvantages of the HC accounting, it is generally regarded as being highly reliable. For this reason HC accounting is required in the preparation of tax returns and for certain government statistical information. Other accounting methods that have been devised in order to overcome the disadvantages of HC accounting increase subjectivity and have not achieved the level of acceptability that HC accounting enjoys. Finally, not the least advantage of HC accounting is that it is inexpensive because data once recorded does not require restatement at current costs or in units of current purchasing power.

The principal disadvantage of HC accounting is that it produces financial statements that can be seriously misleading in times of rising prices. This is due to the inclusion in balance sheets of asset values that may be materially out of date and therefore lower than current values. Consequently, the depreciation charge and cost of sales in the profit and loss account will not reflect the current cost of the assets being consumed.

This would not be too serious a problem if it were relatively easy for the users of accounts to adjust HC figures in order to take into account the effect of changing prices. In practice, this is very difficult to do, even for those financial analysts who are experts in the business of the company concerned, because the assets of a company will suffer different degrees of price change.

The undervaluation of fixed assets is a problem for HC accounting even at low rates of inflation due to the long lives of the assets. Where inflation is high, the cost of sales charged to the profit and loss account can be materially lower than the current replacement cost. Consequently, the profit produced by the HC accounting may be considerably higher than the 'real' profit when the need to replace fixed assets and stock are taken into account.

This overstating of profit can have a number of undesirable consequences. It can lead to setting sales prices too low, at a level which may not produce sufficient cash flows to replace the fixed assets and stock consumed in their production. Secondly, it can lead to dividends being set at a level that effectively distributes some of the company's capital, thus reducing its physical operating capability.

The combination of overstated profit and understated capital employed will doubly enhance the recorded return on capital employed and will provide a falsely optimistic picture of the profitability of the company. This will also have the effect of penalising companies or divisions with newer assets whose return on capital employed will compare unfavourably with those with other assets even where the former are more efficient and, in reality, more profitable.

HC accounting has the further disadvantage that no recognition is given to the loss that is incurred by an entity which holds net monetary assets in a period of rising prices. Equally, it ignores the gain that is produced from holding net monetary liabilities under the same circumstances.

HC accounting makes it difficult to compare the financial performance of a company over time because the comparative figures represent different amounts of purchasing power. As was mentioned above it is often quite difficult for the users of accounts to adjust for this effect with any reasonable degree of accuracy.

In the absence of a generally agreed alternative to HC accounting, companies and analysts have attempted to supplement it with non-financial information which is not, therefore, subject to the effects of changing prices but which is independently verifiable. Such information includes physical measures of output (tonnes, megawatts), physical measures of operating capacity (barrels of oil per day, square feet of shop space) or physical measures of reserves (tonnes of ore or barrels of oil in the ground).

12   CHANGING PRICE LEVELS

Tutorial note. Many candidates did not relate their answer to the quotation given in the question.

Suggested solution

(a)   To: The manager
       From: The management accountant
       Subject: *Accounting for the effects of changing prices*

I refer to your enquiry regarding the article by David Allen on the above subject.

It is generally recognised that the accounts of a company prepared on a historical cost (HC) basis can be very misleading during a period of changing prices. Where prices are rising, an HC balance sheet understates the values of the net assets employed while the profit and loss account overstates the profit.

Profit is usually defined as the amount that is left over after the capital of an enterprise has been maintained. This is, therefore, the amount that can be distributed or consumed without reducing the wealth of the enterprise. The difficulty that arises during periods of increasing prices is that of defining the capital of the enterprise. There are two approaches to this issue and the two quotations from Allen's article reflect each of these approaches.

The first approach regards the enterprise from a purely financial view as a bundle of net monetary value which belongs to the shareholders. Thus, under this approach, the capital of the enterprise is maintained by restating the value of the shareholders' funds at the beginning of the period by the change in the purchasing power of money over the period. This is known as the 'financial capital' or 'proprietorial' approach, and this is the view reflected in quotation (i). It was adopted in PSSAP 7 and is known in the UK as current purchasing power (CPP) accounting.

The alternative view, known as the 'operating capital' or 'entity' view, regards the enterprise as a bundle of operational capability. This could be expressed as the productive capacity of a factory or the output of a mine, for example. Thus, under this view the capital of an enterprise is only maintained if its operating capacity is maintained. In accounting terms this means that the profit is struck after an amount is set aside to reflect the effects of price changes that are specific to the enterprise's actual assets. These specific price changes may be quite different from the general level of price changes used to measure changes in purchasing power.

This approach was adopted in SSAP 16 and is known as current cost accounting. Historical cost profit is decreased (or increased) by adjustments to depreciation and cost of sales to reflect the true amount of resources consumed in the period.

The approach proposed by Allen is a combination of the two above approaches and is known as a 'real terms' approach. The effect of this combined approach is to recognise both the effects of general purchasing power changes in the way an enterprise is financed as well as the effect of specific price changes on the operating capacity in which that finance is invested. A simplified commercial example is shown below in order to illustrate this combined approach.

(b) *Example*

A company has operating assets recorded at £1 million at current cost at the start of the year. There is no gearing in the company and so shareholders' funds (equity) is also £1 million at current cost.

If the RPI is 10% over the year then, to maintain the value of shareholders' funds, £100,000 extra must be retained in the business. This should therefore be deducted from historical cost profit *before* fixing the distribution level for the year.

However, suppose that non-monetary assets (fixed assets and stocks) have increased in value over the period by, say, £150,000, calculated by applying specific price indexes to their balance sheet values to adjust them to current costs at the year end. These *unrealised* holding gains are not recognised in historical cost profit but should be added to the value of equity to offset the general fall in the value of money.

13 MANUFACTURING COMPANY

To: The board of directors
From: Management accountant
Date: 12 December 19X7
Subject: *Accounting for price-level changes*

Introduction

At present we report our accounting results and financial position on an historical cost basis. Our published accounts have shown healthy profits in recent years and we have paid out a large proportion of reported profits in the form of dividends. This report attempts to show how our published results would be affected by changing our accounting convention from the historical cost basis to a basis designed to show the effects of rising prices.

Methods of accounting for price level changes

Three methods which might be considered are:

(a) modified historical cost accounts;
(b) current cost accounts;
(c) current purchasing power accounts.

(a) It is common in practice to prepare modified historical cost accounts; this usually means that up-to-date valuations are included in the historical cost balance sheet for some or all fixed assets, without any other adjustments being made. Surpluses on revaluation are transferred to a revaluation reserve. There is no increase in reported profits or in profits available for distribution.

(b) Current cost accounting (CCA) was widely used in the UK during the first half of the 1980s. It is a system based on the use of replacement costs rather than historical costs, both in the balance sheet valuation of assets, and in the charges for depreciation and cost of sales in the profit and loss account.

   If we had been using CCA over the last few years, our reported profits would have been significantly lower. The machinery we use and the raw materials we incorporate in our products have risen significantly in price over that period. The increases have exceeded the rate of general price inflation. Our balance sheets would have shown higher valuations for stock and fixed assets, but the surpluses would have been transferred to a non-distributable reserve (the current cost reserve) without affecting profit. The profit and loss account would have been adversely affected not only by increased depreciation charges and cost of sales, but also by a *monetary working capital adjustment*. This is an adjustment to reflect the extent to which our short-term monetary assets (debtors less creditors) lose value in times of rising prices.

(c) Current purchasing power (CPP) accounting is a system which measures profit as the increase in the current purchasing power of equity. Profits are stated after allowing for the decline in the purchasing power of money as a result of *general* price inflation. It differs in this from CCA, which attempts to measure the impact on a company of price changes specific to its own business.

In our case, we have seen a 12% rise in the retail price index over the last three years. We are not in general able to increase our prices beyond the rate of general inflation, but we would have to report a loss on holding net monetary assets and this would lead to a decline in our published profits.

Conclusion

Any method of accounting for price-level changes will reflect the erosion of the company's capital base in times of rising prices. Reported profits are likely to be lower and the funds available for distribution as dividends are likely to suffer.

14   CD

Tutorial notes

(a)   This is a question from the CIMA specimen paper. The first step is to prepare historical cost accounts for the year ended 31 March 19X5. These are presented in working 1.

(b)   Note (e) to the question is assumed to mean that CD Limited charges a full year's depreciation on the plant disposed of and shows the loss on disposal as a separate item.

Suggested solution

(a)   CURRENT PURCHASING POWER PROFIT AND LOSS ACCOUNT FOR THE YEAR ENDED 31 MARCH 19X5

	£c'000	£c'000
Sales (4,800 x 132/126)		5,029
Opening stock (250 x 132/120)	275	
Purchases (3,300 x 132/126)	3,457	
	3,732	
Closing stock (index for mid-March 19X5		
275 x 132/131.5)	276	
Cost of sales		3,456
Gross profit		1,573
Monetary expenses:		
Rent (40 x 132/123)	43	
Distribution (900 x 132/126)	943	
Other operating expenses (168 x 132/126)	176	
Interest (28 x 132/132)	28	
		1,190
Profit after monetary expenses		383
Non-monetary expenses:		
Depreciation on premises (10 x 132/126)	10	
Depreciation on plant (180 x 132/120)	198	
Depreciation on vehicles (100 x 132/120)	110	
Loss on disposal (W2)	4	
		322
		61
Loss on monetary items (W3)		4
		57
Tax		42
Retained profit		15

(b) CURRENT PURCHASING POWER BALANCE SHEET
AS AT 31 MARCH 19X5

	£c'000	£c'000
Fixed assets		
Premises (390 x 132/126)	409	
Plant and machinery (918 x 132/120)	1,010	
Vehicles (400 x 132/120)	440	
		1,859
Current assets		
Stock	276	
Cash	522	
	798	
Creditors: amounts falling due within one year		
Taxation	42	
Net current assets		756
Total assets less current liabilities		2,615
Creditors: amounts falling due after more than one year		
Loan		(400)
		2,215
Capital and reserves		
Called-up share capital (2,000 x 132/120)		2,200
Retained profit		15
		2,215

Workings

1. *Historical cost accounts*
   PROFIT AND LOSS ACCOUNT FOR THE YEAR ENDED 31 MARCH 19X5

	£'000	£'000
Sales		4,800
Opening stock	250	
Purchases	3,300	
	3,550	
Less closing stock (3,300 x 1/12)	275	
Cost of sales		3,275
Gross profit		1,525
Monetary expenses		
Rent	40	
Distribution (75 x 12)	900	
Other operating expenses (14 x 12)	168	
Interest (14% x 6/12 x 400)	28	
		1,136
Profit after monetary expenses		389
Non-monetary expenses		
Depreciation on premises (5% x 400 x 6/12)	10	
Depreciation on plant (15% x 1,200)	180	
Profit on disposal of plant (108 - (120 x 85%))	(6)	
Depreciation on vehicles (20% x 500)	100	
		284
Profit before tax		105
Taxation @ 40%		42
Retained profit		63

BALANCE SHEET AS AT 31 MARCH 19X5

	Cost £'000	Dep'n £'000	Net £'000
Fixed assets			
Premises	400	10	390
Plant and machinery	1,080	162	918
Vehicles	500	100	400
	1,980	272	1,708
Current assets			
Stock		275	
Cash *		522	
		797	
Current liabilities			
Taxation		42	
Net current assets			755
			2,463
Long-term liability			
Loan			(400)
			2,063
Capital and reserves			
Share capital			2,000
Retained profit			63
			2,063

	£'000
* Opening cash balance	50
Add: cash profit	389
proceeds on disposal of plant	108
	547
Less increase in stock	25
Closing cash balance	522

2. *Loss on disposal of plant*

	£c'000
Historical cost of plant disposed of was £120,000	
Value in £c at 31 March 19X5 = 120 x 132/120	132
Depreciation in £c at 31 March 19X5	
15% x 120 x 132/120	20
Net book value at 31 March 19X5	112
Less cash received	108
Loss on disposal	4

3. *Loss on monetary items*

(*Note.* In the exam itself it would be advisable to derive this amount as a balancing figure. Complete the balance sheet, entering retained profit as a balance. Then use the figure of retained profit to complete the profit and loss account, entering the loss on monetary items as a balance. This working, however, shows how the figure can be proved.)

	£'000	£c'000
Initial holding of net monetary assets (NMA)	50	
As expressed in £c at 31 March 19X5 (50 x 132/120)	55	
Loss on initial holding of NMA		5
Increase in NMA per HC accounts		
(profit after monetary expenses 389 less increase		
in stock 25)	364	
Increase in NMA per CPP accounts (383-1)	382	
Loss on increase in NMA		18
Gain on long-term loan (400 x 132/126 - 400)		(19)
Net loss on monetary items		4

(*Note.* The £108,000 proceeds on disposal of plant do not affect this calculation because the cash was received on the last day of the year.)

15 TUTORIAL QUESTION: NORWICH

(a) CURRENT COST OPERATING PROFIT FOR 19X6

	£m	£m
Historical cost operating profit		15
Current cost adjustments		
Depreciation adjustment	3	
Cost of sales adjustment	5	
		(8)
Current cost operating profit		7

SUMMARISED CURRENT COST BALANCE SHEET
AS AT 31 DECEMBER 19X6

	£m	£m
Fixed assets		85
Current assets		
Stocks	21	
Debtors	30	
Bank	2	
	53	
Current liabilities	30	
		23
		108
Long-term liability		(20)
		88
Capital and reserves		88

(b) (i) *Interest cover*

HC accounts: 15 ÷ 3 = 5 times
CC accounts: 7 ÷ 3 = 2.3 times

(ii) *Return on shareholders' equity*

HC accounts: 12 ÷ 62 = 19.4%
CC accounts: 4 ÷ 88 = 4.5%

(iii) *Debt/equity ratio*

HC accounts: 20 ÷ 62 = 32.3%
CC accounts: 20 ÷ 88 = 22.7%

(c) (i) *Interest cover*

Companies must maintain their capital base if they wish to stay in business. The significance of the interest cover calculation is that it indicates the extent to which profits after tax are being eaten into by payments to finance external capital. The figures calculated above indicate that only one-fifth of historical cost profit is being absorbed in this way, while four-fifths are being retained to finance future growth. On the face of it, this might seem satisfactory; however, the current cost interest cover is only 2.3 times, indicating that, after allowing for the impact of rising prices, interest payments absorb nearly half of profits after tax.

(ii) *Return on shareholders' equity*

This is the ratio of profits earned for *shareholders* (profits after interest) to shareholders' equity. Once again, the position disclosed by the historical cost accounts is more favourable than appears from the current cost ratio. The historical cost profit is higher than the current cost profit because no allowance is made for the adverse impact of rising prices; and at the same time the denominator in the historical cost fraction is lower because shareholders' capital is stated at historical values rather than their higher current values.

The significance of the ratio is that it enables shareholders to assess the rate of return on their investment and to compare it with alternative investments that might be available to them.

(iii) *Debt/equity ratio*

The significance of this ratio is as a measure of the extent to which the company's net assets are financed by external borrowing and shareholders' funds respectively.

In times of rising prices it can be beneficial to finance assets from loan capital. While the assets appreciate in value over time (and the gain accrues to shareholders), the liability is fixed in monetary amount. The effect of this is that current cost accounts tend to give a more favourable picture of the debt/equity ratio than historical cost accounts. In the ratios calculated above, the amount of debt is £20m in both balance sheets. This represents nearly one-third of the historical cost value of shareholders' funds, but only one-fifth of the equity calculated on a current cost basis.

16   TUTORIAL QUESTION: POYNTON

Tutorial note. This is not a difficult question if you know the requirements of the relevant SSAPs. The trickiest point in part (a) is recognising that, while a *combination* of the FIFO and average cost bases of valuing stock will produce the highest and lowest profits possible arithmetically, it is not possible to mix them in practice. Additionally, a change from FIFO to average cost valuation for opening stock necessitates a prior year adjustment (see note 4).

We have incorporated detailed notes in our solution explaining the difference between the accounting treatments adopted. This is *not* a requirement of the question and you should not therefore have commented on your answer; if you did, you wasted time and effort for which no marks would have been awarded in an exam!

Suggested solution

(a)   POYNTON LIMITED
      SUMMARISED PROFIT AND LOSS ACCOUNTS
      FOR THE YEAR ENDED 30 JUNE 19X8

	Highest £'000	*Lowest* £'000
Turnover	7,230	7,230
Cost of sales (note 1)	4,950	4,966
Gross profit	2,280	2,264
Distribution costs and administrative expenses	1,380	1,380
Amortisation of goodwill (120 ÷ 3) (note 2)	-	40
Development expenditure written off (note 3)	-	60
	1,380	1,480
Retained profit for the year	900	784
Retained profit brought forward (note 4)	625	577
Goodwill written off against reserves (note 2)	(120)	-
	1,405	1,361

SUMMARISED BALANCE SHEET AS AT 30 JUNE 19X8

	Highest		Lowest	
	£'000	£'000	£'000	£'000
Fixed assets				
Intangible assets				
Development costs		60		-
Goodwill		-		80
Tangible assets		2,050		2,050
		2,110		2,130
Net current assets				
Stocks	400		336	
Net monetary assets	295		295	
		695		631
Total assets less current liabilities		2,805		2,761
Capital and reserves				
Share capital		1,400		1,400
Profit and loss account		1,405		1,361
		2,805		2,761

Notes

1. *Cost of sales*

   Cost of sales is charged with (increased by) a decrease in stock over the period and credited with (reduced by) an increase. Profit will therefore be highest if that valuation method is chosen which produces the smallest decrease or highest increase. It is not permissable under the Companies Act 1985 or SSAP 2 to use one method of valuation for opening stock and another for closing stock.

	FIFO	Average cost
	£'000	£'000
Opening stock	350	302
Closing stock	400	336
Increase	50	34

   Here, the FIFO valuation reduces cost of sales by more than the average cost valuation. Cost of sales is therefore as follows.

	Highest	Lowest
	£'000	£'000
Manufacturing costs	5,000	5,000
Less increase in stocks	50	34
	4,950	4,966

2. *Goodwill*

   SSAP 22 allows purchased goodwill to be treated in either of two ways. It can be amortised over its estimated economic life which reduces profit for the year in the same way as depreciation. Alternatively, it can be deducted from reserves. This does not affect profit for the year at all and thus this treatment results in higher reported profit.

3. *Development expenditure*

Under SSAP 13 development expenditure may either be written off as incurred or (if it meets the criteria laid down in the SSAP) it may be treated as a fixed asset and amortised over the life of the product it relates to. Amortisation would begin here in July 19X8 and so none need be charged in 19X7/X8.

4. *Reserves brought forward*

Since last year's accounts showed closing stock at FIFO valuation, this year's should, if average cost valuation is adopted, incorporate a prior year adjustment as required by SSAP 6 because of the change in accounting policy.

	£'000
Profit and loss account as at 1 July 19X7 as previously stated	625
Decrease in profit in respect of closing stock	
(valued lower on average cost basis): 350 - 302	48
Profit and loss account as at 1 July 19X7 restated	577

(b) *Tutorial note.* Obviously, many different asset valuation methods could have been chosen. In our answer we have discussed the revaluation of fixed assets, the choice of consolidation method in preparing group accounts and brand accounting.

Suggested solution

Company law permits but does not require the inclusion in the balance sheet of certain fixed and current assets at valuation. Usually only fixed assets are revalued, most commonly because land and buildings have increased in value. There is no requirement in any current SSAP or in law to revalue all assets or to keep valuations up to date. SSAP 12 does, however, require that depreciation on revalued assets should be calculated on the basis of the revalued amount and not on cost.

Thus, a balance sheet figure for fixed assets may represent a hotch potch of unexpired costs and part-depreciated revaluations, possibly long out of date. Many commentators argue that such figures do not help the reader to understand the state of a company's affairs. Although the financial statements must include details of revaluations and material differences between market and book value of assets, the balance sheet itself often gives no clue either to the historical costs incurred by the company or to the current value of assets. This means that users who wish to assess the company's true worth, gearing and financial security must amass current value information for themselves if they have sufficient information or influence on the company so to do. This is time consuming and expensive and does not give the assurance of objectivity that *audited* current valuations would give.

Additionally, because depreciation may be based on historical costs or out of date valuations, profit is not reduced by the true cost of assets consumed in the period. Profit could be overstated as a consequence and distributions (that is, dividend payments) could erode the company's operating capability by reducing its capital in real terms.

Another area where choice is currently permitted is in consolidation of a business which its parent company has merged with rather than acquired. In such a case, SSAP 23 and the Companies Act permit either the acquisition or the merger method to be applied. This can make a considerable difference to the group accounts.

The acquisition method requires that an acquired company's assets and liabilities should be stated at fair value as at acquisition and that the difference between these fair values and the fair value of consideration should be treated as goodwill, which must either be amortised or written off against reserves. All pre-acquisition profits and other reserves are eliminated from the consolidated accounts.

The merger method requires that the merged companies simply add together their assets, liabilities and reserves at book value and adjust consolidated reserves to eliminate or add the difference between the parent company's investment and the subsidiary's share capital. No pre- and post-acquisition distinction arises and so the combined business's profit and loss account shows combined current and prior year results even if the combination took place part of the way through the year.

Thus, the user of consolidated accounts must refer extensively to the notes to find out:
(i)   which method has been used for which combinations;
(ii)   what fair value adjustments have been made (acquisitions method);
(iii) what the analysis of profit was between businesses in the year of combination (merger method).

Within the same set of accounts, some combinations may have been accounted for by the merger method and some by the acquisition method, in which case a further distinction arises between those in which goodwill is to be amortised and those in which it is eliminated against reserves. This makes it difficult to attach any value to the consolidated accounts.

Finally, *brand accounting* is a recent phenomenon whereby companies with valuable portfolios of branded products (such as Hovis bread or Paxo stuffing) have begun to attribute a value to these brands and to treat them as intangible assets in the balance sheet. There are currently no Companies Act provisions on this practice nor is there an SSAP in issue on the topic. Companies can therefore adopt any valuation method they please and many have chosen not to amortise brands. Most controversially, some have chosen to capitalise brands which have been developed internally and not acquired (which, by implication, have been given an objective valuation on the basis of which a purchase price was fixed). Many valuations are on the basis of estimated future earnings rather than separately identifiable costs incurred in developing brands.

The result is that shareholders' funds are greatly increased and the balance sheet looks stronger. Additionally, goodwill calculated on acquisitions of companies with large brand portfolios becomes much less significant because brands are treated as part of the separable net assets of such companies rather than as part of the goodwill.

The problem for users of accounts is therefore that there is no consistency in this area and, many would argue, insufficient prudence. While some consider that capitalisation of brands results in a more meaningful balance sheet, others feel that brands are *too* intangible and too subject to the whims of fickle consumers to be treated as fixed assets.

17 TUTORIAL QUESTION: NEWTRADE

(a) JOURNAL ENTRIES

		Dr £	Cr £
DEBIT	Plant and machinery	126,580	
	Motor lorries	42,520	
	Motor cars	12,259	
	VAT	25,365	
CREDIT	Suspense		206,724

Being extraction of asset costs from suspense account.

DEBIT	Suspense	40,916	
CREDIT	Government grants		25,316
	Profit and loss		15,600

Being the extraction and capitalisation of capital-based grants, and the crediting to profit and loss of revenue-based grant from suspense account.

DEBIT	Profit and loss	36,272	
CREDIT	Plant and machinery: acc. depreciation		25,316
	Motor lorries: accumulated depreciation		8,504
	Motor cars: accumulated depreciation		2,452

Being the provision for depreciation of assets for the year.

DEBIT	Government grants (20% x £25,316)	5,063	
CREDIT	Profit and loss		5,063

Being the amortisation of capital-based government grants for the year.

Depreciation of a full 20% on cost has been charged on the assumption that the assets have been held for the whole year.

(b) MEMORANDUM

To: Directors
From: Accountant
Date: 10 May 19X3
Subject: *Reasons for journal entries and their effect on the accounts*

(i)   The journal entries were made in order to reflect fairly in the accounts the acquisition and consumption (as measured by depreciation) of the fixed assets, and the receipts of the grants.

(ii)   Since the VAT paid on the acquisition of the plant and machinery and the motor lorries is recoverable, it is appropriate that the costs of the assets net of VAT are capitalised and depreciated systematically over their expected useful lives, and that the VAT is shown as a debtor recoverable within one year.

(iii) The VAT paid on the acquisition of the motor cars is irrecoverable, and therefore is a cost of acquisition. The total cost of acquisition should, in accordance with SSAP 5, be capitalised in the motor cars account, and depreciated systematically over the expected useful lives of the cars. Irrecoverable VAT therefore reduces reported profits.

(iv) The grant received in respect of employment of local labour effectively reduces the cost of employment for the period. It is thus appropriate to credit the grant directly to the profit and loss account of that period, thus increasing profits.

(v) The grant received relating to the acquisition of plant and machinery reduces the effective cost of the related plant and machinery. Since the cost of fixed assets is depreciated over the expected life of the assets, it is consistent that the grant relating thereto should be credited to revenue over the expected useful life of those assets in a similar manner. This is in accordance with SSAP 4, and also with the matching concept detailed in SSAP 2.

(vi) Of the two ways of achieving this (the cost reduction method, and the deferred credit method), the deferred credit method has the following principal advantages:

   (i) assets acquired at different times and locations are recorded on a uniform basis regardless of changes in government policy; and
   (ii) control over the ordering, construction and maintenance of assets is based on the gross value.

The deferred credit method involves the setting up of a government grants deferred credit account, which would be carried in the balance sheet, normally, under 'Accruals and deferred income'.

18 STRACHAN

Tutorial note. As originally set, this question was harder because different rates of tax were in force for each year. However, as amended to current rates it makes a good first revision question on tax in published accounts.

Suggested solution

PROFIT AND LOSS ACCOUNTS (EXTRACTS)

YEAR ENDED 31 DECEMBER	*19X5* £	*19X6* £
Income from fixed asset investments	–	20,000
Tax on ordinary profits (W1)	140,000	285,000
Dividends payable	150,000	50,000

BALANCE SHEETS (EXTRACTS)

AS AT 31 DECEMBER	*19X5* £	*19X6* £
Debtors		
ACT recoverable (£100,000 x $\frac{1}{3}$)	33,333	–
Creditors: amounts falling due within one year		
Proposed dividend	100,000	–
ACT on proposed dividend	33,333	–
Mainstream corporation tax (W2)	123,333	230,000

Workings

1. *Tax on ordinary profits*

	19X5 £	19X6 £
£400,000/£800,000 @ 35%	140,000	280,000
Tax associated with dividends received	-	5,000
	140,000	285,000

2. *Mainstream corporation tax*

	19X5 £	19X6 £
Tax on chargeable profits (W1)	140,000	280,000
Less ACT on dividends *actually paid* in year:		
£50,000 x ⅓	(16,667)	
£150,000 x ⅓		(50,000)
	123,333	230,000

The company has surplus FII of £20,000 to carry forward at the end of 19X6. This will be used to reduce the amount of any ACT payable on dividends paid during 19X7.

19 BINSTEAD

(a)

	£
Net profit before taxation (W1)	708,667
Taxation (W4)	248,917
Net profit after taxation	459,750
Extraordinary item (65% x £15,000)	(9,750)
Net profit for the year	450,000

Workings

1. *Profit before tax*

	£	£
Net trading profit		800,000
Add: dividends received	36,500	
tax credit thereon		
(25/75 x £36,500)	12,167	
		48,667
Less debenture interest payable		(140,000)
Net profit before tax		708,667

2. *Draft corporation tax computation*

	£	£
Net trading profit		800,000
Less interest payable		(140,000)
Add depreciation		245,000
Less capital allowances		(300,000)
		605,000
Add: balancing charge	30,000	
disallowable expenditure	20,000	
		50,000
Net taxable profit		655,000

3. *Movement on deferred tax account*

	£
Timing differences	
Capital allowances	300,000
Balancing charge	(30,000)
Depreciation	(220,000)
	50,000
Transfer to deferred tax a/c @ 35%	17,500

4. *Tax charge in profit and loss account*

	£
On profits for year (35% x £655,000) (W2)	229,250
Add movement on deferred tax a/c (W3)	17,500
Less overprovision for 19X0	
£(120,000 - 110,000)	(10,000)
Add tax credit on dividends received (W1)	12,167
	248,917

(b) Balance on deferred tax account   260,834

Balance on corporation tax account   179,500

Workings

1. *Deferred tax*

	£
Balance on deferred tax account at 31.12.X0.	250,000
Add ACT on 19X0 proposed final dividend	
25/75 x £80,000	26,667
	276,667
Add transfer for year	17,500
	294,167
Less ACT on 19X1 proposed final dividend	
25/75 x £100,000	(33,333)
Balance at 31.12.X1.	260,834

2. *Corporation tax*

	£	£
Corporation tax charge for year		229,250
Tax on extraordinary item (£15,000 @ 35%)		(5,250)
		224,000
Less ACT paid in 19X1 on:		
19X0 final paid	80,000	
19X1 interim paid	50,000	
19X1 preference paid	40,000	
	170,000	
Dividends received	36,500	
	133,500	
ACT paid 25/75 x £133,500		44,500
Balance at 31.12.X1.		179,500

20 TUTORIAL QUESTION: MILLER

Tutorial note. It is extremely unlikely that a question as straightforward as this would appear in an AFA paper now. However, it gives you an opportunity to practise your report writing skills as well as to revise SSAP 9 and SSAP 6.

Suggested solution

To: Board of Directors
From: Accountant
Subject: *Change in the basis of stock valuation*

In the accounts for the year ended 31 December 19X2 stock will for the first time be valued, not at direct cost, but at direct cost plus production overheads. This is the valuation method prescribed by Statement of Standard Accounting Practice 9 *Stocks and long-term contracts*. Compliance with SSAP 9 will mean that we will avoid a qualified report from our auditors.

The effects of the change are set out below.

(i)   In the balance sheet, stock at 31 December 19X2 will be valued at £79,500 compared with a direct cost valuation of £49,500, so stock will be £30,000 greater than if the previous valuation basis had been used.

(ii)   This will be matched by an increase of £30,000 in retained profits, arrived at as follows.

	£
Upward restatement of retained profits at 31.12.X1	36,000
Less reduction in profits reported for 19X2	6,000
Net increase in retained profits	30,000

(iii)   The upward restatement (£36,000) of last year's retained profits arises from valuing last year's stock at £90,000 (previously, £54,000).

(iv)   The reduction in 19X2 profits (£6,000) is the difference between profits on the old basis (£338,800) and profits on the SSAP 9 basis (£332,800).

Workings

1.   Opening stock valued at direct cost only was £54,000. Since direct costs per unit were £9, there must have been 6,000 units in opening stock.

2.   *Production in 19X2*

	£
Direct costs: 11/12 x 54,000 x £9	445,500
1/12 x 54,000 x £10	45,000
	490,500
Production overheads	324,000
	814,500

Production in the year was 54,000 units: £324,000 ÷ £6.

3. *Closing stock*

There must be 5,000 units in stock at the year end: 6,000 + 54,000 - 55,000.

	Units	Direct cost £	SSAP 9 £
December production			
(1/12 x 54,000)	4,500		
Direct cost (@ £10)		45,000	45,000
Production overhead (@ £6)			27,000
	4,500	45,000	72,000
November production (balance)	500		
Direct cost (@ £9)		4,500	4,500
Production overhead (@ £6)			3,000
	5,000	49,500	79,500

21 LONG-TERM CONTRACTS

Tutorial note. The examiner commented that answers to this question were poor. This was due to lack of knowledge and failure to use a report format. The latter shows very poor examination technique; the former is inexcusable given SSAP 9's importance in financial reporting. Go back to your study text if you are in any doubt about the revised SSAP 9 disclosure requirements.

Suggested solution

From: Chief accountant
To: Credit controller
Subject: *Accounting treatment of long-term work in progress*

One of the major difficulties encountered in preparing financial statements is that they express the profit or loss of an entity over an arbitrary time period whereas in reality the activities that produce the profit or loss are continuous. This means that assessments have to be made at the end of the arbitrary accounting periods of the current condition of transactions that are only partially complete at that time.

This is not a problem when the cash-to-cash cycle in a particular business is a short one, since a large number of separate transactions take place over the accounting period and any inaccuracies in the assumptions made will usually more or less cancel each other out.

Where, however, an enterprise undertakes a relatively small number of large, long-term contracts, the profit reported in a particular accounting period will depend to a greater extent on the accounting policy adopted. Debate in the accounting profession on the most appropriate treatment for long-term contracts has centred on the relative importance to be given to *matching* revenues earned in the period with the costs that relate to them and the need to exercise *prudence* in financial reporting. Prudence, according to SSAP 2 will override the matching concept when the two are in conflict. In practice, however, the rules that have been developed to deal with accounting for long-term contracts are based on the matching concept with the prudence principle acting as a safeguard against over-optimistic profit assessment. The aim is to give a fair view of the activities in the period.

The accounting standard that governs long-term contracts is SSAP 9. Its general principle is that an assessment should be made at the end of each year of the profit that has been earned through the work completed under each long-term contract at the year end. This does not mean that profit can only be taken on completed contracts nor that pre-defined stages need to be reached before profit can be recognised. It does mean, however, that an independent assessment made by a quantity surveyor, architect or similar person is normally required by the auditors. There would clearly be scope for manipulation and 'creative accounting' were this assessment to be left entirely to the management of the enterprise concerned.

In order to assess the amount of profit that has been made to date in respect of a contract still under way, the standard requires that an assessment be made of the *final* outcome of that contract. If this cannot be done with a reasonable degree of certainty, then no profit should be taken until such a degree of certainty exists.

Where a contract is running at a loss, any loss to date must be taken in full, as otherwise the value of the contract work in progress carried forward would be greater than its realisable value. This would infringe the prudence principle mentioned earlier. Moreover, even if the contract has not produced a loss to date, if it appears that it will eventually produce a loss, that loss should be provided for in full as soon as it becomes apparent.

The standard presentation in the profit and loss account is to include the appropriate amount of certified work in turnover in the profit and loss account and the corresponding costs in cost of sales.

In the balance sheet, an amount may be included in debtors under the heading 'amounts recoverable on contracts'. This represents turnover to date less progress payments to date (each contract is looked at separately before aggregating these figures). If progress payments to date exceed turnover, then the excess is deducted from any balance remaining on the contract account after the transfer to cost of sales. This transfer includes any necessary provision for losses.

Finally, if there are still excess progress payments, then these should be shown as a creditor. This explains the negative balance on work in progress you mention. Another possible reason is that, if the provision for foreseeable losses exceeds the balance on the contract account, then a provision should be included in the balance sheet.

22 GONERIL, REGAN AND CORDELIA

(a) GONERIL LIMITED
PROFIT AND LOSS ACCOUNT FOR THE
YEAR ENDING 30 JUNE (EXTRACTS)

	19X4 £	19X5 £	19X6 £	19X7 £
Depreciation				
120,000/40	3,000	3,000		
160,000/50			3,200	-
Loss on revaluation*				
£(376,800 - 290,000 - 86,000)			800	
Profit on sale*				
£(320,000 - 290,000)				30,000

154

MOVEMENT ON RESERVES FOR THE
YEAR ENDING 30 JUNE

	19X5 £	19X6 £
Unrealised		
Profit on revaluation £(380,000 - 294,000)	86,000	
Loss on revaluation		(86,000)

BALANCE SHEET AS AT 30 JUNE	19X4 £	19X5 £	19X6 £	19X7 £
Freehold land and buildings				
Cost	300,000	-	-	-
Depreciation	3,000			
Net book value	297,000			
Freehold land and building at valuation		380,000	290,000	-
Reserves				
Unrealised	-	86,000	-	-

REGAN LIMITED
PROFIT AND LOSS ACCOUNT FOR THE
YEAR ENDING 30 JUNE (EXTRACTS)

	19X4 £	19X5 £	19X6 £	19X7 £
Depreciation				
£120,000/40	3,000	3,000		
£114,000/50**			2,280	
Profit on sale*				
£(320,000 - 291,720)				28,280

BALANCE SHEET AS AT 30 JUNE (EXTRACTS)	19X4 £	19X5 £	19X6 £
Freehold land and buildings			
Cost	300,000	300,000	300,000
Depreciation	3,000	6,000	8,280
Net book value	297,000	294,000	291,720

(** Whether or not Regan Limited would take account of the revised estimated life is not clear; it would therefore be equally acceptable to calculate 19X4 depreciation as £120,000/40 as previously.)

CORDELIA LIMITED
PROFIT AND LOSS ACCOUNT FOR THE
YEAR ENDING 30 JUNE (EXTRACTS)

	19X6 £	19X7 £
Deficit on revaluation of investment property*	10,000	
Profit on sale*		
£(320,000 - 290,000)		30,000

MOVEMENTS ON INVESTMENT
REVALUATION RESERVE FOR THE YEAR
ENDING 30 JUNE (EXTRACTS)

	19X5 £	19X6 £
Unrealised surplus £(380,000 - 300,000)	80,000	
Unrealised deficit		(80,000)

BALANCE SHEET AS AT 30 JUNE (EXTRACTS)

	19X4 £	19X5 £	19X6 £	19X7 £
Investment property at valuation	300,000	380,000	290,000	-
Reserves Investment revaluation	-	80,000	-	-

Notes

1. The amounts marked * would be disclosed as exceptional if material in size.
2. If the directors consider that the market value of Regan Limited's property differs substantially from the amount at which it is stated in the balance sheet, and that this difference is significant to shareholders or debenture holders, they should disclose this in their report. This may be necessary in 19X5 and 19X6.

(b) Useful information on this point was contained in the ASC statement published at the time ED 26 (the forerunner to SSAP 19) was produced. Relevant extracts are reproduced below.

'It is not, and never has been, the general practice in the UK and Ireland to provide for annual depreciation of investment properties. Certainly there are cases in which annual depreciation has been or is provided (usually for reasons of great prudence) but it is by no means a general practice. The reason that annual depreciation is not provided on such properties is largely instinctive and has not been clearly rationalised. Subject to consideration of submissions on this Exposure Draft, the ASC believes that this instinctive practice has a sound foundation.

At the outset it should be noted that we are here concerned with investment properties as opposed to properties which form an integral part of the manufacturing or commercial processes of an enterprise. The prime criterion is that of any other general investment; that it can be sold at any time, without interfering with the ordinary operations of the enterprise.

Under general accounting conventions (both historical cost and current cost) fixed assets are subject to annual depreciation charges to reflect, on a systematic basis, the consumption, wearing out and use of the asset in the course of the business of the enterprise. Under those conventions it is also accepted that an increase in the value of such a fixed asset does not remove the necessity to charge depreciation to reflect, on a systematic basis, the consumption of the asset.

It is however persuasively argued that a different treatment is required for a fixed asset which is not held for 'consumption' in the business operations of an enterprise but is held as a disposable investment. In such a case the current value of the investment, and changes in that current value, are of prime importance rather than a calculation of systematic annual depreciation.'

The argument therefore proceeds as follows.

1.   The financial statements of enterprises holding investments are helpful to users of financial statements if the investments are accounted for at current values rather than on the basis of cost or valuation established some time in the past.

2.   Depreciation is only one element which enters into the annual change in the value of a property and as the use of a current value places the prime emphasis on the values of the assets, it is not generally useful to attempt to distinguish, estimate and account separately for the element of depreciation.

3.   Depreciation, although not separately identified, will be taken into account in dealing with changes in current values.

SSAP 19 makes current value accounting for investment properties mandatory. This is because (a) the argument for current value accounting for investment properties is considered highly persuasive; and (b) if this method of accounting is not considered to be essential for the purpose of giving a true and fair view, then under the Companies Act 1985 it would not be permissible at all and annual depreciation would have to be charged. (Failure to charge annual depreciation on a fixed asset with a finite life constitutes a departure from the requirements of the Companies Act 1985, which can be justified only on the grounds that it is essential for the purpose of giving a true and fair view.)

23   DEPRECIATION OF PROPERTY

Tutorial note. Many candidates showed a poor (or non-existent) knowledge of SSAP 19 in the examination.

Suggested solution

From: Finance Director
To: Managing Director
Date: 31 October 19X2
Subject: *Depreciation of Property*

(a)   All fixed assets that have a finite economic life should be depreciated in a systematic manner over that period. While it is recognised that, generally, freehold land has an indefinite economic life, the same is not true of buildings. Even if they are properly maintained, most industrial and commercial buildings will become economically obsolete in time, even if they remain structurally sound.

The failure to provide depreciation on industrial and commercial buildings over their period of use overstates the profits of the company and this could lead to over-distribution of profit.

(b)   An investment property is defined in the relevant accounting standard (SSAP 19) as one which is held for its investment potential and for which a rental is negotiated at arms length (and where construction is complete). It cannot be one which is owned and occupied by a company or its affiliated companies for its own purposes.

This means that our properties, which are used for the purposes of the company's own manufacturing, distribution and administrative activities, do not qualify for treatment as investment properties.

It also means that they could not be made to qualify as investment properties by transferring them to another group company and renting them back.

(c) Under SSAP 19 investment properties are not depreciated but are shown in the accounts at open market value. Increases in market value are credited to an investment revaluation reserve and decreases are charged to it. Falls in market value below the revaluation reserve are taken directly to the profit and loss account. The open market valuation, which is related to rentals, is likely to vary considerably over time and large charges against profits could occur during periods of weakness in the property market. This could lead to greater volatility of earnings than if the properties had been depreciated, but it reflects more accurately the realities of the property market.

24 GOODWILL

Tutorial note. The examiner remarked that 'the treatment of goodwill is a controversial and topical area and it is important that candidates at Stage 3 keep up to date with current accounting problems.'

Suggested solution

To: Managing director
From: Financial controller
Subject: *Accounting for goodwill*

Goodwill arises when the value of a business as a totality is different from the sum of the values of its individual assets and liabilities. Where the total value is less than the sum of the values, goodwill is negative.

Goodwill is generated by the interaction of the assets, the management, the workforce and the suppliers and customers of the business so that in aggregate each element generates more wealth than it would without the others. It is inherent to a greater or lesser extent in any business that is a going concern.

Inherent goodwill (which may include the value of brands) is not usually accounted for in the financial statements of a business because these are based on actual identifiable transactions. Inherent goodwill emerges as a result of these transactions as a whole but not as the result of a particular transaction which can be accounted for. Thus, there is no possibility of an *objective* valuation. This view is generally accepted and recognition of inherent goodwill in accounts is prohibited by SSAP 22 *Accounting for goodwill*.

Where, however, one business is acquired by another the price paid will often be in excess of the fair values of the separable net assets acquired. This excess is known as purchased goodwill and, since a transaction has occurred, an appropriate accounting treatment is required. Opinion varies within the accounting profession, however, on this point and so alternative treatments are allowed within SSAP 22.

One view is that goodwill is an asset which is not different from any other intangible asset. It has been purchased along with the other net tangible assets of the acquired business and the valuation put on it by the acquiring company is explicit. Consequently, according to this view, it is necessary to record this asset in the accounts of the acquiring company and to amortise it over its useful life. This treatment, it is argued, will comply with the matching concept underlying financial reporting and will ensure that the cost of the goodwill is matched with the additional benefits that are expected to arise from the particular mix of net assets, employees, suppliers and customers acquired.

The contrary view is that goodwill is unique and is unlike any other asset because it has no separate existence from the other assets of the acquired business. Moreover, it is argued that, while the value can be determined at the point of acquisition, this is not a suitable basis for recognition in financial statements since its future value is uncertain. In the same way, no rational or reliable assessment can be made of its useful life. Thus, the amount of money spent on purchased goodwill should be regarded as the immediate consumption of some of the acquiring company's capital and should be written off immediately to reserves.

Each of these solutions has it problems. The reliability of the value of goodwill shown as an asset in company accounts is known to be low and many financial analysts will discount this item in assessing the financial position of a company. The economic life of goodwill requires a subjective assessment and could be subject to manipulation. In addition, amortisation reduces earnings per share, thus deterring many directors from choosing this method.

On the other hand, an immediate write off to reserves will weaken the company's balance sheet and will increase the gearing ratio where there is borrowing. Where reserves are insufficient to meet a write off, a company may be deterred from making an acquisition that it otherwise believes makes business sense and it is argued that business decisions should not be based on financial reporting considerations.

On balance SSAP 22 currently prefers the immediate write off to reserves and recommends this treatment. Capitalisation and amortisation is, however, allowed and recent developments suggest that this latter treatment is gaining favour and that a revision of SSAP 22 will prescribe it as the only permitted method. It is certainly true that SSAP 22 has been heavily criticised for failing to provide comparability between companies.

The use of merger accounting may help to avoid recognising goodwill. However, goodwill is so significant that the difference between the purchase price (fair value of equity and the other consideration) and the fair value of net assets acquired should still be disclosed.

Finally, on the subject of disposals, the gain or loss which arises when a business is sold will almost always be reflected in the profit and loss account. This provides an additional argument in favour of capitalisation and amortisation which would ensure symmetrical treatment of acquisitions and disposals.

25   SSAP 24

Tutorial note. This was a very unpopular question in the examination and many candidates tackled it as a last resort. You must be up to date and demonstrate detailed knowledge of the accounting standards. If you are able to do so, then this is a very straightforward question.

Suggested solution

(a)   To: Managing director
       From: Finance director
       Subject: *SSAP 24 Accounting for Pension Costs*

As you are aware, SSAP 24 now regulates the manner in which companies are required to account for the costs of pensions provided for employees. The purpose of this memorandum is to summarise the principles underlying SSAP 24 and the changes that it makes.

The basic principle of SSAP 24 is that the cost of pensions should be provided in a systematic manner over the working lives of the employees concerned. Only where a pension scheme is a defined contribution scheme will this equate in any one year to the amount paid to the trustees. In a defined benefit scheme like ours the contribution rate will vary from time to time depending on the performance of the fund, the overall level of pay increases and changes in the benefits provided.

Over the long run, the cost of providing pensions is expected to be a substantially constant percentage of the current and expected future payroll cost. This percentage is based on the regular actuarial valuation of the pension fund, the primary purpose of which is to assess the ability of the fund to provide the benefits defined in the scheme.

From time to time, the assessment will identify surpluses and deficits in the fund. The accounting treatment required by SSAP 24 is that these surpluses or deficits should be recognised as reductions or increases in the regular cost over the remaining service lives of the employees currently in the scheme. This has the effect of smoothing out these surpluses and deficits which can themselves arise and disappear quite suddenly as a result of the investment performance of the fund.

The accounting treatment is unaffected by any funding decision that the company may decide to make based on the actuarial valuation. Where it is decided to increase the company contribution 'up front' in order to fund a deficit, the difference between the additional contribution and the increased cost, as described above, will not be charged in full to the profit and loss account but will be treated as a prepayment and charged over the period of the deficit. Where, on the other hand, a surplus allows for a contribution holiday this effect will not be recognised immediately in the profit and loss account but will be spread over the period of the holiday.

The overall effect of the changes required by SSAP 24 will be that the change for pensions in the profit and loss account in the future will be less volatile than in the past when we simply charged the contributions to the fund and the balance sheet will more realistically recognise any over or under provision of pensions.

(b) SSAP 24 requires the following disclosures.

(i) The nature of the scheme, ie whether it is a defined benefit or a defined contribution scheme or a combination of both.

(ii) Whether the scheme is funded or unfunded.

(iii) The accounting policy and, where different, the funding policy of the scheme.

(iv) Whether the scheme is regularly valued by a qualified actuary, the date of the most recent actuarial valuation and whether the actuary is an employee or an officer of the company or an affiliated company.

(v) The pension cost for the period, distinguishing between the regular cost and any variations from it, together with an explanation of any material changes from the cost in the previous period.

(vi) Details of any prepayments or accruals provided in the accounts in respect of any differences between the amounts charged in the accounts as pension costs and amounts paid to the fund or directly to pensioners.

(vii) The amount of any deficiency in the fund calculated on the basis of the current funding policy together with details of any action taken or proposed to deal with the deficiency.

(viii) A summary of the results of the most recent actuarial valuation, including the actuarial methods used, assumptions made, the market value of the scheme assets, the level of funding as a percentage of payroll and comments on any material actuarial surplus or deficit.

(ix) Whether the company has a commitment to make any additional payments and the period of such commitment.

(x) The accounting treatment of any refund which is recognised as a credit in the accounts.

(xi) Details of any expected effects on the future pension cost of any material charges in the terms of the pension scheme.

26 TUTORIAL QUESTION: CAXTON

Tutorial note. The point of this question is to make you aware of the importance of *memorising* the Companies Act 1985 formats for published accounts. This is a tedious task but unfortunately an essential one. You need to know what *must* be shown on the face of the accounts, in *exactly* what order and the *exact* wording of the caption. Although in practice many companies take advantage of the Act's permission to adapt the arrangement and headings of items designated by an Arabic number, in the examination you have to prove that you know what the law requires. The examiner will not assume that you are a sophisticated user of published accounts if your answer is not in Companies Act format; he will assume that you don't know the format.

Items designated by Arabic numbers can be shown in the notes to the accounts instead of on the face of the accounts. It would be correct, therefore, to show only the totals for tangible fixed assets, stocks and so on. In an exam answer it is often neater to compress the balance sheet in this way, especially if you are also required to prepare notes. However, if you are not required to prepare notes, then it may be quicker to insert all the items required by the formats into the balance sheet itself. It is rarely worthwhile to relegate profit and loss account captions to the notes as the profit and loss account is shorter.

The following solution includes the CA 1985's letters, Roman numerals and Arabic numbers to show you their usefulness in helping you put the captions in the right order. In the balance sheet no indication is given in the Act as to the best place for a total but our solution shows the commonest choice. In the profit and loss account, three totals are required (3, 14 and 20) but there is no guidance on the sub-totalling of items of income and expenditure. Our solution is a logical grouping of items.

Finally, note particularly that our solution has *full headings* at the start of each statement, with the company's name, the statement's name and the date written out in full. It is usual to write 'LIMITED' rather than 'LTD' but 'PLC' rather than 'PUBLIC LIMITED COMPANY'. A reminder: profit and loss accounts are drawn up *for* a period of stated length *ended* (if it's already over) or *ending* (if it's a forecast) on a specific date; balance sheets are drawn up *as at a specific date*.

CAXTON LIMITED
PROFIT AND LOSS ACCOUNT FOR THE YEAR ENDED
31 DECEMBER 19X1 (Note 1)

		Note	£'000	£'000
1.	Turnover	2		4,679
2.	Cost of sales	2		2,051
3.	Gross profit	1		2,628
4.	Distribution costs	2,3	495	
5.	Administrative expenses	2,3	627	
6.	Other operating income	2,3	(112)	
				1,010
				1,618
8.	Income from participating interests	2,3	100	
11.	Amounts written off investments	2,3	(50)	
12.	Interest payable and similar charges	2,3	(25)	
				25
	Profit on ordinary activities before taxation	4		1,643
13.	Tax on profit on ordinary activities	2		552
14.	Profit on ordinary activities after taxation	2		1,091
15.	Extraordinary income	2	120	
16.	Extraordinary charges	2	66	
17.	Extraordinary profit	2	54	
18.	Tax on extraordinary profit	2	15	
				39
20.	Profit for the financial year	5		1,130
	Dividends payable	6		567
	Retained profit for the financial year	4		563

CAXTON LIMITED
BALANCE SHEET AS AT 31 DECEMBER 19X1 (Note 1)

			Note	£'000	£'000
B	*Fixed assets*		1		
I	Intangible assets		3		
	1.	Development costs	2,3	602	
	2.	Patents	7	59	
	3.	Goodwill	3	120	
					781
II	Tangible assets		3		
	1.	Land and buildings	3	114	
	2.	Plant and machinery	2,3	2,106	
	3.	Fixtures, fittings, tools and equipment	2	98	
					2,318
III	Investments		3,8		850
	Carried forward				3,949

			Note	£'000	£'000
	Brought forward				3,949
C	*Current assets*		3		
	I	Stocks			
		1. Raw materials and consumables	2,3	48	
		2. Work in progress	3	107	
		3. Finished goods and goods for resale	2	94	
	II	Debtors	3	567	
	IV	Cash at bank and in hand	3	127	
				943	
D	*Prepayments and accrued income*		2,9	12	
E	*Creditors: amounts falling due within one year*		2		
		2. Bank loans and overdrafts	3	210	
		4. Trade creditors	3	290	
		5. Bills of exhcnage payable	3	404	
				904	
F	*Net current assets*				51
G	*Total assets less current liabilities*		1		4,000
H	*Creditors: amounts falling due after more than one year*		2		578
I	*Provision for liabilities and charge*		2		
		2. Taxation, including deferred taxation	2,10		320
J	*Accruals and deferred income*				196
					2,906
K	*Capital and reserves*		2		
	I	Called up share capital	2		1,500
	II	Share premium account	2		250
	III	Revaluation reserve	2,3		67
	IV	Other reserves	1,11		
		1. Capital redemption reserve			52
	V	Profit and loss account	2,3		1,037
					2,906

Notes

1. Caption omitted

2. Caption's wording was wrong, make sure you can see the mistake.

3. Captions wrongly ordered, make sure you get the order right.

4. Caption required for reasons of presentation but not required by the CA 1985.

5. Caption attributed to wrong sub-total.

6. Caption not required by CA 1985 but information given usually shown on the face of the profit and loss account.

7. The full CA 1985 caption is 'Concessions, patents, licences, trade marks and similar rights and assets'. This is, for obvious reasons, usually abbreviated.

8. 'Loans' are presumably investments. In the absence of further information, one total is given for investments as a full CA 1985 analysis is not possible without knowing the nature of the investments and loans.

9. Prepayments and accrued income may be either a component of 'Debtors' (CII) or a separate caption D. In the absence of any detailed analysis of 'Debtors', the latter treatment has been adopted.

10. It would be permissible simply to use a caption 'Deferred taxation' on the face of the balance sheet since the CA 1985 requires that this amount should be shown separately in the notes.

11. It would be permissible to omit 'Other reserves', as most published accounts do.

27 CHAPMAN

Tutorial notes.

1. Expenses incurred in the course of a company's ordinary activities must be categorised as cost of sales, distribution costs or administrative expenses. In this solution we take the view that the write-off of research expenditure is best shown under cost of sales; while amortisation of goodwill, depreciation on the building and bad debts are administrative expenses. However, other reasonable assumptions would be equally acceptable.

2. The write-off of development expenditure and the bad debt would probably be separately disclosed, in a full set of accounts, as exceptional items. But the loss in relation to the loan advanced to Groves Ltd falls outside the course of Chapman's normal activities and is therefore an extraordinary item.

3. The ACT relating to the proposed dividend should not appear anywhere in the profit and loss account. Instead, it should be shown in the balance sheet, both as a current liability (because it will need to be paid to the Inland Revenue soon after the balance sheet date) and as a deduction from deferred taxation (because it will reduce the amount of corporation tax payable in later years).

Suggested solution

PROFIT AND LOSS ACCOUNT
FOR THE YEAR ENDED 31 MARCH 19X7

	£'000
Turnover	2,150
Cost of sales (W1)	1,250
Gross profit	900
Distribution costs	36
Administrative expenses (W2)	593
Profit on ordinary activities before tax	271
Taxation	112
Profit on ordinary activities after tax	159
Extraordinary loss	58
Profit for the financial year	101
Dividends	75
Retained profit for the year	26
Retained profits brought forward	736
Retained profits carried forward	762

BALANCE SHEET AS AT 31 MARCH 19X7

	£'000	£'000
Fixed assets		
Intangible assets		
Development costs	14	
Goodwill	30	
		44
Tangible assets		
Freehold property (900-22)	878	
Plant and machinery	1,194	
		2,072
		2,116
Current assets		
Stocks	321	
Debtors (197-50)	147	
Cash at bank and in hand	3	
	471	
Creditors : amounts falling due		
within one year		
Trade creditors	104	
Taxation (W3)	120	
Dividend	75	
	299	
Net current assets		172
Total assets less current liabilities		2,288
Provisions for liabilities and charges		
Deferred taxation (W4)	80	
Provision for loan guarantee	58	
		(138)
		2,150
Capital and reserves		
Called up share capital		1,000
Reserves		
Revaluation reserve (W5)	388	
Profit and loss account	762	
		1,150
		2,150

Explanation of adjustments

1. According to SSAP 22, goodwill may either be written off against reserves immediately after acquisition, or may be amortised over its useful life. Since the directors of Chapman have apparently gone to the trouble of estimating its useful life it is best to assume that amortisation is the preferred method.

2. SSAP 13 and the Companies Act 1985 require that research expenditure should be written off as it is incurred. Development costs, on the other hand, may be carried forward in the balance sheet in certain circumstances. Since we are told that the product is proving a great success we can assume that the £14,000 development costs may be capitalised.

3. Note 5 of the question describes an adjusting post balance sheet event. Evidence arising after the balance sheet date indicates that debtors balances are overstated, and an appropriate adjustment must therefore be made.

4. The debenture issue described in note 6 is a non-adjusting post balance sheet event. It would be mentioned in a note to the accounts.

5. The loan guarantee described in note 7 is a contingent loss. Since it is likely that the loss will be realised at a future date it should be provided for in the accounts.

6. Chapman's law suit against Bridge Ltd is a contingent gain. Since the gain is likely to be realised, it may be referred to by way of a note to the accounts; however, it is not permissible to take credit for the gain by adjusting the accounts.

Workings

1. *Cost of sales*

	£'000
Per draft	1,200
Research expenditure written off	50
	1,250

2. *Administrative expenses*

	£'000
Per draft	527
Amortisation of goodwill ($\frac{6}{12}$ x $\frac{1}{3}$ x £36,000)	6
Additional depreciation	10
Bad debt	50
	593

3. *Taxation*

	£'000
Mainstream liability	95
ACT (£75,000 x $^{25}/_{75}$)	25
	120

4. *Deferred taxation*

	£'000
Balance per draft	105
Less ACT on proposed dividend	25
	80

5. *Revaluation reserve*

	£'000
Revalued amount of freehold property	900
Less net book value at 1 April 19X6 (500 + 12*)	512
	388

* Add back the depreciation for the current year as the revaluation took place on the first day of the period.

28 S PLC

Tutorial note. The examiner commented that the presentation of candidates' answers was poor and that workings were difficult to read and hard to find. It is essential with this type of question that you draw up your pro forma statements and notes *before you start*, leaving plenty of space. Next you should work steadily through the question drawing up your workings as you go and clearly cross-referencing them. Keep your notes and your workings separate to indicate that you know what does *not* need to be disclosed.

Suggested solution

(a) PROFIT AND LOSS ACCOUNT FOR THE YEAR ENDED 31 DECEMBER 19X7

	Notes	£'000	£'000
Turnover			1,574,500
Cost of sales (W1)			850,506
Gross profit			723,994
Distribution costs (W2)			127,062
Administrative expenses (W3)			258,058
			338,874
Interest payable (W4)	2		92,460
Profit on ordinary activities before taxation	3		246,414
Tax on profit on ordinary activities	4		82,500
Profit on ordinary activities after taxation			163,914
Extraordinary charges	5	120,000	
Tax on extraordinary charges		30,000	
			90,000
Profit for the financial year			73,914
Dividends paid and proposed	6		21,000
Retained profit for the financial year			52,914
Retained profit brought forward	7		92,046
Retained profit carried forward			144,960

(b) BALANCE SHEET AS AT 31 DECEMBER 19X7

	Notes	£'000	£'000
Fixed assets			
Tangible assets	8		715,750
Current assets			
Stock (W5)	9	111,100	
Debtors (W6)	10	166,714	
Cash and bank		100	
		277,914	
Creditors: amounts falling due within one year			
Bank overdrafts (W7)		80,754	
Trade creditors		139,950	
Other creditors, including taxation (W8)		128,000	
		348,704	
Net current liabilities			70,790
Total assets less current liabilities			644,960
Creditors: falling due after more than one year	11		440,000
			204,960

	Notes	£'000	£'000
Capital and reserves			
Share capital	12		60,000
Retained profit			144,960
			204,960

(c) NOTES TO THE FINANCIAL STATEMENTS

1. *Accounting policies*

In all material respects these accounts are prepared in accordance with applicable UK accounting standards.

These financial statements are prepared under the historical accounting convention.

Depreciation is provided on freehold buildings at the rate of 2% per annum. No depreciation was provided in 19X6 but retained earnings have been adjusted by an amount of £27,000 representing back depreciation for the years since the acquisition of the property. See also note five.

Research expenditure is written off to profit and loss account in the year in which it is incurred.

2. *Interest payable*

	£'000
Interest paid on loans	
Repayable in less than five years	25,460
Other loans	67,000
	92,460

3. *Wages and salaries*

	£'000
Salaries paid to employees	238,006
Directors' emoluments	714
	238,720

(*Note*. Details of employee numbers and the statutory details of directors emoluments should also be disclosed by way of a note.)

4. *Taxation*

	£'000
UK corporation tax at 35% on profits for the year	85,000
Overprovision in previous years	(2,500)
	82,500

5. *Extraordinary charge*

This relates to the closure of the plant at X, together with the related tax credit.

6. *Dividends paid and proposed*

	£'000
Final dividend proposed (W8)	21,000

7. *Prior year adjustment*

	£'000
Retained profit as at 31 December 19X6 as previously stated	119,046
Prior year adjustment	27,000
Retained profit as at 31 December 19X6 restated	92,046

Until this year, no depreciation was charged on freehold buildings but, with effect from 1 January 19X7 depreciation is charged at the rate of 2% per annum. The above adjustment reflects the backlog depreciation in respect of the nine years since the purchase of the buildings.

8. *Tangible fixed assets*

	Land £'000	Buildings £'000	Plant £'000	Fixtures £'000	Total £'000
Cost					
At 1.1.X7	350,000	150,000	200,000	107,722	807,722
Additions	-	-	100,000	-	100,000
At 31.12.X7	350,000	150,000	300,000	107,722	907,722
Depreciation					
At 1.1.X7	-	-	90,000	18,000	108,000
Provision for the year	-	3,000	45,000	8,972	56,972
Prior year adjustment	-	27,000	-	-	27,000
At 31.12.X7	-	30,000	135,000	26,972	191,972
Net book value					
At 1.1.X7	350,000	150,000	110,000	89,722	699,722
At 31.12.X7	350,000	120,000	165,000	80,750	715,750

9. *Stocks*

Stocks are valued at the lower of cost or net realisable value.

	£'000
Raw materials and consumables	19,700
Work in progress	91,400
	111,100

10. *Debtors*

	£'000
Trade debtors	159,714
Deferred asset: advance corporation tax	7,000
	166,714

11. *Creditors: amounts falling due after more than one year*

	£'000
12½% secured debentures redeemable 19X9	200,000
14% floating charge bank loan repayable in equal instalments over ten years from 31 December 19X7	243,000
	443,000

Total amounts payable after five years:
By instalments 120,000

12. *Share capital*

	Authorised £'000	Issued £'000
Ordinary £1 shares	100,000	60,000

13. *Capital commitments*

The board has authorised capital expenditure of £8 million, but none of this amount has been committed at the date the accounts were signed.

14. *Post balance sheet events*

The board has decided to close a further factory at an anticipated cost of £40 million offset by a likely tax credit of £5 million.

Workings

1. *Cost of sales*		£'000
Per trial balance		670,396
Depreciation on property (2% x £150 million)		3,000
Depreciation on plant (15% x £300 million)		45,000
Research written off		120,000
Transfer of rationalisation costs to extraordinary item		(120,000)
Stock write-down (material B: 3,000 - 2,400)		600
WIP write down		6,000
Factory wages		125,510
		850,506

2. *Distribution costs*	£'000	£'000
Per trial balance		86,560
Provision for doubtful debts		
5% x £168,120,000	8,406	
Less existing provision	620	
		7,786
Warehouse wages		32,716
		127,062

3. *Administrative expenses*	£'000
Per trial balance	165,592
Depreciation on office equipment ((107,722 - 18,000) x 10%)	8,972
Office salaries	79,780
Directors' remuneration	714
Administrative overhead transferred from work in progress	3,000
	258,058

4. *Interest payable*	£'000
Per trial balance	79,960
Debenture interest: second half year	12,500
	92,460

5. *Stocks*		£'000
Stock:	material A (at cost)	12,000
	material B (at NRV)	2,400
	material C (at cost)	5,300
		19,700

	£'000
Work in progress: £40.5m - £6m + £47.9m + £9m	91,400

6. *Debtors*

	£'000
Trade debtors	
As trial balance	168,120
Less provision for doubtful debts	8,406
	159,714
ACT recoverable: 35p x 60 million x $\frac{1}{3}$	7,000
As balance sheet	166,714

7. *Bank loans and overdrafts*

	£'000
Bank loan: current instalment	30,000
Bank overdraft	50,754
	80,754

8. *Other creditors, including taxation*

	£'000
Prior year corporation tax	45,000
Current year corporation tax on ordinary activities	85,000
Tax credit on extraordinary item	(30,000)
Proposed dividend (35p x 60 million)	21,000
ACT payable (as in (W6))	7,000
	128,000

This total is the minimum disclosure required: there is no requirement to disclose corporation tax, ACT or proposed dividend creditors separately.

29 COMPREHENSIVE

Tutorial note. In the examination candidates made some silly mistakes on this question and presentation was poor. Remember that, unless the question states otherwise, you *must* include an accounting policies note.

Suggested solution

(a)   M PLC
      PROFIT AND LOSS ACCOUNT FOR THE YEAR ENDED 31 MAY 19X2

	Notes	£'000	£'000
Turnover			1,105,063
Cost of sales (W1)			775,513
Gross profit			329,550
Distribution costs (W2)			125,100
Administrative expenses (W3)			119,100
			85,350
Other operating income			15,000
Interest payable (W4)			(15,375)
Profit on ordinary activities before taxation			84,975
Tax on profit on ordinary activities	2		27,000
Profit on ordinary activities after taxation			57,975
Extraordinary item	3	14,000	
Tax		4,900	
			9,100
Profit for the year			48,875
Dividends			10,500
Retained profit for the year			38,375
Retained profits brought forward as previously stated		209,309	
Prior year adjustment	4	124,125	
			85,184
Retained profits carried forward			123,559

(b) M PLC
BALANCE SHEET AS AT 31 MAY 19X2

	Notes	£'000	£'000
Fixed assets			
Intangible assets	5		4,500
Tangible assets	6		339,712
			344,212
Current assets			
Stock and work-in-progress		301,000	
Debtors		128,910	
		429,910	
Creditors: amounts falling due within one year	7	139,563	
Net current assets			290,347
Total assets less current liabilities			634,559
Creditors: amounts falling due after more than one year			
10% debentures 19X7-X9	8		75,000
Provisions for liabilities and charges			
Deferred taxation	9		46,000
			513,559
Capital and reserves			
Share capital	10		300,000
Share premium			60,000
Revaluation reserve	11		30,000
Profit and loss account			123,559
			513,559

NOTES TO THE FINANCIAL STATEMENTS

1. *Accounting Policies*

(i) In all material respects these accounts have been prepared in accordance with applicable UK accounting standards.

(ii) The above accounts have been prepared under the historical cost convention, modified where appropriate to include the revaluation of freehold land and buildings.

(iii) Stocks and work-in-progress are valued at the lower of cost net realisable value.

(iv) Research and development expenditure is written off to profit and loss account in the year that it is incurred.

(v) Goodwill is written off immediately against reserves. This is a change of accounting policy from that approved in previous years: see also note 4.

(vi) Tangible and intangible assets, other than freehold land and goodwill are depreciated over their estimated useful economic lives at rates based on actual cost or revalued amount less estimate residual values. The rates applied are based on:

- for patents: 10 years
- for freehold buildings: 50 years
- for leasehold buildings: period of the lease.

2. *Taxation*

	£'000
Corporation tax @ x%	15,000
Deferred taxation	12,000
	27,000

3. *Extraordinary item*

	£'000
Costs incurred in connection with the closure of a business segment	14,000
Estimated tax relief on closure costs	4,900

4. *Prior year adjustment*

	£'000
Goodwill previously capitalised written off due to change in accounting policy	124,125

5. *Intangible fixed assets*

	£'000
Patents at cost (acquired during the year)	5,000
Depreciation	(500)
	4,500

6. *Tangible fixed assets*

	Freehold land £'000	Freehold buildings £'000	Invest- ment properties £'000	Plant and machinery £'000	Fixtures and fittings £'000	Total £'000
Cost or valuation						
At 1 June 19X1	50,000	95,000	42,500	168,750	37,500	393,750
Revaluation		10,000	20,000	-	-	30,000
At 31 May 19X2	50,000	105,000	62,500	168,750	37,500	423,750
Depreciation	-	2,100	-	70,125	11,813	84,038
Net book value	50,000	102,900	62,500	98,625	25,687	339,712

The freehold buildings have revalued on an open market basis as at 31 May 19X2 by Messr A, B and C, Chartered surveyors. If these buildings were to be sold at this valuation, an additional tax liability of £3,000,000 would arise.

The investment properties have also been valued on an open market basis as at 31 May 19X2 for Messrs A, B and C. They are rented on a commercial basis to a third party that is unconnected with the company. Their estimated market value is £62.5 million.

7. *Creditors: amounts falling due within one year*   £'000

Creditors	73,125
Bank overdraft	38,438
Corporation tax (15,000 – 3,600 – 4,900)	6,500
Proposed dividends	10,500
ACT payable	3,500
Debenture interest payable	7,500
	139,563

8. *Debentures*

The 10% debentures are secured on the freehold land and buildings.

9. *Deferred taxation*

	£'000
At at 1 June 19X1	37,500
Charge for the year	12,000
ACT recoverable	(3,500)
At 31 May 19X2	46,000

10. *Share capital*

	Authorised	Issued and fully paid
	£'000	£'000
Ordinary shares of £1 each	1,000,000	300,000

11. *Revaluation reserves*

	£'000
Revaluation as at 31 May 19X2	
Investment properties	20,000
Freehold buildings	10,000
	30,000

Workings

1. *Cost of sales*   £'000

Opening stocks	247,738
Purchases	545,450
Closing stocks	(301,000)
Depreciation: building (75%)	1,575
patent	500
Wages	187,500
Overheads	93,750
	775,513

2. *Distribution costs*   £'000

As trial balance	87,600
R & D expenditure	37,500
	125,100

3. *Administrative expenses*   £'000

As trial balance	118,575
Depreciation on building (25%)	525
	119,100

		£'000
4.	*Interest expense*	
	Overdraft interest as trial balance	7,875
	Debenture interest £75,000,000 @ 10%	7,500
		15,375

30 WALSH

(a) WALSH PLC: PROFIT AND LOSS ACCOUNT FOR THE YEAR ENDED 31 MARCH 19X7

	Notes	£m	£m
Turnover	1		750
Change in stocks of finished goods and in work in progress			(80)
Own work capitalised			11
			681
Raw materials and consumables (20+80–30)		70	
Staff costs	2	276	
Depreciation and other amounts written off tangible and intangible fixed assets		100	
Other operating charges		120	
			566
			115
Income from fixed asset investments (14x100/75)			19
			134
Interest payable			23
Profit on ordinary activities before taxation			111
Tax on profit on ordinary activities (35+5)			40
Profit on ordinary activities after taxation			71
Extraordinary income	3	4	
Tax on extraordinary profit		(2)	
			2
Profit for the financial year			73
Dividend proposed			50
Retained profit for the financial year			23
Retained profits brought forward			10
Retained profits carried forward			33

176

(b) WALSH PLC: BALANCE SHEET AS AT 31 MARCH 19X7

	Notes	£m	£m
Fixed assets			
Intangible assets	4	720	
Tangible assets	5	310	
Investments	6	100	
			1,130
Current assets			
Stocks	7	200	
Debtors (5+5+(ACT) 17)	8	27	
		227	
Creditors: amounts falling due within one year			
Bank overdraft		80	
Trade creditors		120	
Other creditors including taxation and social security	9	104	
		304	
Net current liabilities			(77)
Total assets less current liabilities			1,053
Creditors: amounts falling due after more than one year			
4% debenture 19Y4/19Y6	10	250	
Provisions for liabilities and charges			
Pension provision		70	
			(320)
			733
Capital and reserves			
Called up share capital			700
Profit and loss account			33
			733

NOTES TO THE ACCOUNTS

1. *Turnover*

   The company's turnover represents amounts receivable for goods supplied in one class of business in the UK, net of trade discounts, VAT and similar taxes.

2. *Staff costs*

	£m
Wages and salaries	264
Social security costs	10
Other pension costs	2
	276

3. *Extraordinary income*

   This represents the profit on disposal of a restaurant.

4. *Intangible assets*

	£m
Goodwill at written-down value	520
Patents at written-down value	200
	720

Amortisation of intangible assets for the year	50

5. *Tangible assets*

	£m
Land and buildings (200-1)	199
Plant and machinery (100+11)	111
	310

Depreciation of tangible assets for the year	50

6. *Investments*

The investments are a holding of shares in a related company.

7. *Stocks*

	£m
Raw materials and consumables	30
Finished goods	120
Work in progress	50
	200

8. *Debtors*

An amount of £17m included in debtors is a non-current asset, being ACT recoverable in future years.

9. *Other creditors*

	£m
Proposed dividend	50
ACT on proposed dividend (25/75 x 50)	17
Taxation (35+2)	37
	104

10. *Debenture*

The debenture is secured by a floating charge over all of the company's assets.

11. *Contingent liability*

The company faces a court case over pollution traceable to its production process. If the case is lost compensation payments estimated to amount to £100m will become payable.

(c) The company is obviously experiencing liquidity problems. The quick ratio is dangerously low (27/304 = 0.09) and the current ratio is not much more healthy (227/304 = 0.75). The balance sheet overall is weak (there are net current liabilities) and the major assets are intangibles which should presumably be written off. The ability of the company to stay in business must be in doubt, since creditors are owed for 1½ years of material purchases. Despite all this the company proposes to pay out most of its post-tax profits as dividend; it might be wiser to improve liquidity by passing the dividend payment for this year.

31 CONSOLIDATED FINANCIAL STATEMENTS

Tutorial note. Answers to this type of question must be well-structured and argued logically; avoid rambling answers.

Suggested solution

The individual accounts of a parent company are inadequate by themselves for the information needs of shareholders and other interested parties.

(a) The parent company accounts do not reveal the true size and importance of the economic entity in which shareholders have invested.

(b) They show investments in subsidiaries at historical cost, which may be a very poor indication of the resources actually controlled by the group.

(c) Parent company profit will consist only of its own operating profit, other investment income and so on and dividends received from subsidiaries. Shareholders will not know the amount of profits retained by subsidiaries.

(d) Creditors cannot assess, from the parent company accounts alone, the liquidity and solvency of the group as a whole.

The preparation of group accounts helps to overcome these difficulties and therefore provides fuller information than would be available from the parent company accounts. The statement in the question cannot be strictly justified: since individual accounts must still be prepared for each group company, the consolidated accounts are an *additional* source of information which can only be helpful to accounts users.

However, it is true that group accounts taken by themselves suffer from serious shortcomings.

(a) They conceal the liquidity and solvency position of individual group companies. Similarly, the losses of some group companies may be concealed by the overall profitability of the group.

(b) They aggregate assets which may be very disparate in nature.

(c) The do not reveal the extent of intra-group trading and intra-group indebtedness.

(d) They are unsuitable for detailed ratio analysis because they do not indicate which sectors of the group's activities are generating a high level of return and which are less satisfactory.

Some of these objections have been reduced in recent years by statutory provisions on the disclosure of segmental information, but the Companies Act 1985 does not go very far in this direction. SSAP 25 *Segmental reporting* has increased the amount of information to be disclosed in this way although the basis of inter-segmental pricing need not be disclosed.

32   CONSOLIDATION AND REALITY

Tutorial note. It is important to concentrate on relevant topics in this question (goodwill, fair values, brands) and not get sidetracked by current cost accounting.

Suggested solution

It is not the purpose of a balance sheet drawn up under the historical accounting convention to show the value of a company, or in the case of a consolidated balance sheet, a group of companies. There are a number of reasons for this which reflect both the techniques of historical cost accounting and its limitations. These reasons include:

(i)   the effect of inflation;
(ii) the effect of the prudence principle;
(iii) the different treatment of monetary and non-monetary items; and
(iv) items which are not included.

The first reason that a consolidated historical cost balance sheet will not show the value of a group is that it will not reflect the effect of inflation on the value of non-monetary assets. Such assets are recorded in the accounts at their original acquisition costs which, for long-lived assets during periods of significant inflation, will often be a small proportion of their current value. Sometimes, certain assets are revalued to their current value, but this process is not mandatory and is often applied on a selective and infrequent basis. Thus, even balance sheets in which assets have been revalued do not necessarily reflect a realistic valuation.

This effect is compounded by the prudence principle which requires that a dimunition in value that is expected to be permanent should be reflected in a write-down in the carrying value of assets, but which does not require recognition of any corresponding increase. Moreover, the depreciation of fixed assets and the amortisation of intangibles such as goodwill is usually undertaken on a prudent basis in order to avoid the resulting balance sheet values exceeding realisable amounts. The current proposals for accounting for goodwill reinforce this approach by requiring purchased goodwill to be amortised even where the directors consider that no dimunition in value has occurred. Thus, it is more likely than not that, even where accounts are prepared on a current cost basis, the prudence principle would act so as to depress balance sheet values of assets.

The prudence principle also gives rise to different treatment of monetary and non-monetary items. Since monetary items, particularly liabilities, actually reflect amounts of money, rather than merely being the monetary equivalent of physical things, they can more closely represent real value. While the prudence principle encourages the making of provisions against debtors, it requires that the full historical value of liabilities is recorded in the accounts. This applies even where inflation has reduced the real value of liabilities in relation to the non-monetary assets purchased with the funds borrowed. Thus the prudence principle tends to overstate the value of liabilities as well as to understate the value of assets.

Historical cost accounts usually only record the results of transactions that have taken place the only major exception being revaluations of property. Consequently, the balance sheet does not reflect internally generated goodwill which may reflect a superior customer base, good employee relations, particularly skilled staff or management or the ownership of a famous brand. Each of these items may generate super-profit, additional earnings over and above those that might be expected to flow merely from the ownership of the firm's recorded physical assets. The additional value that might flow from these additional earnings is often reflected in the prices paid for companies in takeovers which frequently exceed the book value as reflected in the companies' accounts. Indeed, it is common for the value of a company as reflected in the market price of its shares to exceed its book value by a considerable margin.

When a group consists largely of recently acquired companies, the requirement to include the assets of the subsidiaries at fair value could improve the likelihood that the resulting consolidated balance sheet reflects a realistic valuation. However, there is no consensus as to how to apply the fair value concept nor is there any requirement to continue to adjust these assets to fair value in subsequent years. When the merger method is used, fair values need not be used for consolidation.

In summary, therefore, it is unlikely that a consolidated balance sheet prepared on the accounting principles will provide a realistic valuation for that group.

33 TUTORIAL QUESTION: AYE AND BEE

Tutorial note. This is a simpler question than any you are likely to meet with in the examination. It is designed as a gentle introduction to the basic principles of consolidation, illustrating the calculation and accounting treatment of goodwill.

Suggested solution.

(a) AYE PLC: CONSOLIDATED BALANCE SHEET AS AT 31 DECEMBER 19X4

	£'000	£'000
Tangible fixed assets		
Buildings		6,000
Plant		3,939
Vehicles		716
		10,655
Current assets		
Stock	3,408	
Debtors (less £23,000 inter-company)	2,746	
Cash	41	
	6,195	
Creditors: amounts falling due within one year		
Overdraft	2,016	
Trade creditors (less £23,000 inter-company)	1,941	
Tax	758	
Dividend	280	
	4,995	
Net current assets		1,200
Total assets less current liabilities		11,855
Creditors: amounts falling due after more than one year		
10% debentures	4,000	
15% debentures	500	
		4,500
Minority interest (W4)		522.5
		6,832.5

	£'000	£'000
Capital and reserves		
Called up share capital		
Ordinary shares of 50p each		5,000.0
Reserves		
Share premium account	500	
General reserve (W2)	1,055	
Unappropriated profit (W3)	277.5	
		1,832.5
		6,832.5

(b) Aye plc has made a profit of 15/115 x £23,000 = £3,000 on its sale of goods to Bee plc. Bee plc has not yet sold goods to an outside party and the profit is therefore unrealised as far as the group is concerned. The adjustment necessary is to reduce:

(i)   the balance of unappropriated profit; and
(ii) the value of stocks
by £3,000.

Workings

1. *Goodwill*

	£'000
Net assets acquired (72.5)	
Share capital (nominal value)	725
General reserve	290
	1,015
Cost of shares acquired	1,450
Goodwill to be written off	435

2. *General reserve*

	£'000	£'000
Reserve: Aye plc		1,200
Bee plc		800
		2,000
Deduct		
Cost of control of Bee plc (72.5% x £400,000)	290	
Minority interest (27.5% x £800,000)	220	
Goodwill written off (W1)	435	
		(945)
Consolidated balance sheet		1,055

3. *Unappropriated profit*

	£'000
Profit: Aye plc	205
Bee plc	100
	305
Deduct minority interest (27.5% x £100,000)	(27.5)
Consolidated balance sheet	77.5

4. *Minority interest*

	£'000
Bee plc	
Share capital	275.0
General reserve (W2)	220.0
Unappropriated profit (W3)	27.5
	522.5

34 BATH

Tutorial note. This question introduces the complication of dividends proposed by the subsidiaries but not yet accrued for by Bath Limited. Notice that in the profit and loss ledger account the balances entered for each company should be *after* accruing for proposed dividends. In this case, that means an adjustment to Bath Limited's draft accounts figure.

Suggested solution

BATH LIMITED: CONSOLIDATED BALANCE SHEET AS AT 31 DECEMBER 19X1

	£	£
Fixed assets		
Intangible assets		
Goodwill arising on consolidation (W1)		164,160
Tangible assets		
Freehold property at NBV	267,000	
Plant and machinery at NBV	395,800	
		662,800
Investment		52,000
		878,960
Current assets		
Stocks and work in progress (W2)	598,560	
Debtors	340,200	
Cash at bank and in hand	73,700	
	1,012,460	
Creditors: amounts falling due		
within one year		
Bank overdraft	72,300	
Trade creditors	385,400	
Proposed dividend	30,000	
Other creditors (W3)	170,600	
	658,300	
Net current assets		354,160
Total assets less currnct liabilities		1,233,120
Minority interests (W4)		(258,880)
		974,240
Share capital and reserves		
Called up share capital		750,000
Share premium account		15,000
Profit and loss account (W5)		209,240
		974,240

183

Workings

1. *Goodwill arising on consolidation*

	Total £	*Jankin* £	*Arthur* £
Net assets acquired			
Share capital	320,000	80,000	240,000
Reserves (W5)	118,120	15,520	102,600
	438,120	95,520	342,600
Cost of shares acquired	657,000	153,000	504,000
∴ Goodwill	218,880	57,480	161,400
Amortisation (25%)	(54,720)	(14,370)	(40,350)
CBS	164,160	43,110	121,050

2. *Stocks and work in progress*

	£
Per question: Bath	206,000
Jankin	99,000
Arthur	294,200
	599,200
Add stock in transit (at cost to group)	960
Less profit in stock held by Jankin	(1,600)
Stocks in consolidated balance sheet	598,560

3. *Other creditors*

	£	£
Taxation		158,000
Dividends payable to minorities		
Jankin (20% x £15,000)	3,000	
Arthur (40% x £24,000)	9,600	
		12,600
		170,600

4. *Minority interests*

	£	£
In Jankin: share capital		20,000
reserves (20% x £22,400)		4,480
		24,480
In Arthur: share capital	160,000	
reserves (40% x £186,000)	74,400	
		234,400
		258,880

5.

PROFIT AND LOSS ACCOUNT

	£	£		£	£
Minorities (W4)			Bath: at 1.1.X1		191,000
Jankin		4,480	19X1 profit		37,000
Arthur		74,400	Jankin div		
		78,880	(80%x£15,000)		12,000
			Arthur div.		
			(60% x £24,000)		14,400
Cost of control					254,400
Arthur					
at 1.1.X1	132,000		Less unrealised profit		(1,840)
to 30.6.X1	27,000				252,560
total pre-acq'n	159,000		Jankin		
group share			At 1.1.X1	19,400	
(60%)	95,400		19X1 profit	3,000	
divi. paid					22,400
from pre-acq'n profits					
(6/12 x £14,400)	7,200		Arthur		
	102,600		At 1.1.X1	132,000	
Jankin (80%			19X1 profit	54,000	
x £19,400)	15,520				186,000
		118,120			
Goodwill					
amortised (W1)		54,720			
Consolidated balance sheet		209,240			
		460,960			460,960

35 ABC

Tutorial note. Common errors were as follows.

- Treating the associated company as a subsidiary (in other words, equity accounting was not used)
- Revaluation of stock was not charged to cost of sales
- Goodwill arising on consolidation was not amortised
- Intra-group trading accounts were not cancelled
- Balance sheet layouts were not known

Suggested solution

ABC PLC
CONSOLIDATED BALANCE SHEET OF AS AT 31 DECEMBER 19X7

	£'000	£'000
Fixed assets		
Tangible assets (W2)		36,669
Interest in associated company (W3)		1,925
		38,594
Current assets		
Stocks (14,629 + 6,834 + 200)	21,663	
Debtors (12,105 + 4,216 - 500)	15,821	
Cash at bank and in hand (384 + 244)	628	
	38,112	
Creditors: amounts falling due within one year		
Trade creditors (10,196 + 3,894)	14,090	
Taxation (1,054 + 480)	1,534	
	15,624	
Net current assets		22,488
Total assets less current liabilities		61,082
Creditors: amounts falling due after one year (20,000 + 5,000)		25,000
		36,082
Minority interest (W4)		4,865
		31,217
Capital and reserves		
Share capital		10,000
Profit and loss account (W5)		21,217
		31,217

Workings

	£'000	£'000
1. *Goodwill*		
(a) DEF		
Consideration		7,000
Rights issue*		1,200
		5,800
Assets acquired		
Share capital	4,000	
Reserves	3,000	
Additional value of stock	800	
Additional value of transport	1,000	
	8,800	
of which ABC's share is 60%		5,280
Goodwill		520

This will have been fully amortised by 31 December 19X7.

	£'000
* Share capital acquired in rights issue: $5,000 \times \frac{1}{5} \times 60\%$	600
Share premium: 1,000 x 60%	600
	1,200

		£'000	£'000
(b)	**GHI**		
	Consideration		1,500
	Assets acquired		
	Share capital	1,000	
	Reserves	4,000	
		5,000	
	of which ABC's share is 25%		1,250
	Goodwill		250
	Amortisation (19X6 62.5 + 19X7 62.5)		125
	Net book value		125

2. *Tangible assets*

	£'000	£'000
Fixed assets of ABC plc		26,427
Fixed assets of DEF plc		9,832
		36,259
Add additional value of fixed assets of DEF		
Excess value at 30 June 19X4	1,000	
Depreciation 19X4 - X7 (200 + 160 + 128 + 102)	(590)	
		410
		36,669

3. *Interest in associated company*

	£'000
Cost of investment	1,500
Less goodwill amortised (see W1)	(125)
Add post-acquisition reserves (25% x (6,200 - 4,000))	550
	1,925

4. *Minority interest (DEF)*

	£'000	£'000
Share capital	5,000	
Share premium	1,000	
Retained profits	5,752	
Fixed asset revaluation	1,000	
Additional depreciation	(590)	
	12,162	
of which minority interest is 40%		4,865

5. *Group reserves*

	£'000
ABC reserves	20,795
Add: group share of post acquisition profits of GHI (2,200 x 25%)	550
group share of post acquisition profits of DEF (2,752 x 60%)	1,651
Less: group share of stock revaluation (800 x 60%)	(480)
group share of additional depreciation (590 x 60%)	(354)
goodwill written off (520 + 125)	(645)
unrealised profit on sale of stock by ABC to DEF	(300)
	21,217

Note. The surplus on revaluation of stock when DEF was acquired is a pre-acquisition profit, realised on its subsequent sale and therefore excluded from group reserves (because the surplus is already in DEF's retained profits).

36 PQR PLC

Tutorial note. Some candidates showed a lack of understanding of the concepts underlying consolidation by leaving the investment in a subsidiary on the group balance sheet. Problems and omissions included fair value revaluations, the goodwill write-off, identification of pre-acquisition profits and cancellation of the inter-company charge.

Suggested solution

(a) PQR PLC: CONSOLIDATED BALANCE SHEET AS AT 31 DECEMBER 19X9

	£m	£m
Fixed assets		
Intangible assets: goodwill (W1)		360
Tangible assets (W2)		3,323
		3,683
Current assets		
Stock (W3)	650	
Debtors (W4)	412	
Cash and bank (234 + 26 + 19)	279	
	1,341	
Creditors: amounts falling due within one year		
Trade creditors (W5)	315	
Tax payable (112 + 47 + 27)	186	
Dividends payable	100	
	601	
Net current assets		740
Total assets less current liabilities		4,423
Minority interests (W6)		(498)
		3,925
Capital and reserves		
Share capital		500
Retained profit (W7)		3,425
		3,925

Workings

1. *Goodwill*

	£m	£m	£m
STU Ltd			
Consideration			1,452
Net assets acquired			
Share capital 80% of £200m		160	
Retained profit 80% of £800m		640	
Stock revaluation 80% of £50m		40	
Plant revaluation 80% of £200m		160	
			1,000
			452
VWX Ltd			
Consideration given: 80% x £500m		400	
Net assets acquired			
Share capital 60%* of £100m	60		
Retained earnings 60%* of £320m	192		
		252	
			148
Total goodwill (gross)			600
Two years amortisation @ 20% pa			(240)
Net goodwill			360

* *Note.* 80% x 75% = 60%

2. *Tangible fixed assets*

	£m	£m
PQR plc		1,840
STU Ltd		863
VWX Ltd		520
STU Ltd: plant revaluation	200	
additional depreciation	(100)	
		100
		3,323

3. *Stock*

	£m
PQR plc	350
STU Ltd	212
VWX Ltd	108
STU Ltd stock amortisation	(20)
	650

4. *Debtors*

	£m
PQR plc	213
STU Ltd	127
VWX Ltd	82
Less intra-group items	(10)
	412

5. *Trade creditors*

	£m
PQR plc	162
STU Ltd	101
VWX Ltd	52
Intra-group items: accrued management charge	10
inter-company adjustment	(10)
	-
	315

6. *Minority interests*

	£m	£m
STU Ltd on acquisition		
Share capital: 20% x £200m		40
Retained profit: 20% x £1,330m		266
Stock revaluation: 20% x £50m		10
Plant revaluation: 20% x £200m		40
		356
VWX Ltd on acquisition		
Share capital: 40% x £100m	40	
Retained profit: 40% x £510m	204	
		244
20% investment in STU Ltd		(100)
Share of additional depreciation		(20)
Dividends due by subsidiaries		
STU Ltd: 20% of £50m	10	
VWX Ltd: 40% of £40m	16	
		26
Intra-group unrealised profit in stock: 20% x £20m		(4)
Management charge: 40% x £10m		(4)
		498

7. *Retained profit*

	£m	£m
PQR plc		3,215
STU Ltd 80% x £530m		424
VWX Ltd 60% x £190m		114
Fair value adjustment: stock amortisation		(50)
additional depreciation		(80)
Goodwill amortisation		(240)
Intra-group dividends		
STU Ltd 80% x £50m	40	
VWX Ltd 60% x £40m	24	
		64
Intra-group unrealised profit on stock: 80% x £20m		(16)
Management charge: 60% x 10		(6)
		3,425

(b) Under acquisition accounting, the purchase of one company, or part of it, by another is treated as a transaction. It is a basic assumption of this approach that this transaction will have taken place on a commercial basis and that the acquiring company will have given and received consideration which properly reflects the values of the net assets acquired.

Consequently, the consideration given is valued at its fair value. When this consideration is cash, the value is obvious; where, however, the consideration consists of shares or other securities, an assessment needs to be made of their fair market value at the time of the transaction.

Correspondingly, the net assets acquired should be valued at their fair market value, to reflect the true nature of the transaction. The principal advantage of this method is that a fair assessment can be made of the goodwill paid, which is the difference between the fair value of the consideration given and the fair value of the separable net assets received. This method is, therefore, consistent with the purchase of the net assets if they had been acquired individually instead of as part of an ongoing business.

Thus, the assets acquired will be reflected in the consolidated accounts at a realistic valuation rather than at an historic value as held in the accounts of the acquired company. One disadvantage of this fair value calculation is that these assets will not necessarily be recorded in the consolidated balance sheet on the same basis as identical assets owned by the parent (acquiring) company.

It follows from the above that depreciation will be charged on the fair value and this will represent a fairer charge to post-acquisition profits than that based on the book value of the acquired company. Equally, the profit or loss on subsequent disposal will be more realistic, being based on the real acquisition cost of those assets to the group.

37 WHITESIDE

WHITESIDE GROUP: CONSOLIDATED BALANCE SHEET AS AT 31 DECEMBER 19X6

	£'000	£'000
Fixed assets		
Intangible assets		
Goodwill (W2)		199
Tangible assets		
Land (add £350,000)	2,350	
Equipment (less £25,000)	1,615	
		3,965
Investments		
Shares in related company (W4)		222
		4,386
Current assets		
Stock (less £100,000)	1,198	
Debtors	1,975	
Bank	1,298	
	4,471	
Creditors: amounts falling due within one year		
Trade creditors	2,201	
Net current assets		2,270
Total assets less current liabilities		6,656
Creditors: amounts falling due		
after more than one year		
Loan (19X8)		1,000
Minority interests (W3)		941
		4,715

		£'000
Capital and reserves		
Called up share capital		2,000
Reserves (W5)		2,715
		4,715

1. *Group structure*

Whiteside

80% |

McClair

75% |

Olsen	minority interest (direct)	25%
	minority interest (indirect)	15%
		40%

2. *Goodwill*

	£'000	£'000
Assets acquired		
Share capital		
McClair		600
Olsen		300
		900
Reserves: pre-acquisition profits		
McClair: per accounts	1,450	
land	350	
group share (80%)		1,440
Olsen: 60% x £940,000		565
		2,904
Cost of investment in McClair	2,500	
Group share of investment in Olsen (80% x £1,500,000)	1,200	
		3,700
Goodwill		896
Reserves: goodwill written off (6/8)		597
Balance: CBS (2/8)		199
		896

3. *Minority interest*

	£'000	£'000
Share capital		
McClair (20% x £750,000)	150	
Olsen (40% x £500,000)	200	
		350
Reserves		
McClair (20% x £1,750,000)	350	
Olsen (40% x £1,290,000)	515	
		866
Revaluation surplus (20% x £350,000)		70
		1,286
Minority share of investment in Olsen (20% x £1,500,000)		(300)
Stock: minority share of unrealised profit (40% x £100,000)		(40)
Unrealised profit (20% x £(125,000 - 100,000))		(5)
Consolidated balance sheet		941

4. *Investment in associated company*

	£'000	£'000
Net assets of O'Brien		
Share capital	100	
Retained profits £(420,000 - 50,000)	370	
	470	
Group share (30%)		141
Premium paid on acquisition of shares in O'Brien		
Net assets at date of acquisition		
£(100,000 + 300,000)	400	
Group share (30%)	120	
Cost of investment	250	
Premium on acquisition	130	
Amortisation (3/8 x £130,000)	49	
		81
		222

5. RESERVES

	£'000		£'000
Minority interest		Whiteside	2,970
McClair	350	McClair	1,750
Olsen	516	Olsen	1,290
Cost of control		O'Brien: group share of post-	
McClair	1,440	acq'n profits	
Olsen	564	(30% x £(120,000 - 50,000))	21
Stock (60% x £100,000)	60	Group share of revaluation surplus	
Equipment		(80% x £350,000)	280
(80% x £(125,000 - 100,000))	20		
Amortisation of premium on			
acq'n of O'Brien	49		
Amortisation of goodwill on			
acq'n of McClair	597		
Balance: CBS	2,715		
	6,311		6,311

38 GREATER COMBINATIONS

Tutorial note. This is a question which tests your knowledge of disposals of shares in subsidiary companies. Note in particular working 3 which illustrates how to compute the extraordinary gain/loss arising and the treatment of the subsidiary company's reserves no longer consolidated.

Suggested solution

(a) Consolidated balance sheet at 30 November 19X9

	£'000
Fixed assets	
Intangible assets: patents and trademarks	95
Tangible assets	700
	795
Net current assets (W1)	1,010
Total assets less current liabilities	1,805
Provisions for liabilities and charges	
Taxation, including deferred taxation (W2)	(182)
	1,623
Minority interests (25% x 360)	(90)
	1,533
Capital and reserves	
Called up share capital: £1 ordinary	500
Capital reserve on consolidation	60
Other reserves and unappropriated profits	973
	1,533

(b) Detailed analysis of movements in group 'reserves and unappropriated profits'.

	GC £'000	Coop £'000	Total £'000
At 1 December 19X8			
GC (800 - 60)	740		
Coop (post-acquisition only)			
(260 - 16 - £(100 x 0.80))		164	904
Profits in six months to 31.5.X9	67.5	18	85.5
	807.5	182	989.5
Effect of disposal at 31.5.X9 (W3)	35.0	(45.5)	(10.5)
	842.5	136.5	979.0
Profits in six months to 30.11.X9	67.5	13.5	81.0
Proposed dividends			
GC	(75)		(75)
Coop	15	(15)	-
Provision for unrealised profit (net)	(12)		(12)
At 30 November 19X9	838	135	973

Workings

		£'000	£'000
1.	*Net current assets*		
	Greater Combinations Ltd: per question		700
	Cooperative Ltd: per question		330
			1,030
	Add dividend receivable (75% x 20)		15
			1,045
	Less: provision for unrealised intra-group profit	20	
	corporation tax liability on gain	15	
			35
			1,010

		£'000
2.	*Deferred taxation*	
	Greater Combinations Ltd: per question	100
	Cooperative Ltd: per question	90
		190
	Less tax effect of provision for unrealised profit	
	(20 @ 40%)	8
		182

		£'000
3.	*Effect of disposal*	
	Sale proceeds (25,000 @ £3)	75
	Less cost (25,000 @ £1)	25
	Gain	50
	Tax at effective rate of 30%	15
	Holding company's extraordinary gain	35
	Less share of post-acquisition retained reserves	
	up to date of disposal (25% x 182)	45.5
	Group extraordinary loss	(10.5)

39 DUXBURY

Tutorial note

The extraordinary charges (and the associated tax) are shown *after* minority interests in the profit and loss account. This means that only the group's share of the charges must be shown.

Suggested solution

(a) DUXBURY PLC: CONSOLIDATED PROFIT AND LOSS ACCOUNT
FOR THE YEAR ENDED 31 DECEMBER 19X6

	£'000	£'000
Turnover (17,000 + 7,400 − 400)		24,000
Cost of sales (W1)		11,570
Gross profit		12,430
Distribution costs (2,400 + 200)		2,600
Administrative expenses (1,780 + 300)		2,080
		7,750
Income from shares in associated company (600 x 25%)		150
Profit on ordinary activities before taxation		7,900
Tax on profit on ordinary activities		
Group	3,700	
Share of associated company (200 x 25%)	50	
		3,750
Profit on ordinary activities after taxation		4,150
Minority interest (W2)		612
Group profit on ordinary activities after taxation		3,538
Extraordinary charges (W3)	273	
Tax on extraordinary loss	135	
		138
Profit for the financial year		3,400
Dividends		300
Retained profit for the financial year		3,100
Retained profits brought forward (W4)		10,200
Retained profits carried forward		13,300

(b) *Retained profits in the consolidated balance sheet*

	£'000
As part (a)	13,300
Less Moran's retained profits (added to value of investment)	
(100 + 150 − 50 − 7.5 − 25)	168
	13,132

Workings

	£'000
1. *Cost of sales*	
Duxbury	8,000
Albiston (1,050 + 1,700 + 1,300 − 380)	3,670
Less intercompany purchase	(400)
Add unrealised profit in stock valuation	200
Add pre-acquisition profit on disposal of stock (200 − 100)	100
	11,570

2. *Minority interest*
40% of Albiston Ltd's post-tax profit less the provision for
   unrealised profit = 40% x (1,730 − 200)   612

3. *Extraordinary items*	*Gross*	*Tax*
	£'000	£'000
Duxbury	200.0	100.0
Albiston: 60% x 100/50	60.0	30.0
Moran: 25% x 50/20	12.5	5.0
	272.5	135.0

4. *Retained profits brought forward*		
	£'000	£'000
Duxbury		9,500
Albiston		
Post-acquisition profits: 6,000 - 5,000	1,000	
Group share (60%)		600
Moran		
Post-acquisition profits: 2,000 - 1,600	400	
Group share (25%)		100
		10,200

40 PROJECTION

Tutorial note. Candidates who did not rely on rote learning did well on this question. However, problems were experienced with the more difficult adjustments, particularly in the calculation of the minority interest. *Candidates must understand the concept and principles underlying consolidations.* Candidates also had problems with, or did not attempt, part (b).

Suggested solution

(a) FORECAST CONSOLIDATED PROFIT AND LOSS ACCOUNT
FOR ABC AND SUBSIDIARY FOR YEAR ENDING 31 DECEMBER 19X1

	£m
Turnover (W1)	917.5
Cost of sales (W2)	534.0
Gross profit	383.5
Distribution costs (W3)	96.0
Administrative expenses (W4)	63.0
Interest	12.0
Net profit before tax	212.5
Taxation (W5)	74.9
Net profit after tax	137.6
Minority interest (W6)	7.5
Net profit attributable to members of ABC	130.1
Dividends payable (W7)	36.5
Retained profit for the year	93.6

Workings

1. *Turnover*			£m
ABC	800 x 105%		840.0
DEF	200 x 105%		210.0
Less intra-group sales (see below)			(132.5)
			917.5

		£m
Intra-group sales		
ABC's cost of sales		525.0
ABC's stock increase (5% of opening stock):		
5% x 20% x 500		5.0
ABC's purchases in total		530.0
25% is purchased from DEF		132.5

2. *Cost of sales*

	£m
ABC : 500 x 105%	525
DEF : 120 x 105%	126
	651
Less intra-group purchases (see below)	117
	534

Intra-group sales as above	132.5
Profit on stock	
ABC closing stock = 525 x 20% = 105	
Of which 25% from DEF = 26.25	
Of which DEF profit = 40%	(10.5)
Increase in value of DEF opening stock for consolidation purposes only	(5.0)
	117.0

3. *Distribution costs*

	£m
Additional depreciation on sales vehicles	
15 x 20% per annum	3.0

4. *Administrative expenses*

	£m
Consideration	100.0
Net assets bought (80% x 75)	60.0
Goodwill	40.0
Amortisation @ 20% per annum	8.0

5. *Taxation*

	ABC £m	DEF £m
Turnover	840.0	210
Cost of sales	(525.0)	(126)
Distribution costs	(90.0)	(3)
Administrative expenses	(50.0)	(5)
Dividend from DEF (W7)	10.6	–
Interest	(12.0)	–
Pre-tax profit	173.6	76
Tax @ 30%	52.1	22.8

6. *Minority interest*

	£m
DEF profit after tax (W5)	53.2
Intra-group profit on stock (W2)	(10.5)
Opening stock adjustment (W2)	(5.0)
Adjusted DEF profit	37.7
Of which 20% is minority interest	7.5

7. *Dividends* £m

ABC: (173.6 - 52.1) x 30% (30/100) 36.5

DEF: (76.0 - 22.8) x 25% (10/40) 13.3

Of which 80% is ABC's: 10.6

(b) ABC plc's earnings per share

19X0
Profit after tax	£100m
Number of shares	200m
Earnings per share	50p

19X1

(i) *Basic earnings per share*

Net profit attributable to members of ABC	£130.1m
Shares in issue and ranking for dividend	200m
Basic earnings per share	65.1p

(ii) *Fully diluted earnings per share*

	£m	£m
Net profit as above		130.1
Interest saved		
£40m @ 12%	4.80	
Less tax @ 30%	1.44	
		3.36
		133.46
Number of shares = 200m + 40m =		240m
Fully diluted earnings per share		55.6p

41 THOPAS

Tutorial note. The main problem here is the balance sheet figure for 'investment in associated company'. W1 shows the calculation of goodwill on acquisition of Prudence, and its amortisation in 19X3 and 19X4. This enables us to calculate the investment figure in W2.

Suggested solution

(a) THOPAS GROUP CONSOLIDATED BALANCE SHEETS AS AT 31 DECEMBER

	19X4		19X3	
	£'000	£'000	£'000	£'000
Fixed assets				
Intangible assets				
Goodwill on consolidation		100.0		200.0
Tangible assets		5,030.0		4,327.0
Investment in associated				
company (W2)		622.5		632.5
		5,752.5		5,159.5
Current assets				
Stock	527		342	
Debtors	216		194	
Bank	48		73	
	791		609	
Creditors: amounts falling				
due within one year	204		201	
Net current assets		587.0		408.0
Total assets less current liabilities		6,339.5		5,567.5
Minority interests		(490.0)		(440.0)
		5,849.5		5,127.5
Capital and reserves				
Ordinary share capital		2,000.0		1,500.0
Revaluation reserve		500.0		–
Profit and loss account (W3)		3,349.5		3,627.5
		5,849.5		5,127.5

(b) CONSOLIDATED PROFIT AND LOSS ACCOUNT
FOR THE YEAR ENDED 31 DECEMBER 19X4

	£'000	£'000
Turnover		7,660.0
Cost of sales		6,238.0
Gross profit		1,422.0
Distribution costs and administrative		
expenses: 1790 + 135 (W1)		1,925.0
		(503.0)
Share of profit of associated company		
(25% x £980,000)		245.0
Loss on ordinary activities		(258.0)
Taxation		
Group	150	
Share of associated company	(110)	
		40.0
Loss after taxation		(218.0)
Minority interest		(60.0)
Loss attributable to shareholders retained		
for year		(278.0)
Retained profits brought forward		3,627.5
Retained profits carried forward		3,349.5

(c) CONSOLIDATED STATEMENT OF SOURCE AND APPLICATION OF FUNDS
     FOR THE YEAR ENDED 31 DECEMBER 19X4

	£'000	£'000
Source of funds		
Loss before taxation, after minority interest (278 + 40)		(318)
Adjustment for items not involving the		
movement of funds		
Amortisation of goodwill ((200 - 100) + 135)	235	
Depreciation	558	
Profit on disposal of fixed assets	(65)	
Minority interest in retained profits (490 - 440)	50	
Profits retained by associated company (245 - 110 - 10)	(125)	
		653
Total generated from operations		335
Other sources of funds		
Issue of shares		500
Proceeds on disposal of fixed assets		65
Tax recovered*		40
Total sources of funds		940
Application of funds		
Purchase of fixed asssets		761
		179
Movements in working capital		
Increase in stocks		185
Increase in debtors		22
Increase in creditors		(3)
		204
Decrease in net liquid funds		(25)
		179

* There is no tax liability or asset brought forward or carried forward. The tax credit of £40,000 in the consolidated profit and loss account must be assumed to have been received in cash during the year.

Workings

1. *Goodwill on acquisition of Prudence Limited*

	£'000
Share of value of assets acquired (assumed to be at fair value)	
Nominal value of shares acquired	37.5
Pre-acquisition profits	37.5
	75.0
Consideration paid	750.0
Goodwill at 31 December 19X2	675.0
Amortisation in 19X3 (20% x £675)	135.0
Unamortised balance at 31 December 19X3	540.0
Amortisation in 19X4	135.0
Unamortised balance at 31 December 19X4	405.0

2. *Investment in associated company*

	19X4 £'000	19X3 £'000
Group share of net assets of Prudence Ltd		
Share capital	37.5	37.5
Retained profits	180.0	55.0
	217.5	92.5
Goodwill on consolidation (W1)	405.0	540.0
	622.5	632.5

3. *Retained profits*

	19X4 £'000	19X3 £'000
Thopas and Melibee consolidated	3,477.0	3,745.0
Group share of Prudence (post-acq'n only)		
25% x (220 - 150)		17.5
25% x (720 - 150)	142.5	
	3,619.5	3,762.5
Less consolidation adjustment: amortisation of goodwill in respect of Prudence	270.0	135.0
	3,349.5	3,627.5

42 CRERAND

(a) JOURNAL ENTRIES

			Dr £	Cr £
(i)	*Transactions with French supplier*			
1 May	DEBIT Purchases		29,630	
	CREDIT Creditors			29,630
	Being purchase of materials (Fr 280,000 @ 9.45)			
1 Aug	DEBIT Creditors		31,579	
	CREDIT Bank			31,579
	Being payment to French supplier (Fr 300,000 @ 9.5)			
1 Nov	DEBIT Purchases		33,684	
	CREDIT Creditors			33,684
	Being purchase of materials (Fr 320,000 @ 9.5)			
31 Dec	DEBIT Creditors		674	
	CREDIT Exchange gain			674
	Being exchange gain (see W1) on transactions with French supplier			

(ii)   *Investment in Belgian customer*

(*Tutorial note.* The normal accounting treatment of non-monetary assets, such as trade investments, denominated in foreign currencies, is to record them at their original sterling cost and leave their carrying value unchanged thereafter. An exception to this rule occurs when the acquisition of the asset is financed by a foreign currency loan in order to protect against exchange fluctuations. In this case, the exchange differences arising on the asset and on the loan are taken into account by netting them off together and transferring the net amount to reserves.)

			Dr £	*Cr* £
1.	DEBIT	Investments (3,600,000 @ 60.10 - 3,600,000 @ 62.50)	2,300	
	CREDIT	Loan (180,000 @ 3.05 - 180,000 @ 3.12)		1,324
		Exchange reserve		976

*Exchange difference on Belgian investment
and DM loan*

			Dr £	*Cr* £
2.	DEBIT	Debtors	632	
	CREDIT	Income from fixed asset investments		632

*Being dividend of B Fr 38,000 (@ 60.10)
receivable from Belgian investment*

(iii) *Investment in Italian hotel*

			Dr £	*Cr* £
31 Dec	DEBIT	Property and fittings	244,131	
	CREDIT	Net current assets	49,765	
		Loan		187,793
		Branch current account		106,103

Being translation of balances relating to foreign branch, using year-end rate. (Note. The 'surplus retained' is amalgamated with the 'head office capital account'.)

		Dr	*Cr*
DEBIT	Bank	69,450	
CREDIT	Exchange loss	2,665	
	Branch current account		72,115

*Being translation at average rate of remittances
from foreign branch*

		Dr	*Cr*
DEBIT	Exchange reserve	3,986	
CREDIT	Branch current account		3,986

*Being unrealised loss on translation of branch
balance sheet (W2)*

(b) BALANCE SHEET EXTRACTS

		19X7 £	19X6 £
Fixed assets			
Tangible assets			
Property and fittings		244,131	253,658
Investments			
Other investments		59,900	57,600
Current assets			
Debtors			
Accrued income		632	?
Creditors: amounts falling due within one year			
Trade creditors		36,269	5,208
Creditors: amounts falling due after more than one year			
Bank loans (W3)		246,809	252,814

(*Note.* In addition, it would be necessary to disclose the net current assets of the Italian hotel under appropriate headings. In total, these assets would be disclosed at £49,765 in 19X7, £40,976 in 19X6.)

(c) Trading transactions with the French supplier would be translated using the temporal method. The exchange gain of £674 would be taken to profit and loss account. (SSAP 20, para 8)

The net exchange gain (£976) arising on translation of the Belgian investment and the German loan by which it is financed would be taken to reserves. (SSAP 20, para 29)

The exchange loss of £2,665 arising from the remittances received from the Italian hotel would be taken to profit and loss account. (SSAP 20, para 12)

The exchange loss of £3,986 on translating the Italian branch balance sheet using the closing rate method would be taken to reserves. (SSAP 20, para 19)

Workings

1. FRENCH SUPPLIER

	Fr.	£		Fr.	£
Bank	300,000	31,579	Balance b/f	50,000	5,208
∴ Exchange gain	–	674	Purchases	280,000	29,630
Balance c/f	350,000	36,269	Purchases	320,000	33,684
	650,000	68,522		650,000	68,522

2.

BRANCH CURRENT ACCOUNT

	Lira(000)	£		Lira(000)	£
Balance b/f	204,000	99,512	Bank	150,000	72,115
Profit for year	172,000	82,692	Balance c/f	226,000	106,103
			Exchange loss	–	3,986
	376,000	182,204		376,000	182,204

3. *Bank loans*

	19X7	19X6
	£	£
Deutschemark loan	59,016	57,692
Lira loan	187,793	195,122
	246,809	252,814

43 OXFORD

(a) CONSOLIDATED BALANCE SHEET AT 31 DECEMBER 19X5

	£'000	£'000
Fixed assets		
Tangible assets (3,240 + (4,860 @ 3.6))		4,590
Current assets		
Stocks (1,990 + (8,316 @ 3.6))	4,300	
Debtors (1,630 + (4,572 @ 3.6))	2,900	
Cash at bank and in hand (240 + (2,016 @ 3.6))	800	
	8,000	
Creditors: amounts falling due within one year		
(5,030 + (4,356 @ 3.6)) – (75% x 2,304 @ 3.6))	5,760	
Net current assets		2,240
Total assets less current liabilities		6,830
Creditors: amounts falling due after		
more than one year		(1,920)
		4,910
Capital and reserves		
Called up share capital (£1)		118
Other reserves-capital reserve (W1)		250
Profit and loss account		3,472
		3,840
Minority interests (25% x (15,408 @ 3.6))		1,070
		4,910

(b) CONSOLIDATED PROFIT AND LOSS ACCOUNT
FOR YEAR ENDED 31 DECEMBER 19X5

	£'000
Turnover (40,425 + (97,125 @ 3.75))	66,325
Cost of sales (35,500 + (77,550 @ 3.75))	56,180
Gross profit	10,145
Distribution and administration (4,400 + (5,850 @ 3.75))	5,960
Profit on ordinary activities before taxation	4,185
Tax on profit on ordinary activities	
(300 + (4,725 @ 3.75))	1,560
Profit on ordinary activities after taxation	2,625
Minority interests (25% x (9,000 @ 3.75))	600
Profit for the financial year (see note)	2,025
Dividends	700
Retained profit for the year	1,325

STATEMENT OF RESERVES FOR THE YEAR ENDED 31 DECEMBER 19X5

	£'000
Profit and loss account at 1 January 19X5	1,885
Retained profit for the year	1,325
Exchange differences (W2)	262
Profit and loss account at 31 December 19X5	3,472

Note. Of the profit for the financial year, £982,000 has been dealt with in the accounts of Oxford plc. Oxford plc has taken advantage of the legal dispensation not to publish its own profit and loss account.

Workings

1.	*Goodwill*		£'000
	Cost of investment		470
	Less share of net assets acquired	DM'000	
	Share capital	1,348	
	Profit and loss account	2,876	
		4,224	
	Group share (75%) @ 4.40		720
	Goodwill (capital reserve)		(250)

2.	*Exchange differences*	£'000	£'000
	Net assets of Bonn at 31 December 19X5		
	(15,408 @ 3.6)		4,280
	Less net assets of Bonn at 31 December 19X4		
	(10,160 @ 4.0)		2,540
	Increase over the year		1,740
	Less retained profit for the year		
	Profit after tax (9,000 @ 3.75)	2,400	
	Dividends: interim (1,448 @ 3.92)	(369)	
	final (2,304 @ 3.60)	(640)	
			1,391
	Exchange differences		349
	Group share (75%)		262

3.	*Proof of reserves*		£'000	£'000
(i)	At 31 December 19X5			
	Oxford per question			502
	Add dividend receivable (75% x (2,304 @ 3.6))			480
				982
	Bonn			
	Net assets at 31.12.X5 (15,408 @ 3.6)		4,280	
	Less net assets at acquisition (4,224 @ 4.4)		960	
	Post acquisition retained reserves		3,320	
	Group share (75%)			2,490
				3,472
(ii)	At 31 December 19X4			
	Oxford (502 – (198))			700
	Bonn			
	Net assets at 31.12.X4 (10,160 @ 4.0)		2,540	
	Less net assets at acquisition		960	
	Post acquisition retained reserves		1,580	
	Group share (75%)			1,185
				1,885

44 T GROUP

Tutorial note. The examiner said that part (b) of this question was badly answered, with candidates differentiating between monetary and non-monetary items rather than the use of closing rate or temporal method.

Suggested solution

To: The Managing Director
From: Group accountant
Subject: *Foreign currency translation*

With reference to our recent acquisition of a foreign subsidiary, this memorandum outlines how its financial statements will be translated into pounds sterling. This area of accounting practice is covered by SSAP 20 *Foreign currency translation*.

(a) *Foreign currency translation methods*

There are two permitted methods for translating the accounts of foreign subsidiaries for the purpose of consolidating their results with those of the rest of the group. These are the *temporal method* (whereby each item is translated at the rate applicable when the underlying transaction occurred) and the *closing rate method* (by which each item is translated at the rate at the balance sheet date).

SSAP 20 requires the temporal method to be used in respect of foreign operations which are essentially an extension of the activities of the UK parent (perhaps acting as a selling agent for products produced in the UK). The closing rate method is used where the overseas operation is autonomous. The operations of our new subsidiary fall into the latter category. The chosen method must be applied consistently.

(b) *Treatment of foreign currency exchange differences*

Foreign currency exchange differences are of two types, *transaction* differences and *translation* differences. Transaction differences occur when the sterling revenue or costs are recorded initially at the rate at the time the transaction occurs but this rate has changed by the time cash has been received or paid. Transaction differences are regarded as part of the normal business of the company or the finalisation of otherwise provisionally recorded transactions and are, therefore, charged or credited directly to profit and loss account. When the foreign operations are regarded as merely an extension of the UK operations (and therefore the temporal method is used) all foreign exchange gains and losses are regarded as transaction differences and are taken directly to profit and loss.

Translation gains and losses, on the other hand, are those that arise from the conversion of the accounts of an autonomous overseas operation into sterling for consolidation purposes. The investing company does not regard itself as having undertaken each of the foreign currency denominated transactions. It has made a net investment in the foreign operation in the expectation of receiving foreign currency returns by way of dividends and interest on loans. Where the foreign operation has taken on foreign currency debt this is considered to be matched against a corresponding amount of the foreign currency assets. Thus gains in the sterling value of the assets due to an appreciation in the foreign currency will be matched by losses on the increased sterling equivalent of the loans. Thus, the exposure of the UK holding company is limited to its net investment in the overseas subsidiary.

While transaction differences are considered to have been realised when the transactions to which they relate have been completed, translation differences are not considered to be realised until the net investment or part of it is disposed of. Consequently, translation gains and losses are retained in the reserves section of the balance sheet and only released to income when the associated net assets are sold or written off. This is an example of reserve accounting.

Where the acquisition of an overseas subsidiary is financed by foreign currency borrowings, there is a matching of foreign currency exposure although if there is more than one currency involved, this is not a complete match. Where the subsidiary is autonomous, and therefore the closing rate method is used, the translation difference on the borrowings may be offset *in reserves* against that on the investment in subsidiary. However, any excess gain or loss on the borrowings over that in the subsidiary must be taken to the profit and loss account. This concession can be applied both in T plc's accounts and in the T Group accounts.

(c) *Disclosure*

Disclosure must be made of the method used for translating foreign currencies and, if different methods are used for different subsidiaries, this fact must be disclosed. If, as allowed by SSAP 20, the profit and loss accounts of foreign subsidiaries are translated at the average rate for the period instead of the rate at the end of the period this should be disclosed.

Exchange gains on net foreign currency borrowings or holdings should be disclosed together with an analysis between the amount taken to profit and loss account and the amount taken to reserves.

The net movement on reserves due to exchange differences must be shown in the analysis of reserves contained in the notes to the accounts.

45. FOREIGN EXCHANGE

Tutorial note. You must be able to show a sound knowledge of the contents of the SSAPs in the examination. The examiner said that few students knew the basic rules of SSAP 20.

Suggested solution

From: Finance Director
To: Managing Director
Date: 31 October 19X2
Subject: *Accounting for foreign currency transactions*

(a) Where a company has operations that are conducted overseas by a subsidiary company, that subsidiary will usually conduct its business in the local currency of its country. Consequently, it will maintain its accounting records and present its financial statements in that currency.

   For the purposes, however, of including the accounts of the overseas subsidiary in the consolidated accounts of the parent company, it is necessary to translate the accounts of the subsidiary into the reporting currency of the parent. Under the provisions of SSAP 20 there are two methods of doing this, the closing rate/net investment method (adopted by company 1) and the temporal method (adopted by company 2).

   The closing rate/net investment method is used where the overseas subsidiary is regarded as a largely autonomous unit in which the foreign currency exposure of the parent is represented by its net equity investment (including shareholder loans) in that company. The net investment is translated each year at the rate of exchange ruling at the end of that year and any difference which arises due to different exchange rates is regarded as an unrealised loss or gain to the parent and is taken to reserves. These losses or gains are only regarded as realised when all or part of the investment is liquidated at which time the appropriate proportion of the reserve will be transferred to the profit and loss account.

   Where, however, the overseas operations are regarded as an integral part or an extension of the operations of the parent, the temporal method is used. Under this method, each transaction is recorded at the actual rate applicable on the date of the transaction, as though the parent had converted the necessary funds on that date in order to undertake the transaction itself. An approximation of this method can be used where it is not practicable to identify each transaction underlying the accounts of the subsidiary (usually an average rate for the period is used). Since these transactions are treated as though they were those of the parent, losses and gains that arise due to the movement in exchange rates are regarded as realised and taken directly to the profit and loss account.

(b) From the foregoing it will be seen that the choice between the closing rate/net investment method and the temporal method should be based on the nature of the overseas operation and its relationship to the parent. This choice cannot be based on the relative desirability of the results of applying either method.

   The basic determination to be made is whether or not the overseas subsidiary acts in an autonomous manner or whether it is an extension of the parent. SSAP 20 requires the use of the closing rate/net investment method (presuming autonomy) unless the opposite can be demonstrated. Generally the determining fact will be the economic environment in which the subsidiary operates; if it is predominantly that of the parent, then the temporal rate method may be used. In determining which economic environment it operates in, consideration should be given to:

(i) the extent to which the cash flows of the subsidiary have an impact on the parent;
(ii) the extent to which the functioning of the subsidiary is dependent directly on the parent;
(iii) the currency in which the majority of the trading transactions are denominated; and
(iv) the major currency to which the operation is exposed in its financing structure.

For example, the overseas subsidiary of an oil company that buys its crude oil on the open market, refines it and sells the product in its local market and is partly financed by local currency borrowings would use the closing rate/net investment method. On the other hand, the overseas marketing subsidiary of a manufacturing company which buys all its product from the parent and is financed by the parent in the parent's own currency would normally use the temporal method.

46 TUTORIAL QUESTION: NEWMAN

NEWMAN LIMITED
CONSOLIDATED BALANCE SHEET AS AT 30 SEPTEMBER 19X8

(a) *Acquisition method*

	£'000	£'000
Freehold properties		325
Other fixed assets (3,650 + 420)		4,070
Net current assets (1,160 + 51)		1,211
		5,606
Capital and reserves		
Ordinary share capital (W1)		2,500
Reserves		
As at 1 October 19X7	2,600	
Share premium on new issue of shares (W1)	400	
Retained profit for the year	210	
Goodwill written off (W2)	(104)	
As at 30 September 19X8		3,106
		5,606

(b) *Merger method*

	£'000	£'000
Freehold properties		210
Other fixed assets		4,070
Net current assets		1,211
		5,491
Capital and reserves		
Ordinary share capital (W1)		2,500
Reserves		
As at 1 October 19X7 (2,600 + 221)	2,821	
Retained profit for the year (210 + 160)	370	
Merger reserve	(200)	
		2,991
		5,491

Workings

1. *Newman Ltd's share capital*

	£'000
Shares in issue before combination	2,000
Issued to shareholders in Gilbert Ltd	
$5/3 \times 300,000$	500
	2,500

Share premium on new issue = £400,000 (£900,000 - £500,000).

2. *Goodwill arising on consolidation*

	£'000
Consideration given	900
Fair value of Gilbert's assets (325 + 420 + 51)	796
Goodwill arising on consolidation	104

In accordance with SSAP 22's preferred treatment, goodwill has been written off against reserves.

	£'000

3. *Merger adjustment*

	£'000
Nominal value of shares issued	500
Nominal value of shares acquired	300
Merger adjustment	200

This adjustment is needed because, under the merger method, the amount at which Newman Ltd records its investment in the shares of Gilbert Ltd is the nominal value of shares issued as consideration (£500,000). No share premium need be recorded because merger relief is available under s 131 CA 1985. The shares acquired, however, against which the investment of £500,000 is to be cancelled, have a nominal value of £300,000. The £200,000 imbalance is simply deducted from reserves to make the balance sheet balance.

47   STEPNEY

STEPNEY PLC: CONSOLIDATED BALANCE SHEET AS AT 31 DECEMBER 19X7

	£'000	£'000
Fixed assets		85,675
Current assets (W1)	30,496	
Current liabilities	17,933	
Net current assets		12,563
Total assets less current liabilities		98,238
Share capital		15,000
Profit and loss account		83,238
		98,238

CONSOLIDATED PROFIT AND LOSS ACCOUNT
FOR THE YEAR ENDED 31 DECEMBER 19X7

	£'000	£'000
Turnover		56,852
Cost of sales (W4)		24,305
Gross profit		32,547
Distribution costs		5,967
Administrative expenses		3,757
Profit on ordinary activities before taxation		22,823
Tax on profit on ordinary activities		7,316
Profit on ordinary activities after taxation		15,507
Extraordinary losses		2,616
Profit for the financial year		12,891
Dividend		2,000
		10,891
Merger adjustment (W2)		(1,000)
Retained profit for the financial year		9,891
Retained profits brought forward		
As previously reported (52,047 + 21,520)	73,567	
Prior year adjustment (W2)	(220)	
As restated		73,347
Retained profits carried forward		83,238

Workings

1. *Current assets*

	£'000	£'000
Stepney		22,685
Brennan		8,623
		31,308
Adjustment in respect of Brennan's closing stock		
FIFO cost	3,826	
Average cost	3,014	
		(812)
		30,496

2. *Merger adjustment*

	£'000
Nominal value of shares issued by Stepney	2,000
Nominal value of shares acquired by Stepney	1,000
Difference to be deducted from group reserves	1,000

3. *Cost of sales*

	£'000	£'000
Stepney		18,221
Brennan		
Unadjusted	5,492	
Adjustment in respect of stock valuation		
(3,826 − 3,014) − (2,748 − 2,528)	592	
		6,084
		24,305

48   RESTART

(a)   (i)   REDUCTION AND RECONSTRUCTION ACCOUNT

19X7		£	19X7		£
1 Oct	9% preference shares	240,000	1 Oct	8% preference shares	320,000
	Ordinary shares (25p each)	80,000		Ordinary shares	320,000
	Patents and trade marks	10,000		Freehold properties	120,000
	Provision for doubtful debts	30,000		Loans from directors	30,000
	Plant and machinery	50,000			
	Shares in subsidiary	20,000			
	Development cost	24,000			
	Ordinary shares (to directors)	30,000			
	Profit and loss account	220,000			
	Capital reserve (bal)	86,000			
		790,000			790,000

ORDINARY SHARE CAPITAL ACCOUNT

19X7		£	19X7		£
1 Oct	Reduction and reconstruction account	320,000	30 Sept	Balance b/d	240,000
				Bank	80,000
		320,000			320,000
				Reduction and reconstruction account	80,000
	Balance c/d	330,000		Directors' loans	30,000
	1,320,000 shares of 25p each)			Bank	220,000
		330,000			330,000

8% PREFERENCE SHARE CAPITAL ACCOUNT

19X7		£	19X7		£
1 Oct	Reduction and reconstruction account	320,000	30 Sep	Balance b/d	320,000

9% PREFERENCE SHARE CAPITAL ACCOUNT

19X7		£	19X7		£
1 Oct	Balance c/d (400,000 shares of 75p each)	300,000	1 Oct	Reduction and reconstruction account	240,000
				Bank	60,000
		300,000			300,000

BANK ACCOUNT

19X7		£	19X7		£
1 Oct	Ordinary share capital	80,000	30 Sep	Balance b/d	104,000
	Ordinary share capital	220,000	1 Oct	Balance c/d	256,000
	Cumulative preference share capital	60,000			
		360,000			360,000

(ii)   RESTART LIMITED
BALANCE SHEET AS AT 1 OCTOBER 19X7 (as reduced)

	£	£	£
Fixed assets			
Intangible assets			
Patents & trade marks (as revalued)			24,000
Tangible assets			
Freehold properties (as revalued)		190,000	
Plant and machinery (as revalued)		70,000	
			260,000
Investment			
Shares in group company			100,000
			384,000
Current assets			
Stock		124,000	
Debtors			
Trade debtors (less provision of £30,000)	130,000		
Amounts owed by group company	42,000		
		172,000	
Cash at bank		256,000	
		552,000	
Creditors: amounts falling due within one year		220,000	
Net current assets			332,000
Total assets less current liabilities			716,000

	£	£
Capital and reserves		
Authorised share capital	700,000	
Called up share capital		
400,000 9% cumulative preference shares of 75p allotted and fully paid		300,000
1,320,000 ordinary shares of 25p each allotted and fully paid		330,000
Capital reserve		86,000
		716,000

(b) In a scheme of capital reduction and company reconstruction the principal aim is to place the company on a sound footing, enabling it to make profits and to pay dividends, without requiring it to cover previous losses. Assets are revalued or eliminated, and paid up capital which is not represented by assets is written down.

Since preference shares are usually preferential for repayment of capital as well as for the payment of dividends, if the company goes into liquidation, the ordinary shareholders are last in line for any distribution. Therefore, the principle is for losses to be borne by the ordinary shareholders, while the preference shareholders may, at the most, agree to forego arrears of preference dividend. Any reduction of their capital would presumably have to be compensated by a higher rate of return.

Debenture holders and other creditors might agree to reduce their claim, or receive shares or new debentures instead of cash, if it appears such action may produce a more advantageous result than would arise on the liquidation of the company.

It is evident, therefore, that the ordinary shareholder must bear the bulk of any losses and the consequent reduction in capital, since the write down of their equity simply recognises and adjusts an existing situation. By retaining their equity interest the ordinary shareholders remain entitled to the residue of the profit, which it is hoped will be made in the future.

49 ROBERT

(a) JOURNAL ENTRIES

			Dr £	Cr £
(i)	DEBIT	Share capital	20,000	
		Reserves	6,500	
	CREDIT	Shareholder's account		26,500
		Being transfer of shareholders' funds		
(ii)	DEBIT	Realisation account	26,500	
		Creditors	26,000	
	CREDIT	Freehold property at cost		12,000
		Plant at NBV		17,000
		Development expenditure		10,000
		Stock		7,500
		Debtors		2,000
		Bank		4,000
		Being transfer to realisation account of assets and liabilities taken over		
(iii)	DEBIT	Robert Ltd	69,444	
	CREDIT	Realisation account		69,444
		Being purchase consideration due from Robert Ltd (W1)		
(iv)	DEBIT	Realisation account	42,944	
	CREDIT	Shareholders' account		42,944
		Being profit on realisation		

(v) DEBIT   Shareholders' account   18,000
     CREDIT Robert Ltd   18,000

     Being preference shares issued by
     Robert Ltd

(vi) DEBIT   Shareholders' account   38,583
      CREDIT Robert Ltd   38,583

      Being ordinary shares issued by
      Robert Ltd (75% x (69,444-18,000))

(vii) DEBIT   Shareholders' account   12,861
      CREDIT Robert Ltd   12,861

      Being cash paid by Robert Ltd in
      respect of balance of purchase consideration

(b) Purchase consideration for Alpha Ltd

	£
Preference shares: 35,000 of £1 each at par	35,000
Ordinary shares (75% of balance): 150,000 of 25p each issued at 30p	45,000
Cash (25% of balance)	15,000
Total (W1)	95,000

Since there are 30,000 shares in Alpha Ltd the preference shares will be distributed 1 for 1 leaving 5,000 to be sold at par. The final distribution to shareholders of Alpha Ltd will therefore be:

	All share holders (30,000 shares)	*Holder of 100 shares (÷ 300)*
	£	£
Preference shares: 30,000 of £1 each	30,000	100.00
Ordinary shares: 150,000 of 25p each	45,000	150.00
Cash	20,000	66.70
	95,000	316.70

(c) ROBERT LTD
BALANCE SHEET AS AT 31 DECEMBER 19X2

	£	£
Fixed assets		
Intangible assets		
Development costs	10,000	
Goodwill (W2)	83,544	
		93,544
Tangible assets		
Land and buildings	53,000	
Plant and machinery	39,500	
		92,500
		186,044
Current assets		
Stocks	21,750	
Debtors	11,650	
Cash at bank and in hand (W3)	33,350	
	66,750	
Creditors: amounts falling due		
within one year		
Trade creditors	45,000	
Net current assets		21,750
Total assets less current liabilities		207,794
Capital and reserves		
Called up share capital (W5)		181,996
Share premium account (W5)		25,798
		207,794

Workings

1. *Purchase consideration*

		Alpha		Beta	
Year	Weight	Profit	Hash	Profit	Hash
		£	£	£	£
19X0	1	8,000	8,000	17,000	17,000
19X1	2	14,000	28,000	13,000	26,000
19X2	3	16,500	49,500	6,500	19,500
	6		85,500		62,500

∴ Weighted average profit (÷ 6)   14,250   10,417

∴ Purchase consideration (÷ 15%)   95,000   69,444

2. *Goodwill*

	Alpha £	Beta £	Total £
Fair value of assets acquired			
Freehold property	35,000	18,000	53,000
Plant	17,500	22,000	39,500
Development expenditure	-	10,000	10,000
Stock less provision	14,250	7,500	21,750
Debtors less provision	9,700	1,950	11,650
Bank	(14,000)	4,000	(10,000)
Creditors	(13,000)	(26,000)	(39,000)
Provision for warranty claims	(6,000)	-	(6,000)
	43,450	37,450	80,900
Purchase consideration	95,000	69,444	164,444
∴ Goodwill	51,550	31,994	83,544

3. *Bank account*

	£		£
Balance from Beta	4,000	Balance from Alpha	14,000
Share issue (balance)	71,211	Net payments to shareholders:	
		Alpha	15,000
		Beta	12,861
		Balance c/d 31.12.X2 (W4)	33,350
	75,211		75,211

4. *Cash required for liquidity ratio of 1:1*

	£
Combined creditors in Robert Ltd	39,000
Provision for warranty claims	6,000
Combined debtors in Robert Ltd	(11,650)
Cash balance required	33,350

5. *Share capital of Robert Ltd*

	Preference shares £	Ordinary shares £	Share premium £
Shareholders of Alpha	35,000	37,500	7,500
Shareholders of Beta	18,000	32,153	6,430
External issue (W3)	-	59,343	11,868
	53,000	128,996	25,798

218

50 PQR

Tutorial note. This is a fairly straightforward question. Make sure you provided *journals*, not just the reconstruction accounts, as required by the question.

(a)		Dr £'000	Cr £'000
DEBIT	Ordinary share capital	1,000	
CREDIT	10% Preference share capital		1,000

Being the conversion of the ordinary share capital into 10% preference share capital

DEBIT	Loan from parent company	388	
CREDIT	Reconstruction account		388

Being the write off of the loan from the parent company

DEBIT	Cash	1,000	
CREDIT	Ordinary share capital		1,000

Being the issue of new ordinary shares to the management (200) and venture capital company (800)

DEBIT	Cash	600	
CREDIT	Tangible assets: property		250
	Reconstruction account		350

Being the sale of factory at a surplus

DEBIT	Tangible assets: property	320	
CREDIT	Reconstruction account		320

Being the revaluation of the remaining factory

DEBIT	Reconstruction account	175	
CREDIT	Cash		175

Being the costs of redundancy

DEBIT	Cash	150	
	Reconstruction account	10	
CREDIT	Fixed assets: plant and equipment		160

Being the sale of surplus plant at a loss

DEBIT	Fixed assets: plant and equipment	300	
CREDIT	Cash		300

Being the purchase of additional plant

DEBIT	Reconstruction account	150	
CREDIT	Patents		150

Being the write off of worthless patents

DEBIT	Reconstruction account	35	
CREDIT	Stocks		35

Being write off of obsolete stocks

DEBIT	Reconstruction account	15	
CREDIT	Debtors		15

Being write off of bad debts

	£'000	£'000
DEBIT Reconstruction account	556	
CREDIT Retained profits		556

Being write off of balance on profit and loss account:
retained losses

	£'000	£'000
DEBIT Reconstruction account	60	
CREDIT Cash		60

Being the costs of the reconstruction

	£'000	£'000
DEBIT Reconstruction	57	
CREDIT Capital reserves		57

Being the transfer of the surplus on reconstruction
to capital reserves

RECONSTRUCTION ACCOUNT

	£'000		£'000
Redundancy costs	175	Loan from parent company written off	388
Loss on sale of surplus plant	10	Profit on sale of factory	350
Write off of patents	150	Revaluation of remaining factory	320
Write off of obsolete stocks	35		
Write off of bad debts	15		
Write off of past losses	556		
Costs of reconstruction	60		
Balance: surplus on reconstruction transferred to capital reserve)	57		
	1,058		1,058

(b) BALANCE SHEET OF PQR LTD AS AT 1 JANUARY 19X8

	£'000	£'000
Fixed assets		
Land and buildings at valuation		450
Plant and equipment (420 - 160 + 300)		560
		1,010
Current assets		
Stocks (255 - 35)	220	
Debtors (124-15)	109	
Cash at bank and in hand	1,108	
	1,437	
Creditors: amounts due in less than one year	(390)	
Net current assets		1,047
		2,057
		£'000
Capital and reserves		
Ordinary share capital		1,000
10% preference share capital		1,000
Capital reserve		57
		2,057

Note. Attached to the balance sheet should be a note to the effect that capital commitments at 1 January 19X8 amounted to £500,000.

51 MOSES

(a) To: Marketing director
From: Finance director
Date: 2 November 19X7
Subject: *Information available from published financial statements*

Introduction

This report is intended to set out the information available from the financial statements published by our competitors.

Contents of published financial statements

The financial statements of limited companies include a profit and loss account, a balance sheet, a statement of source and application of funds and notes to the accounts. The directors' report is also sometimes considered to be included in the term 'financial statements'.

Information available

Information relevant to the marketing function would include the items listed below.

(i) *Turnover and profit*. The profit and loss account will show total turnover and a note will disclose an analysis of the total figure between different classes of business and different geographical markets. The analysis between different classes of business must also be provided in respect of the figure for profit before taxation by all companies. All public companies and the largest private companies must also disclose net profit (and net assets) analysed between classes of business and geographical location of operations, to comply with SSAP 25 *Segmental reporting*.

(ii) *Overheads*. Details must be given of distribution costs, administrative expenses and staff costs.

(iii) *Fixed assets*. The figures for intangible assets may indicate the extent of a competitor's investment in the development of new products. The funds statement will usually specify the amount actually expended on development during the year. Details of tangible fixed assets are also available, analysed between land and buildings, plant and machinery and fixtures and fittings. This may provide an indication of the value of shops, warehouses and distribution vehicles.

(iv) *Current assets*. Information will be available not only on the level of finished goods stocks and debtors, but also on stock turnover and debtors collection period. Comparative figures may indicate trends in stock and debtors levels.

(v) *Business development*. The directors' report will contain a review of the development of the company's business during the year, details of any activities in the field of research and development, and a note of likely future developments.

(b) *Limitations of the information available*

    (i)   Published financial statements normally disclose the minimum information required by statute and accounting standards. They are not as detailed as internal management accounts. It may be impossible, for example, to determine the exact nature of fixed assets held: a total figure for freehold premises may include amounts in respect of factory, warehouse and offices.

    (ii)   Financial statements are usually published long after the period to which they relate. The information in them may be outdated. This problem is made worse by the fact that most accounts are prepared on an historical cost basis, rather than using current costs.

    (iii)   There may be problems of comparability if our competitors use accounting policies different from our own.

    (iv)   Segmental analyses need not be given if the directors consider them too commercially sensitive.

52 SEGMENTAL ANALYSIS

(a)   A group of companies may undertake a wide variety of business activities in a number of business segments in different parts of the world. The consolidated accounts of such a group combines the balance sheets and profit and loss accounts of the subsidiaries that undertake these activities as though the group were a simple company. While this process of consolidation provides the users of the accounts with an overview of the group's activities it also has the effect of obscuring much useful detail. The provisions of the Companies Acts and SSAP 25 on segmental disclosure are intended to expose that detail which may relate both to business segment and to geographical location.

Users of the accounts are interested in the contribution to group profit from each business segment because each has different characteristics as regards risk, profitability and growth potential. A segmental analysis allows users to judge the efficiency of management by comparing the results of individual business segments with corresponding segments of competitor firms for a given period and over time.

In addition, users will be able to see how the contribution from each segment changes over time and can decide whether the development of the group's portfolio of businesses has their support. This may be particularly relevant to the analysis of a group that is making a particular effort to diversify. Quite often, the objective of diversification is to reduce risk; this may not, however, be popular with the shareholders since this will usually involve a reduction in return. The motive for risk reduction may be to safeguard the position of the management; but shareholders who wish to reduce their own risk can do so by diversifying their own portfolios.

Segmental financial information will usually also provide geographical detail regarding the location of assets and the source of profits. Such information is particularly useful in assessing the political and exchange rate risk to which an international group is exposed. At the same time, it can provide an indication of whether the group is positioned to benefit from likely economic expansion in certain parts of the world, for example the developing countries of the Pacific Rim.

From a geographical analysis it may be possible to deduce how much of any change in profit is attributable to exchange differences and to forecast the likely state of possible future changes in exchange rates.

Employees and trades unions are interested in divisional financial performance because the capacity of the employer to pay increased wages will be dependent on the financial position and profitability of the individual divisions and not of the whole group.

Governments and international bodies make use of segment information in compiling statistics about international trade and in developing their policies in regard to international companies.

(b) A group may resist disclosing detailed segment information for reasons of confidentiality, cost or the difficulty of presenting and interpreting such information.

The principal reason is usually confidentiality. The disclosure of the relative profitability of business segments or geographical location may provide useful information to competitors and may allow them to target their actions more accurately. For example, the disclosure of high margins in a particular business segment could attract new entrants to the business and thus depress such margins.

The disclosure of geographical information could lead to the terms of individual contracts or fiscal arrangements becoming known and this may be unwelcome to the contracting party or government.

The cost of collecting, interpreting and presenting segment information may be considerable for a large and diverse group. In order to ensure that the information is relevant and consistent, special procedures may need to be established, computers programmed and staff assigned specifically to prepare the information and present the results. Where the analysis presented is different from the analysis used internally, this additional cost may be regarded as unnecessary and a waste of the group's resources.

A group may also resist the disclosure of this information if it considers that its disclosure will not materially aid the understanding of the group's results by the users of the accounts. There is no standardisation of the analysis to be used and the structure of the group's business may change from year to year. Consequently, the decision as to what to disclose needs constant review. It is a common experience that the more information is disclosed, the more is demanded. Frequently, the demand for information comes not from the shareholders but from the financial analyst/commentator community and management may not consider that all such requests for additional information are legitimate. Moreover, more harm may be done to the company's reputation due to misunderstood or misinterpreted segment information than would result from mere speculation about undisclosed detail.

While management may claim confidentiality, cost or difficulty as the principal reasons for disinclination to disclose segment information, it will sometimes be the case that the real reason is the desire to hide inefficiency or vulnerability to takeover. The usual losers in a takeover are the management of the target company and a conflict of interest may always be possible.

53 CONSOLIDATED FUNDS STATEMENT

To: The Chairman
From: The Group Accountant
Copy: Group Finance Director
Date: 2 December 19X1
Subject: *Source and Application of Funds Statement for 19X1*

With reference to your memorandum of 24 November on the above subject, the answers to your queries are set out below.

1. The item 'income from associated company' in the consolidated profit and loss account reflects the group's share of the profits of XY Ltd. Of this, however, only the dividend received from XY of £75,000 has been received by the group in cash and this is, therefore, the amount that is shown in the group source and application of funds statement. The balance of £1,150,000 has been retained by XY Ltd to finance the expansion of its operations.

    The group's share of XY's tax charge for the year amounts to £525,000. This is included with the group tax charge in the profit and loss account because the group's share of XY's profit is included on a pre-tax basis. However, the payment of this tax does not represent a flow of funds out of the group.

2. The amount shown in the profit and loss account for minority interests represents the proportion of the total group profit that is attributable to the minority shareholders in the subsidiaries, companies that are not wholly owned. This is done so that the consolidated profit and loss account can show the group profit that is attributable to the shareholders of the parent company.

    The corresponding amount in the statement of source and application of funds represents only the dividends paid in the year (last year's final and this year's interim) to the minority shareholders in the non-wholly owned subsidiaries.

3. I imagine the difficulty you have with these figures is because the movements in the statement of source and application of funds is not the same as the difference between the two balance sheet figures. These are reconciled below.

Stocks	£'000
Closing stock	20,750,000
Opening stock	15,250,000
Movement	5,500,000
Less stocks acquired as part of S Ltd: this is included in the item 'purchase of S Ltd'	(1,375,000)
Movement on stocks in statement of source and application of funds	4,125,000
Fixed assets	
Closing fixed assets	26,500,000
Opening fixed assets	21,125,000
Net movement	5,375,000
Add back depreciation charged in 19X1	2,750,000
Gross movement	8,125,000
Less fixed assets acquired as part of S Ltd	3,250,000
Movement on fixed assets in statement of source and application	5,375,000

Taxation	£'000
Taxation payable at 1 January 19X1	6,125,000
Amount provided in 19X1	9,875,000
Taxation payable at 31 December 19X1	(11,375,000)
Mainstream corporation tax paid	4,625,000
Add advance corporation tax paid	750,000
Total taxation paid per statement of source and application of funds	5,375,000

Summary of Acquisition of S Ltd
The purpose of this summary is to provide information for the shareholders of the parent company regarding this acquisition and how it was financed. It shows that the group paid £3,500,000 (of which only £1,000,000 was in cash) for an 80% share in net assets amounting to £3,750,000 in total (ie £3,000,000 group share). The difference of £500,000 represents the goodwill of the business acquired.

4. As you have noted, SSAP 10 contains only the relevant general principles and provides guidelines for their application in practice. At the time it was issued, statements of source and application of funds were regarded as experimental and the intention of the standard was to allow companies to develop a presentation that best suited their own circumstances. The general approach that we have taken is intended to provide as informative a statement as we can without disclosing information of a commercially sensitive nature not incurring unnecessary preparation costs. In future we will produce a cash flow statement rather than a statement of source and application of funds statement as SSAP 10 has now been replaced by FRS 1 *Cash flow statements*.

I should be happy to discuss any of the above matters with you further.

54 TUTORIAL QUESTION: CASH FLOW STATEMENTS

(a) ARC LIMITED
CASH FLOW STATEMENT FOR THE YEAR ENDED 31 DECEMBER 19X1

	£'000	£'000
Net cash inflow from operating activities		2,390
Returns on investments and servicing of finance		
Interest received	40	
Interest paid	(280)	
Dividends paid	(5,100)	
Net cash inflow from returns on investments and servicing of finance		(5,340)
Taxation		
Corporation tax paid (including advance corporation tax)	(3,200)	
Tax paid		(3,200)
Investing activities		
Payments to acquire tangible fixed assets	(11,800)	
Receipts from sales of tangible fixed assets	1,000	
Net cash outflow from investing activities		(10,800)
Net cash inflow before financing		(16,950)
Financing		
Repurchase of debenture loan	150	
Net cash inflow from financing		150
Increase in cash and cash equivalents		(16,800)

Notes to the cash flow statement

1. Reconciliation of operating profit to net cash inflow from operating activities

	£'000
Operating profit	20,640
Depreciation charges	5,050
Loss on sale of tangible fixed assets	700
(Increase)/decrease in stocks	(10,000)
(Increase)/decrease in debtors	(18,200)
Increase/(decrease) in creditors	4,200
Net cash inflow from operating activities	2,390

2. Analysis of changes in cash and cash equivalents during the year

	£'000
Balance at 1 January 19X1	600
Net cash inflow/outflow	(16,800)
Balance at 31 December 19X1	(16,200)

3. Analysis of the balances of cash and cash equilvalents as shown in the balance sheet

	19X0 £'000	19X1 £'000	*Change in year* £'000
Cash at bank and in hand	600	–	(600)
Bank overdrafts	–	(16,200)	(16,200)
	600	(16,200)	(16,800)

4. Analysis of changes in finance during the year

	Debenture loan £'000
Balance at 1 January 19X1	600
Cash inflow/(outflow) from financing	150
Balance at 31 December 19X1	750

Workings

1. *Depreciation*

	£'000	£'000
Depreciation at 31 December 19X9		10,750
Depreciation at 31 December 19X8	9,500	
Depreciation on assets sold	3,800	
		5,700
Charge for the year		5,050

2. *Loss on sale of fixed assets*

	£'000	£'000
Proceeds on sale		1,000
Net book value: cost	5,500	
depreciation	(3,800)	
		1,700
Loss on sale		700

		£'000	£'000
3.	*Dividends paid*		
	Dividends payable at 31 December 19X8		3,000
	Declared 19X9: preference		100
	ordinary interim		2,000
	ordinary final		6,000
			11,100
	Less payable at 31 December 19X9		6,000
	∴ Paid in year		5,100
4.	*Purchase of fixed assets*		
	Balance at 31 December 19X9		23,900
	Balance at 31 December 19X8	17,600	
	Cost of assets sold	(5,500)	
			12,100
			11,800

(b) The main change introduced by FRS 1 compared to the requirements of SSAP 10 is fairly obvious.

'The FRS requires reporting activities to report cash flows rather than accrual based funds flows'.

The FRS exempts a large number of companies from preparing cash flow statements, namely all those which fall under the definition of a small- or medium-sized company. SSAP 10 required all companies with a turnover or gross income of over £25,000 to prepare a statement of source and application of funds (SSAF). Another onerous duty is thereby removed from smaller companies.

The FRS is much more prescriptive in terms of the way information is presented. One of the most important examples of this is the way the purchase price or sale consideration of a subsidiary must be shown in one line under 'investing activities'. In a SSAF a 'line-by-line' approach could be used to diffuse the information.

The cash flow statement and the required notes to the statement clearly show the user the relationship between profit and cash flows. This is important as it is a concept that non-accountants often find difficult to grasp. In (a) above, note 1 shows the cost to the company of the expansion in trading during the year in terms of the increased burden of working capital and depreciation charges. (Compare the profit of £20.64m with the net cash inflow from operations of £2.39m.) The statement itself shows the costs of expansion in terms of taxation, dividend and interest costs.

The cash flow statement will not only help the shareholders, investors and other users of financial statements. The management of the company may also benefit. In this example, the company will obviously require new funding if its trading expansion is to continue. It should be easier to convince existing and potential investors of the need for finance by showing them the cash flow statement.

55 VALUE

Tutorial note. It is simplest to insert a balancing figure for bought-in materials and services.

Suggested solution

(a) VALUE LIMITED
CONSOLIDATED VALUE ADDED STATEMENT
FOR THE YEAR ENDED 30 JUNE 19X2

	£'000	£'000
Turnover		6,861
Bought-in materials and services		
(balancing figure)		5,268
Value added		1,593
Other income *		27
		1,620
Applied the following way		
To pay employees (1,071 + 3)		1,074
To pay providers of capital		
Interest on loans	43	
Dividends	141	
		184
To pay government		
Corporation tax		105
To provide for maintenance and		
expansion of assets		
Depreciation	71	
Retained profit	186	
		257
		1,620

* Rent £12,000 + interest received £3,000 + surplus on property disposal £4,000 + surplus on sale and leaseback £8,000.

(b) There are no statutory or professional requirements relating to value added statements. Examples of items which could have been treated differently are as follows.

   (i)   Depreciation has been shown as a separate application of value added. An alternative is to include it as a cost of goods and services in arriving at the value added.

   (ii) The payments to government have been shown to be only the corporation tax on profits. An alternative view is that all money exchanges with national and local government be shown. Then VAT, PAYE, NI and local business rates would be included in this item.

   (iii) The amount shown as payable to employees is considered by some commentators to be made up of two elements: a basic payment for the work done, which should be included as part of the cost of goods and services, and other benefits to employees, for example, bonus payments, pensions, welfare and social costs and profit sharing schemes, which are an application to employees of the value added.

56 C PLC

Tutorial note. The examiner was concerned about two problems candidates had with this answer. The more worrying was the failure of many candidates to attempt part (b), a standard rider to ratio analysis questions. Make sure you can cope with such questions. Secondly, he commented that there is still a widespread misconception that any divergence from a current ratio of 2:1 and an acid test ratio of 1:1 is problematic. Don't forget that these ratios are affected by the nature of a business and different sectors have different norms.

To: The board
From: Management accountant
Subject: *Analysis of F plc's profitability and liquidity*

(*Note.* This report should be read in conjunction with the appendix, which contains relevant ratios.)

(a) Sales have effectively remained static over the three year period, a fall of some 13% between 19X6 and 19X7 having been reversed in 19X8. The gross margin, at between 45% and 52% is relatively high, but this has deteriorated over the period, because of increases in labour costs and overheads.

Administrative and distribution costs, however, are very high in relation to turnover and have reduced the margin to 3%, 2% and a net loss in 19X8. Because of the relatively high level of these costs, net profit is very sensitive to small percentage changes. Net profits of this size must be regarded as very unsatisfactory and, in the absence of constructive action, the prospects of the company are doubtful.

Return on capital employed has declined from 5.9% to a negative 4.3%. Even the positive returns in 19X6 and 19X7 are unsatisfactory, representing a discount against the return available on a risk-free investment. In the event that the net realisable value of the assets exceeds the book value, the return is even less satisfactory.

One of the reasons for the low return is poor utilisation of both fixed and current assets. Fixed assets produce turnover of less than three times, suggesting that certain of the fixed assets are very unproductive. This should be analysed further, if possible. It seems that no fixed assets have been purchased in the period and the depreciation rate is very low, suggesting a long average life. It is interesting that fixed assets should be so significant, given the high labour costs, suggesting that fixed assets are perhaps not being used efficiently.

Stocks are very high in relation to usage, materials stocks representing some 5-6 months consumption. This would indicate that some stocks are not turning over at all and may be obsolete. Work in progress represents some $3\frac{1}{2}$ months production, again suggesting that certain items may no longer be saleable and require writing off.

Debtors appear to be better controlled, representing some 7-8 weeks sales, although this indicator has deteriorated over the period. This may require some investigation particularly as this has not been accompanied by an improvement in the gross margin which might otherwise have suggested that longer credit was being granted in order to sustain higher prices.

The current ratio is barely adequate at around 1.4 and reflects the very high stock levels. The acid test ratio at around 0.5 indicates that the company is facing a serious liquidity crisis. The overdraft would appear to be permanent and the company would benefit from a fresh capital injection, including some long-term loan finance. Whether this is feasible will depend on the level of equity and the existence of any preference shares and whether there are realistic prospects of a return to profitability in the near future. For this to happen, it would seem that both distribution and administrative costs would need to be reduced considerably and asset utilisation improved. The disposal of slow moving stocks and underused fixed assets might assist in a re-financing exercise.

(b) The principal shortcomings of the above analysis are the lack of detail underlying the figures and the lack of a benchmark against which to measure the company's performance.

Firstly, the accounts from which the conclusions have been drawn are necessarily summarised and some or all of the following detail would be useful in order to develop the analysis.

- Accounting policies on inclusion of overheads in cost of sales and WIP.

- Whether these (and other) accounting policies have changed over the period.

- An analysis of stocks between raw materials, WIP and finished stocks.

- Are any of the stocks or WIP part of a long-term contract and does the creditors figure include any progress payments in respect of it?

- How large is the overdraft and how has it changed over the period?

- Are additional overdraft facilities available?

- Is it possible to take additional credit from suppliers without damaging the company's credit rating?

- A segmental analysis of debtors and sales is needed.

Secondly, although ratios are a useful way to summarise information they may mislead, in the absence of full information. F plc's liquidity may be better than it appears if it has a large overdraft facility. Also, the balance sheet may have been subject to window dressing and there may be off balance sheet finance.

Thirdly, on their own, the accounts of F plc do not indicate how well the company is doing compared to its competitors. While the above analysis indicates a poor and deteriorating performance, if the whole industry is depressed this could represent a *relatively* good performance. Thus the indicators shown in the appendix should be compared to the averages for the industry or those of comparable rivals.

Finally, the 19X8 accounts may be out of date and the situation could have changed dramatically in the intervening months. This is one aspect of a general proviso about ratio analysis: it can only suggest where to direct further enquiry, it cannot provide the basis for decisions.

Appendix

	19X6	*19X7*	*19X8*
Return on capital employed	5.9%	4.1%	(4.3%)
Asset turnover (turnover: fixed assets)	2.67	2.43	2.86
Gross margin/sales	52%	49%	45%
Net profit/sales	3%	2%	(2%)
Stock turnover: raw materials/materials	174 days	228 days	183 days
WIP/cost of sales	117 days	119 days	106 days
Debtors: sales	46 days	57 days	55 days
Current ratio	1.44	1.44	1.41
Acid test	0.48	0.52	0.52

57 METEOR

(a) From: Management accountant
   To: Board of JKL plc
   Subject: *GHI plc*

Set out below are the results of my analysis of the summarised accounts of GHI plc for the years 19X7 to 19X9. The ratios derived from the analysis are attached as Appendix I. I have examined GHI from three viewpoints: growth, profitability and financial position.

Growth

Turnover doubled between 19X7 and 19X8 and more than doubled again in 19X9. Assets have also increased at roughly the same rate over the three years. Gross profit, however, has not increased proportionately, by 72% and 87% respectively and net profit after tax by 77% and 137%.

This rate of growth is much faster than is likely to have occurred organically and it would appear that GHI has been making acquisitions (buying turnover and profits) in order to reach a size at which it can achieve economies of scale and a good market share.

Profitability

Profitability has fallen over the three years which is consistent with the rush for growth noted above.

Gross margin has fallen from 32% in 19X7 to 29% in 19X8 and to 21% in 19X9. Net margin has also fallen from 14% to 12% to 10% over the same period. This fall may also be due to sales mix and needs to be compared with the industry average as GHI may be moving from a niche position to having a wider product range.

Distribution costs as a proportion of sales rose between 19X7 and 19X8 from 11% to 13% but fell back to 9% in 19X9. Administration costs have fallen from 7% of sales in 19X7 to 4% in 19X8 and 2% in 19X9. These ratios indicate that GHI may now be achieving the economies of scale that is presumably the object of its expansion.

Return on capital employed has fallen from 17% in 19X7 to 11% in 19X8 and to 10% in 19X9. The effect, however, of the high level of gearing has been to produce a significant increase in the return on shareholders funds, from 22% in 19X7 to 48% in 19X9.

It is not possible to deduce from the figures provided the full reasons for the changes in profitability and additional research is required into, inter alia, the following:

- changes in sales mix;
- changes in the composition of distribution and administration expenses, particularly whether advertising expenditure has been curtailed;
- analysis of turnover by outlet and per square foot of selling space;
- extent of reliance on particular suppliers.

Financial position

The current ratio has improved considerably over the period, from 0.54 in 19X7 to 1.1 in 19X9. This is still rather low, however, particularly since more than half the current assets consists of stock.

The quick ratio has also improved from 0.2 in 19X7 to 0.49 in 19X9 but this is still precariously low due to the large overdraft. On the assumption that this overdraft will continue to be available, the creditors are just covered by debtors.

Clearly the expansion has been financed entirely by borrowing since, in addition to the overdraft, loans of £10 million have been raised in the past two years. The gearing level has increased from zero in 19X7 to 79% in 19X9. GHI, therefore, has taken on a considerable amount of financial risk which, while enhancing return to shareholders at present, makes it vulnerable to a downturn in trade.

The rate of turnover of stock has deteriorated over the period and in 19X9 represented 102 days sales compared with 83 days in 19X7. This may reflect the lag effect of stocking up during the period of expansion, but may indicate a lack of attention to the need to maintain stock turnover in order to increase sales.

Debtors have also increased disproportionately from 8 days sales in 19X7 to 64 days sales in 19X9. This is not consistent with a cash retail business and suggests that GHI has introduced a consumer credit facility.

(b) An examination of the full annual report and accounts of GHI would yield the following additional information.

- A segmental analysis of turnover and income which might indicate whether GHI had branched out into consumer finance. This analysis, however, is largely at the discretion of the company, and it is not likely that it would disclose commercially valuable information.

- Details of the debenture loan including the security given, the rate of interest and the term.

- Details of the overdraft including whether or not it is secured.

- Details of whether and when the property was last revalued. This could give some indication of its current value.

- Details of fixed assets including estimated economic lives and the extent to which they are depreciated.

- Details of capital commitments.

- Details of the taxation charge, which has fallen as a proportion of the pre-tax income from 43% to 33% over the three years.

- A statement of source and application of funds which will show more clearly how the expansion in capital employed has been financed and the current liquidity position.

Appendix

	19X7	*19X8*	*19X9*
Growth in turnover	-	92%	164%
Growth in assets	-	158%	147%
Gross profit/sales	32%	29%	21%
Net profit/sales	14%	12%	10%
Distribution costs/sales	11%	13%	9%
Administration expenses/sales	7%	4%	2%
Return on capital employed	17%	11%	10%
Return on shareholders' funds	22%	28%	48%
Current ratio	0.54	0.67	1.10
Quick ratio	0.20	0.21	0.49
Gearing	nil	51%	79%
Level of stockholding:days	83	132	102
Level of debtor:days	8	43	64

58   M PLC

From:	Finance Director
To:	Board of Directors
Date:	31 October 19X9
Subject:	*Profitability and financial position of M plc from 19X5 to 19X8*

(a) *Purpose*

The purpose of this report is to provide an assessment of the trading performance, operational efficiency and financial position of M plc for the four years ended 31 December 19X8. This analysis is based on the published accounts for this period.

(b) *Growth*

	19X6	*19X7*	*19X8*
Increase in sales	11%	7%	3%
Increase in fixed assets	45%	29%	-4%
Increase in net assets	7%	3%	4%

From the above it can be seen that, while fixed assets increased significantly over the period, there was little real growth in either net assets or sales turnover. This suggests that the increased fixed asset has not produced corresponding increases in turnover and has been financed at least partly by additional loans.

(c) *Profitability*

	19X5	19X6	19X7	19X8
Gross margin	35%	34%	32%	29%
Net margin	14%	12%	7%	6%
Distribution costs/sales	5%	5%	6%	7%
Administration costs/sales	15%	15%	17%	13%
Return on capital employed	44%	36%	20%	15%
Return on equity	38%	39%	22%	15%
Dividend payout ratio	86%	84%	89%	77%

Each of the above indicators of profitability show a declining trend which should be a cause for concern. The reduction in the gross margin from 35% in 19X5 to 29% in 19X8 could be due to a changed sales mix which could be satisfactory if the total turnover were increasing; since it is not, it indicates an increasing inability to pass on higher costs of raw materials and production costs in prices.

This trend is compounded by the steeper fall in the net margin. The reason for this is the marked increase in the ratio of distribution costs to sales and (apart from 19X8, which may have been untypical) no reduction in the ratio of administration costs/sales. Either these costs are somewhat out of control or the expansion in sales has not been adequate to deliver any economies of scale in these departments.

The above trends are reflected in the sharp fall in ROCE and the almost equally significant fall in the return on shareholders equity. Unless this trend is arrested M plc will have considerable difficulty in the future in attracting or replacing its financing.

In spite of declining profitability the payout ratio remains very high, and suggests that inadequate funds are being retained to finance growth.

(d) *Operating efficiency/working capital management*

	19X5	19X6	19X7	19X8
Sales/fixed assets	7.6	5.8	4.9	5.2
Stocks/turnover: days	50	51	45	38
Debtors/turnover: days	66	73	79	82
Trade creditors/cost of sales: days	35	34	29	25

As mentioned above, the operational efficiency of fixed assets, as measured by the sales generated has fallen markedly over the period. The improvement in 19X8 reflects lower fixed assets rather than a relative increase in turnover. Even allowing for the time lag between investment and increased sales, this suggests that the asset base is not being worked hard enough.

Stock turnover is, however, improving which indicates that active stock management is being undertaken. Debtors, on the other hand, have increased by a quarter in relation to turnover. Whether the current level is acceptable can only be judged by comparing the amount of credit given with the industry norm, which may also have increased over the period. The amount of credit taken from suppliers is lower in 19X8 than it was in 19X5 and this seems inconsistent with the debtors position. It is possible, however, that purchases and sales are made in different markets which have experienced different trends and comparison with the industry norm is necessary.

(e) *Financial condition*

	19X5	19X6	19X7	19X8
Current ratio	2.4	2.0	1.9	2.2
Acid test	1.4	1.2	1.2	1.5
Gearing	-	11%	20%	21%
Total debt/equity ratio	43%	67%	86%	77%
Interest cover (times)	34	9	3.5	2.6

The short term liquidity position appears satisfactory compared to the generally accepted norms of two for the current ratio and one for the acid test ratio. At present, however, the company does not have any cash and is operating on an overdraft. This means that continued liquidity depends on the ability to turn debtors into cash quickly; clearly this has been a problem in the past as the average credit period granted has increased. The ability of M plc to pay its debts as they become due could be critically affected by the solvency or liquidity of a major customer.

The gearing ratio has increased to a level which is not unreasonably high, but the ratio of debt to equity has increased considerably as new long term loans have been taken on, the overdraft increased (although the overdraft has fallen in the last year under consideration) and only a small proportion of profits retained. Accordingly the interest cover has fallen to 2.6 times which may be considered dangerously low. M plc is unlikely to be able to take on any more interest bearing debt and consideration should probably be given to a further injection of equity capital.

In summary, M plc has gone through a period of stagnant profitability with falling rates of growth in sales. This has adversely affected the balance sheet as long term debt and a substantial overdraft have been taken on to finance an expansion of fixed assets and some working capital problems. Some improvements in the working capital problem have been seen in the last year (a fall in stock levels and in the overdraft level), however, an improvement in the debtor collection rate is necessary to ease the liquidity problem further.

59   PILUM

Tutorial note. The question does not state whether the net basis or the nil basis is to be used. The suggested solution below gives both.

Suggested solution

(a)

	Earnings	
	Net basis	*Nil basis*
	£	£
Profit before tax	2,530,000	2,530,000
Less taxation	1,127,000	1,058,000
Profit after tax	1,403,000	1,472,000
Less preference dividends	276,000	276,000
Earnings	1,127,000	1,196,000
Earnings per share	$\dfrac{1,127,000}{4,140,000}$	$\dfrac{1,196,000}{4,140,000}$
	27.2p	28.9p

(b) Shares in issue at 31 December 19X4
4,140,000 + 4,140,000/4 = 5,175,000

∴ EPS

$$\frac{1,127,000}{5,175,000} \qquad \frac{1,196,000}{5,175,000}$$

$$\underline{21.8p} \qquad \underline{23.1p}$$

(c) The first step is to calculate the theoretical ex-rights price. Consider the holder of 5 shares.

	No.	£
Before rights issue	5	9.00
Rights issue	1	1.20
After rights issue	6	10.20

The theoretical ex-rights price is therefore £10.20/6 = £1.70.

The number of shares in issue before the rights issue must be multiplied by the fraction:

$$\frac{\text{Market price on last day of quotation cum rights}}{\text{theoretical ex-rights price}} = \frac{£1.80}{£1.70}$$

Number of shares in issue during the year

	Proportion of year		Shares in issue	Fraction	Total
1 1.X4 - 30.9.X4	9/12	x	4,140,000	x 1.8/1.7	3,287,647
1.10.X4 - 31.12.X4	3/12	x	4,968,000		1,242,000
					4,529,647

EPS on net basis $= \dfrac{1,127,000}{4,529,647}$

$= \underline{24.9p}$

EPS on nil basis $= \dfrac{1,196,000}{4,529,647}$

$= \underline{26.4p}$

(d) The maximum number of shares into which the loan stock could be converted is 90% x 1,150,000 = 1,035,000. The calculation of fully diluted EPS should be based on the assumption that such a conversion actually took place on 1 January 19X4. Shares in issue during the year would then have numbered (4,140,000 + 1,035,000) = 5,175,000 and revised earnings would be as follows.

	£	*Net basis* £	*Nil basis* £
Earnings from (a) above		1,127,000	1,196,000
Interest saved by conversion	115,000		
Less attributable taxation	57,500		
		57,500	57,500
		1,184,500	1,253,500
∴ EPS		1,184,500	1,253,500
		5,175,000	5,175,000
		22.9p	24.2p

(e) EPS in this case must be calculated on these assumptions.

(i) All the options had been exercised on 1 January 19X4. The number of shares in issue throughout the year would then have been (4,140,000 + 460,000) = 4,600,000.

(ii) The proceeds on exercise of the options (460,000 x £1.70) = £782,000 had been invested on 1 January 19X4 in 2½% consolidated stock. At a price of £25 for £100 nominal value of stock, a nominal amount of £782,000 x 100/25 = £3,128,000 could have been purchased.

Revised earnings would be as follows.

	£	*Net basis* £	*Nil basis* £
Earnings from (a) above		1,127,000	1,196,000
Notional interest on consolidated stock (2½% x £3,128,000)	78,200		
Less attributable taxation	39,100		
		39,100	39,100
		1,166,100	1,235,100
		1,166,100	1,235,100
∴ EPS		4,600,000	4,600,000
		25.3p	26.8p

60 R PLC

Tutorial note. The main problem here is the rights issue. If you had difficulty with that part of the question, make sure you can follow the suggested solution. Also, don't skimp on part (b): this was the worst answered part of the question in May 1989.

(a) *Earnings*

Profit and loss accounts	*19X7*	*19X8*
	£'000	£'000
Trading profit before taxation	1,700	2,400
Taxation on ordinary activities	(700)	(1,000)
Profit after taxation	1,000	1,400
Extraordinary items	(400)	(600)
	600	800
Preference dividends	(100)	(100)
Profit attributable to ordinary shares	500	700

Earnings	=	profit attributable to ordinary shareholders before extraordinary items but after preference dividends

For 19X7	=	500 + 400 = £900,000
For 19X8	=	700 + 600 = £1,300,000

Weighted average number of shares in issue
For 19X7 (prior to rights issue) = 2,000,000
For 19X8 (after rights issue), we need to calculate the theoretical ex-rights price (TERP).

		£
Before issue	2,000,000 shares @ £2	4,000,000
Issue	500,000 shares @ £1.50	750,000
Gives	2,500,000 shares @ £1.90	4,750,000

The weighted average number of shares in year of rights issue is calculated by multiplying the number of shares in issue before the rights issue by the bonus fraction (market price before issue ÷ TERP):

$$(2,000,000 \ \times \ \frac{2.00}{1.90} \ \times \ \frac{6}{12} \ ) \ + \ (2,500,000 \ \times \ \frac{6}{12} \ ) = 2,302,632 \text{ weighted average shares}$$

(i)   19X7 $\dfrac{£900,000}{2,000,000}$ =   45p per share

(ii)   19X8 $\dfrac{£1,300,000}{2,302,632}$ =   56p per share

(iii)   *Adjusted earnings per share for 19X7* to be shown as a comparative figure in the 19X8 accounts (assuming that the prior year adjustment relates to 19X7 (ie *the* prior year, not *a* prior year)):

	£
Earnings as originally shown	900,000
Less: prior year adjustment	200,000
Adjusted earnings	700,000

∴ Adjusted earnings per share   = $\dfrac{£700,000}{2,000,000} \ \times \ \dfrac{1.90}{2.00}$

=   33p per share

(b) The limitations of earnings per share as a measure of corporate performance include the following.

(i) The figure for earnings is based on accounting conventions and policies which may change over time and reduce comparability where prior year adjustments are not made.

(ii) Earnings per share are not comparable between companies. This can partly be remedied by the calculation of a price/earnings ratio but this ratio will vary considerably from time to time due to general and specific stock market fluctuations.

(iii) It is a short-term measure and can be affected by, for example, short-term cost reductions that may not be in the long-term best interests of the company. Equally, it can be adversely affected by the need to write certain costs off immediately, such as research, which may benefit the company in the long term.

(iv) No account is taken of the capital employed in the business.

(v) Since extraordinary items are excluded, it does not provide a comprehensive measure of the profits earned.

(vi) The exclusion of extraordinary items provides opportunities for manipulation. It is claimed that unusual credits are often treated as exceptional and included in earnings per share while unusual debits are treated as extraordinary and excluded.

(vii) Earnings per share measures only profitability whereas a full appreciation of financial performance would require measurement of gearing, company's liquidity, interest and dividend cover and business efficiency (gross margin, expense ratios, market share and so on).

STAGE 3
ADVANCED FINANCIAL ACCOUNTING

Time allowed - 3 hours

Number of questions on paper - 5

Answer the <u>two</u> questions in section A

and <u>two</u> questions from section B

Marks indicated at the end of each question

DO NOT OPEN THIS PAPER UNTIL YOU ARE READY TO START

UNDER EXAMINATION CONDITIONS

SECTION A

Answer both questions

1   You are given the following information.

Profit and loss accounts for the year ended 31 December 1990

	ABC Ltd £'000	DEF Ltd £'000	GHI Ltd £'000
Turnover	3,000	1,600	1,000
Cost of sales	(2,000)	(900)	(550)
Gross profit	1,000	700	450
Investment income	9	–	–
Administration expenses	(300)	(200)	(150)
Selling and distribution costs	(200)	(150)	(100)
Profit on ordinary activities before taxation	509	350	200
Taxation	(150)	(100)	(50)
Profit on ordinary activities after taxation	359	250	150
Extraordinary items	(50)	(30)	(10)
	309	220	140
Dividends: paid	(50)	–	(30)
Dividends: proposed	(50)	(100)	(50)
Retained profit for current year	209	120	60
Retained profit at beginning of year	800	350	190
	1,009	470	250

Notes

(1)   ABC Ltd acquired a 30% interest in the ordinary shares (and voting power) of GHI Ltd on 1 January 1988. At that date the retained profits of GHI Ltd were £100,000.

(2)   ABC Ltd acquired a 60% interest in the ordinary shares (and voting power) of DEF Ltd on 31 March 1990.

(3)   It may be assumed that the profits of DEF Ltd accrue evenly over time.

(4)   The investment income of £9,000 in the accounts of ABC Ltd represents a dividend received from GHI Ltd.

(5)   The stock of GHI Ltd at 1 January 1990 contained £100,000 of goods which had been purchased from ABC Ltd. These items had cost ABC Ltd £50,000 to manufacture.

(6)   The board of directors has decided to include the full year's turnover of DEF Ltd in the 1990 consolidated profit and loss account.

Required:

(a)   Show in working schedule format the adjustments needed to produce the consolidated profit and loss account for the ABC Group for the year ended 31 December 1990.

(30 marks)

(b) Explain the composition of the retained profit of the ABC Group for the year ended 31 December 1990 in terms of the amounts retained by ABC Ltd, DEF Ltd and GHI Ltd. **(5 marks)**

(c) Prepare in a format suitable for inclusion in the annual report of the ABC Group the consolidated profit and loss account for the year ended 31 December 1990. **(5 marks)**

(40 marks)

2   You are the management accountant of SR plc. PQ plc is a competitor in the same industry and it has been operating for 20 years. Summaries of PQ plc's profit and loss accounts and balance sheets for the previous three years are given below.

Summarised profit and loss accounts for the year ended 31 December

	1988 £m	1989 £m	1990 £m
Turnover	840	981	913
Cost of sales	554	645	590
Gross profit	286	336	323
Selling, distribution and administration expenses	186	214	219
Profit before interest	100	122	104
Interest	6	15	19
Profit on ordinary activities before taxation	94	107	85
Taxation	45	52	45
Profit on ordinary activities after taxation	49	55	40
Dividends	24	24	24
Retained profit for year	25	31	16

Summarised balance sheets at 31 December

	1988 £m	1989 £m	1990 £m
Fixed assets			
Intangible assets	36	40	48
Tangible assets at net book value	176	206	216
	212	246	264
Current assets			
Stocks	237	303	294
Debtors	105	141	160
Bank	52	58	52
	606	748	770
Creditors: amounts falling due within one year			
Trade creditors	53	75	75
Other creditors	80	105	111
	133	180	186
Creditors: amounts falling due after more than one year			
Long-term loans	74	138	138
	207	318	324
Shareholders' interest			
Ordinary share capital	100	100	100
Retained profits	299	330	346
	606	748	770

You may assume that the index of retail prices has remained constant between 1988 and 1990.

You are required to write a report to the finance director of SR plc:

(a) analysing the performance of PQ plc and showing any calculations in an appendix to this report; **(20 marks)**

(b) summarising five areas which require further investigation, including reference to other pieces of information which would complement your analysis of the performance of PQ plc. **(10 marks)**

(30 marks)

SECTION B

Answer two questions only

3 In recent years several large listed companies have purchased their own ordinary shares.

You are required to summarise:

(a) the accounting requirements for a public listed company when it purchases its own shares; **(9 marks)**

(b) six advantages of a company purchasing its own shares. **(6 marks)**

(15 marks)

4 Discuss the advantages and disadvantages of earnings per share as a measure of corporate performance. **(15 marks)**

5 Fair value is a concept underlying external financial reporting.

Required:

(a) Explain why fair value accounting is required. **(4 marks)**

(b) Explain how the fair value concept is applied. **(5 marks)**

(c) List three areas of application of fair value accounting. **(6 marks)**

(15 marks)

TEST PAPER
SUGGESTED SOLUTIONS

DO NOT TURN THIS PAGE UNTIL YOU

HAVE COMPLETED THE TEST PAPER

SECTION A

1   *Tutorial note.* This is not a very easy question. The main confusion is caused by the inclusion of DEF Ltd's full year results. Some of those results are pre-acquisition, and therefore an adjustment must be made later on in the profit and loss account to remove the pre-acquisition net profit. The examiner tried to make life easier by asking for a consolidation schedule as the first part of the question, but you need to adopt a logical and methodical approach to get the answer right.

Suggested solution

(a)   ABC GROUP
      CONSOLIDATED PROFIT AND LOSS ACCOUNT
      WORKING SCHEDULE FOR THE YEAR ENDED 31 DECEMBER 1990

	ABC Ltd £'000	DEF Ltd £'000	GHI £'000	Adj £'000	Consolidated £'000
Turnover	3,000	1,600			4,600
Cost of sales	2,000	900			2,900
Gross profit	1,000	700			1,700
Investment income	9		(9)		
Administration expenses	300	200			500
Selling and distribution costs	200	150			350
	509	350			850
Share of profits of related co (W1)			75		75
Profit before taxation	509	350			925
Taxation					
Holding company and subsidiary	150	100			250
Associated company (W1)			(15)		15
Profit after taxation	359	250			660
Minority interest (W3)				(100)	100
					560
	359	250			
Extraordinary items (W1, W2)	(50)	(30)	(3)	12	(71)
	309	220			489
Pre-acquisition profit		(x 60% x 3/12)		(33)	(33)
					456
Dividend: paid	50				50
proposed	50	100		100	50
Retained profit for the year	209	120	48	(21)	356
Retained profit b/f	800	350	12	(350)(W2)	812
Retained profit b/f	1,009	470	60	371	1,168

TEST PAPER: SUGGESTED SOLUTIONS

Workings

1. *Share of associated company profit*

	Total £'000		Group share £'000
Profit before tax	200		
Provision unrealised profit	50		
	250	x 30%	75
Taxation	(50)	x 30%	(15)
Extraordinary items	(10)	x 30%	(3)
Dividends received and receivable	(80)	x 30%	(24)
Share of retained profits			33
GHI retained profit			190
Less stock adjustment			(50)
			140

			£'000	
Retained profit b/f				
Pre-acquisition	100	x 30% =	30	
Post-acquisition	40	x 30% =	12	Group retained profit
	140			

2. *Adjustments in relation to subsidiary*

Minority share of extraordinary item = 40% x £30,000 = <u>12,000</u>

				£'000
Retained profit b/f				
Pre-acquisition	350	x	40% =	210
Post-acquisition	350	x	60% =	140
				350
Proposed dividends				
Minority interest	100	x	40% =	40
Pre-acquisition profits	100	x	25% x 60% =	15
Group retained profit	100	x	75% x 60% =	45
				100
Retained profit				
Minority interest	120	x	40% =	48
Pre-acquisition profits	120	x	25% x 60% =	18
Group retained profit	120	x	75% x 60% =	54
				120

3. *Minority interest*

DEF Ltd	£'000
Proposed dividend	40
Retained profit	48
Extraordinary item	12
	100

(b) Retained profit of ABC Group at 31 December 1990

	£'000	£'000
ABC		209
DEF: dividend accrued	45	
retained post acquisition	54	
		99
GHI retained 1990 (33 + 12 + 3)		48
Group retained profit at 31 December		356

(c) ABC GROUP
CONSOLIDATED PROFIT AND LOSS ACCOUNT
FOR THE YEAR ENDED 31 DECEMBER 1990

	Note	£'000
Turnover	1	4,600
Cost of sales		2,900
Gross profit		1,700
Administration expenses		500
Distribution costs		350
Income from shares in related companies		75
Net profit before taxation		925
Taxation	2	265
Net profit after taxation		660
Minority interests		100
		560
Extraordinary items	3	(71)
Pre-acquisition profit		(33)
Profit after taxation		456
Dividends paid and payable		100
Retained profit for the year		356
Retained profit brought forward		812
Retained profit carried forward		1,168

Notes

1. The results of the subsidiary DEF Ltd have been included for the full year, although the share holding was only acquired on 31 March 1990.

2. Taxation includes £15,000, the group share of the tax charge of GHI Ltd, a related company.

3. Extraordinary items includes £3,000, the group's share of extraordinary item charged in the accounts of GHI Ltd, a related company.

2 *Tutorial note.* This is not a difficult question. The structure of the question guides you through the form of the report and the question is conveniently split into the analysis of the figures (part (a)) and the suggestions for further investigations (and perhaps remedies) in part (b). Quite a lot of ratios have been calculated here, but you should be careful not to calculate those you will not use. You are not being asked to explain in great depth all the numbers in the question. You are simply asked what you would investigate and what further information you would require.

TEST PAPER: SUGGESTED SOLUTIONS

Suggested solution

(a) To: Finance Director
     From: Management accountant
     Subject: *Performance of PW plc 1988 to 1990*

An appendix is attached to this report which shows the ratios calculated as part of the performance review.

  1. *Profitability*
      The gross profit margin has remained relatively static over the three year period, although it has risen by approximately 1% in 1990. ROCE, while improving very slightly in 1989 to 21.5% has dropped dramatically in 1990 to 17.8%. The net profit margin has also fallen in 1990, in spite of the improvement in the gross profit margin. This marks a rise in expenses which suggests that they are not being well controlled. The utilisation of assets compared to the turnover generated has also declined reflecting the drop in trading activity between 1989 and 1990.

  2. *Trading levels*
      It is apparent that there was a dramatic increase in trading activity between 1988 and 1989, but then a significant fall in 1990. Turnover rose by 17% in 1989 but fell by 7% in 1990. The reasons for this fluctuation are unclear. It may be the effect of some kind of one-off event, or it may be the effect of a change in product mix. Whatever the reason, it appears that improved credit terms granted to customers (debtors payment period up from 46 to 64 days) has not stopped the drop in sales.

  3. *Working capital*
      Both the current ratio and quick ratio demonstrate an adequate working capital situation, although the quick ratio has shown a slight decline. There has been an increased investment over the period in stocks and debtors which has been only partly financed by longer payment periods to trade creditors and a rise in other creditors (mainly between 1988 and 1989).

  4. *Capital structure*
      The level of gearing of the company increased when a further £64m was raised in long term loans in 1989 to add to the £74m already in the balance sheet. Although this does not seem to be a particularly high level of gearing, the debt/equity ratio did rise from 18.5% to 32.0% in 1989. The interest charge has risen to £19m from £6m in 1988. The 1989 charge was £15m, suggesting that either the interest rate on the loan is flexible, or that the full interest charge was not incurred in 1989. The new long-term loan appears to have funded the expansion in both fixed and current assets in 1989.

APPENDIX

Working	1988	1989	1990
(1) Gross profit margin	34.0%	34.3%	35.4%
(2) ROCE	21.1%	21.5%	17.8%
(3) Profit margin	11.9%	12.4%	11.4%
(4) Assets turnover	1.78	1.73	1.56
(5) Gearing ratio	15.6%	24.3%	23.6%

TEST PAPER: SUGGESTED SOLUTIONS

		1988	1989	1990
(6)	Debt/equity ratio	18.5%	32.0%	30.9%
(7)	Interest cover	16.7	8.1	5.5
(8)	Current ratio	3.0	2.8	2.7
(9)	Quick ratio	1.2	1.1	1.1
(10)	Debtor's payment period (days)	46	52	64
(11)	Stock turnover period (days)	156	171	182
(12)	Creditor's turnover period	35	42	46

Workings (all in £m)

		1988	1989	1990
(1)	Gross profit margin	$\dfrac{286}{840}$	$\dfrac{336}{981}$	$\dfrac{323}{913}$
(2)	ROCE *	$\dfrac{100}{473}$	$\dfrac{122}{568}$	$\dfrac{104}{584}$
(3)	Profit margin	$\dfrac{100}{840}$	$\dfrac{122}{981}$	$\dfrac{104}{913}$
(4)	Assets turnover	$\dfrac{840}{473}$	$\dfrac{981}{568}$	$\dfrac{913}{584}$
(5)	Gearing ratio	$\dfrac{74}{74 + 399}$	$\dfrac{138}{138 + 430}$	$\dfrac{138}{138 + 446}$
(6)	Debt/equity ratio	$\dfrac{74}{399}$	$\dfrac{138}{430}$	$\dfrac{138}{446}$
(7)	Interest cover	$\dfrac{100}{6}$	$\dfrac{122}{15}$	$\dfrac{104}{19}$
(8)	Current ratio	$\dfrac{394}{133}$	$\dfrac{502}{180}$	$\dfrac{506}{186}$
(9)	Quick ratio	$\dfrac{157}{133}$	$\dfrac{199}{180}$	$\dfrac{212}{186}$
(10)	Debtors' payment period	$\dfrac{105}{840} \times 365$	$\dfrac{141}{981} \times 365$	$\dfrac{160}{913} \times 365$
(11)	Stock turnover period	$\dfrac{237}{554} \times 365$	$\dfrac{303}{645} \times 365$	$\dfrac{294}{590} \times 365$
(12)	Creditors' payment period	$\dfrac{53}{554} \times 365$	$\dfrac{75}{645} \times 365$	$\dfrac{75}{590} \times 365$

* ROCE has been calculated here as:

$$\frac{\text{Profit on ordinary activities before interest and taxation (PBIT}}{\text{Capital employed}}$$

where capital employed = shareholders' funds plus creditors falling due after one year and any long term provision for liabilities and charges. It is possible to calculate ROCE using net profit after taxation and interest, but this admits variations and distortions into the ratio which are not affected by *trading* activity.

(b) Areas for further investigation include the following.

   (i) *Long-term loan*
        There is no indication as to why this loan was raised and how it was used to finance the business. Further details are needed of interest rate(s), security given and repayment dates.

   (ii) *Trading activity*
        The level of sales has fluctuated in quite a strange way and this requires further investigation and explanation. Factors to consider would include pricing policies, product mix, market share and any unique occurrence which would affect sales.

   (iii) *Further breakdown*
        It would be useful to break down some of the information in the financial statements, perhaps into a management accounting format. Examples would be:

        ● sales by segment, market or geographical area;
        ● cost of sales split, into raw materials, labour and overheads;
        ● stocks broken down into raw materials, work in progress and finished goods;
        ● expenses analysed between administrative expenses, sales and distribution expenses.

   (iv) *Accounting policies*
        Accounting policies may have a significant effect on certain items. In particular, it would be useful to know what the accounting policies are in relation to intangible assets (and what these assets consist of), and whether there has been any change in accounting policies.

   (v) *Dividend policy*
        The company has maintained the level of dividend paid to shareholders (although it has not been raised during the three year period). Presumably the company would have been able to reduce the amount of long-term debt taken on if it had retained part or all of the dividend during this period. It would be interesting to examine the share price movement during the period and calculate the dividend cover.

Tutorial note. Other matters raised could have included:

(1) working capital problems, particularly stock turnover and control over debtors; and
(2) EPS (which cannot be calculated here as the number of shares is not given) and other related investor statistics, such as the P/E ratio.

3   *Tutorial note.* If you have studied this topic to a reasonable extent you will do well as it only asks for the basic rules to be followed when carrying out such a transaction. The second part of the question should present no problems, as long as you apply common sense when considering the effects of such a purchase of shares and what it may achieve.

Suggested solution

(a)   The accounting requirements for a public listed company when it purchases its own shares are as follows.

The basic accounting entry to effect the purchase (or redemption) is to debit the share capital account and credit cash with the nominal value of the shares (if they are being purchased at nominal value). Alternatively, the entry can be made to a share purchase or redemption account, which will be cleared by a cash payment when all the necessary journal entries have been made.

This transaction has caused the 'creditors' buffer' (capital and reserves excluding debenture capital) to shrink by the nominal value of the shares purchased. This is not permitted, and to rectify the situation a transfer is made from distributable profits to a capital redemption reserve (CRR) equal to the nominal value of the shares.

The purchase must therefore be made out of distributable profits, or alternatively out of the proceeds of a fresh issue of shares. Where such shares are issued, the transfer to the CRR need only be the excess (if any) of the nominal value of the shares purchased over the proceeds of the new issue. Any premium on purchase must be charged to distributable profits, unless the shares were originally issued at a premium and there is a fresh issue of shares. In this case any premium may be charged to the share premium account.

In this last case, there is an additional restriction because it is not possible to have a debit balance on the share premium account. This means that the amount that may be charged to the share premium account is limited to the lower of:

(i)   the premium received on the original issue of the shares now being purchased; or

(ii)   the proceeds of the fresh issue of shares; or

(iii)   the current balance on the share premium account, after accounting for any premium on the fresh issue of shares.

Other rules regarding the transaction are as follows.

(i)   The articles of association of the company must allow the purchase.

(ii)   The shares must all be fully paid on redemption.

(iii)   The shares purchased by the company must be cancelled.

(iv)   There must be shares remaining in issue after the purchase which are not redeemable.

(v)   The company must make a return to the registrar within 28 days of the purchase stating all the details (nominal value of the shares, date of transaction, amount paid and so on).

In summary, the journal entries are as follows.

		£	£
DEBIT	Ordinary share capital	X	
CREDIT	Bank		X

Being the payment for the nominal value of the shares purchased

		£	£
DEBIT	Profit and loss account	X	
CREDIT	Capital redemption reserve		X

Being the transfer of the nominal value of the purchased shares to the CRR to maintain the creditor's buffer

		£	£
DEBIT	Profit and loss account	X	
CREDIT	Bank		X

Being any premium on redemption or purchase

(b) The following are advantages which a company gains when purchasing its own shares.

(i) The purchase allows the distribution of surplus cash, enabling the shareholders of the company to find other (perhaps better) uses for their money.

(ii) Companies with employee share schemes may wish to buy the employees' shares when they leave employment with the company.

(iii) It is possible to buy out dissident shareholders, which will allow the company to develop in the way the majority of the shareholders wish. Fewer shareholders also means that the company is less vulnerable to takeover.

(iv) By reducing the number of shares on the market, the value of the remaining shares may rise as part of the supply and demand mechanism, thus improving the marketability of the shares. (Note the effect on EPS and therefore the P/E ratio.)

(v) Companies which have messy and complicated capital structures may be able to simplify matters by buying whole classes of shares and issuing only one class in return.

(vi) It may be possible to reduce the level of overall dividend paid out, thus reducing ACT payable as well. Retaining earnings in the business would encourage growth.

4   *Tutorial note.* You will do well in this question by considering the way EPS is calculated and the complications which can arise. Knowledge of the financial press and the use EPS is put to in evaluating performance would be of great value in this question. It is necessary to show knowledge of the rudimentary parts of SSAP 3: the description of EPS and the disclosure requirements.

Suggested solution

Earnings per share (EPS) is used by many analysts and other users as a fundamental tool in understanding and interpreting company accounts. It is the measurement of the performance of a business by unit of the investment made by shareholders. As well as being a a figure used in its own right, the EPS is also used as a basis for other calculations, namely the P/E ratio and dividend cover, which are also important performance indicators.

The calculation and disclosure of the EPS of a company is laid out in SSAP 3. Only public companies need to show the EPS. The basic definition of EPS is:

$$\frac{\text{Earnings}}{\text{Number of equity shares in issue}}$$

However, SSAP 3 defines EPS as: 'the profit in pence attributable to each equity share, based on the (consolidated) profit of the period after tax and after deducting minority interests and preference dividends, divided by the number of equity shares in issue (and ranking for dividend in respect of the period).'

Advantage of EPS as a measure of corporate performance

(i)   EPS is better than dividend cover as a measure because it includes all profits whether retained or distributed.

(ii)   EPS is calculated only after charging what is due to other bodies, namely interest to lenders or preference share holders and tax to the government. The remaining figures are concerned only with what the shareholder 'owns'.

(iii)   As the rules for calculating EPS are so strict, the figure produced each year is consistent, and therefore comparable with previous years.

(iv)   The EPS is not difficult for most shareholders to understand as a concept, even if they do not understand all the calculations. As such, it is a powerful indicator. This is demonstrated by the prominence of the EPS on the face of the profit and loss account.

Disadvantages of EPS as a measure of corporate performance

(i)   Differences in capital structure (in terms of the number of shares in issue) do not allow the comparison of EPS between one company and another.

(ii)   The variable nature of parts of the taxation charge makes it necessary to calculate EPS on both a 'net' and 'nil' basic, reducing the comparative value of the figures from year to year.

(iii)   EPS alone cannot show the value of the asset per share which have produced the earnings per share. The P/E ratio must be calculated to indicate how the stock market rates a share.

(iv)   The complications of capital transactions such as bonus issues and rights issues dilutes the usefulness of the EPS as a measure.

5   *Tutorial note.* The best way of answering this question is to think of those SSAPs which mention 'fair value'. It is most often used in acquisition and equity accounting but it is worth remembering that fair values may be applicable to all kinds of purchases. This will help you to think of their examples.

Suggested solution

(a)   Fair value accounting is a concept which is important in several SSAPs, namely 1, 14, 21, 22 and 23. The most frequent application of fair value is where it is necessary to compare the fair value of the consideration paid for an acquisition with the fair value of the assets purchased. The difference between the two will represent goodwill.

This application of fair value is necessary as assets should be recorded at 'cost to the group', not at the historical cost recorded when the asset was bought by the subsidiary. If the fair value is not used, then goodwill will be overstated and post-acquisition profits will be distorted because depreciation charges will be based on outdated values.

(b)   A fair value exercise is carried out on or near the date of acquisition. The fair value of the consideration is easy to calculate if there is only cash involved. However, if shares are involved, then the fair value must be computed by applying the market price of shares at the date of the bid to those shares which are part or all of the consideration. If loan stock is offered then market values apply again, with adjustments made for any conversion rights. The costs of the acquisition should also be included in the consideration.

The fair value of the individual assets acquired is calculated as the total of what the purchaser would have had to pay for each one on the open market. The fair value exercise need not be applied to assets which will not be retained in the group (which will be resold immediately).

The fair value exercise must be based on circumstances at the date of acquisition, but the parent company has some time to assess values and make adjustments, up to the date on which the board approves the first set of accounts after the acquisition.

(c)   Fair value accounting is applied:

(i)   to the purchase of subsidiary companies under SSAPs 14 and 22;

(ii)   to the purchase of associate companies under SSAPs 1 and 22;

(iii) as a guide in SSAP 21 to establish the existence of a finance lease. If the present value of the lease payments amount to more than 90% of the fair value of the asset, then a finance lease is presumed to exist.